Impact ERA
Limitations and Possibilities

THE EQUAL RIGHTS AMENDMENT
Proposed Amendment XXVII

(Proposed by Congress on March 22, 1972)

Section 1. Equality of rights under the law shall not be denied or abridged by the United States or by any State on account of sex.

Section 2. The Congress shall have the power to enforce, by appropriate legislation, the provisions of this article.

Section 3. This amendment shall take effect two years after the date of ratification.

Impact ERA
Limitations and Possibilities

edited by
The Equal Rights Amendment Project
of the
California Commission on the Status of Women

LES FEMMES PUBLISHING
Millbrae, California

Published by LES FEMMES Publishing, 231 Adrian Road,
Millbrae, California 94030.

First printing: April, 1976
Made in the United States of America

Library of Congress Cataloging in Publication Data

Main entry under title:

Impact ERA.

    Includes bibliographical references and index.
    1. Women's rights—United States—Addresses, essays, lectures.
    I. California. Equal Rights Amendment Project.
HQ1426.I56   301.41'2'0973   76-4908
ISBN 0-89087-919-2

1 2 3 4 5 6 7 8 – 80 79 78 77 76

Table of Contents

Contributors

JANELL ANDERSON teaches political science at California State University, Sacramento. She is also doing graduate work in political science at the University of California, Davis.

CAROLYN SHAW BELL is a Professor of economics at Wellesley College and has written numerous articles.

ANNE K. BINGAMAN is a lawyer and also teaches at the University of New Mexico Law School. She is presently a Ford Foundation Fellow with a grant to study marital property rights.

BARBARA A. BROWN is a lawyer at the Women's Law Project in Philadelphia.

JANET SALTZMAN CHAFETZ is a Professor of sociology at the University of Houston. She is the author of *Masculine/Feminine or Human?*

BEVERLY CHIÑAS is a Professor of anthropology at California State University, Chico.

RUTH B. COWAN is a Professor of political science at New York City Community College of the City University of New York. She is also President of the Women's Caucus of the American Political Science Association.

MARY C. DUNLAP is a lawyer with Equal Rights Advocates, Inc. in San Francisco and is presently working under a Carnegie Foundation grant for the training of Title VII advocates at Stanford University.

CHARLES L. ELKINS is an Assistant Professor of English at Florida International University.

CYNTHIA FUCHS EPSTEIN is a sociologist at the Columbia Bureau of Applied Social Research. She is the author of *Woman's Place: Options and Limits of Professional Careers* and co-editor with William J. Goode of *The Other Half: Roads to Women's Equality.*

MARC FEIGEN FASTEAU is a lawyer and author of *The Male Machine.*

ANN E. FREEDMAN is a lawyer at the Women's Law Project in Philadelphia.

JO FREEMAN is Assistant Professor of political science at the State University of New York, College at Purchase. She has been a member of the Task Force on Women and Employment sponsored by the Twentieth

Century Fund and of the Committee on the Status of Women of the Midwest Political Science Association. She has written and lectured extensively on feminism, most recently *The Politics of Women's Liberation: A Case Study of an Emerging Social Movement and its Relation to the Policy Process.*

HARRIET N. KATZ is a lawyer at the Women's Law Project in Philadelphia.

DALE ROGERS MARSHALL is an Associate Professor of political science at the University of California, Davis.

ANNE S. MINER is the Affirmative Action Officer of Stanford University. Previously she had been consultant to the President of Stanford on the Employment of Women.

JEAN MUNDY is a clinical psychologist and Professor of psychology at Long Island University, Zekendorf Campus.

ELOISE C. SNYDER is a Professor of sociology at the University of Pennsylvania.

NAOMI WEISSTEIN is a Professor of psychology at the State University of New York at Buffalo. She is the author of numerous articles, the most anthologized being "Psychology Constructs the Female."

LENORE J. WEITZMAN is an Assistant Professor of sociology at the University of California, Davis. Under a National Science Foundation grant, she presently directs the Divorce Law Research Center for the Study of Law and Society.

Preface and Acknowledgments

The California Commission on the Status of Women has been funded by the Rockefeller Foundation to make a national study of the societal impact of conformance of laws to the Equal Rights Amendment, with the goal of promoting public understanding of the issues involved. Several assumptions underlie the formulation of this project: (1) widespread discrimination on the basis of sex exists in all aspects of our national life and is reinforced by a network of legal protections; (2) the ERA will set forth with unequivocal clarity the principle that equality of rights under the law shall not be denied or abridged on account of sex and mandate legal change at every governmental level; (3) the resultant legal changes will have broad societal impact, with the major institutions such as marriage, family, government, education, and commerce undergoing substantial change as a direct result of requirements to bring federal, state, and local laws into conformance with the ERA; and (4) the process of social change may be facilitated by a wide public knowledge of the issues involved and the alternatives which exist. Assuming, then, the existence of legal backing for sex discrimination, the approaching ratification of the ERA, the far-reaching effects of its implementation, and the possibility of orderly social change, the Commission has developed a project which will assist in the process of change.

The project has a dual dimension. It includes code reviews and the development of guidelines for model codes in the areas of family, employment, education, and criminal justice to be used as models for conformance in all states. But pinpointing areas of necessary legal change is in itself a preface to the examination of the impact of such change on selected key societal institutions. This second dimension of the project is meant to generate an understanding of the interaction of social and legal change in order to develop models for legal change which will simultaneously provide required conformance to the ERA, make adequate provision for orderly institutional change, and give due recognition to human needs.

Fundamental change of the proportion implied here need not be accompanied by chaos if systematic and well-thought-out approaches are used rather than hasty and simplistic ones. The Commission's project seeks to

ix

move beyond the inadequacies of a piecemeal approach by addressing the totality of the problem.

All across the country, some of America's finest minds contributed their time and knowledge to the ongoing development of the project, a necessarily broad-based effort requiring a comprehensive sense of society's interactions as well as a frequently specific focus on individual factors. It is with very real pleasure that we acknowledge and thank those individuals and institutions who have given so unstintingly to our project.

Major recognition must be given to Peter Wood, Charles Warren Fellow, Harvard, and Marjorie Fine Knowles, Associate Professor, University of Alabama School of Law, for their special understanding, encouragement and support. They were there at the beginning and, sharing our vision of society's horizons, never faltered in the journey with us.

For their expertise in specific fields which lent invaluable assistance in focusing the implications of the ERA on present societal institutions, we wish to thank a number of women. They include: Barbara Allen Babcock, Associate Professor of law, Stanford University; Anne K. Bingaman, Assistant Professor, University of New Mexico Law School; Barbara A. Brown and Ann E. Freedman of the Women's Law Project, Philadelphia; Mary Dunlap and Wendy Webster Williams of Equal Rights Advocates, San Francisco; Herma Hill Kay, Professor of law, University of California at Berkeley; Dale Rogers Marshall, Associate Professor of political science, University of California, Davis; Bernice Sandler, Executive Associate, Association of American Colleges; and Lenore Weitzman, Assistant Professor of sociology, University of California, Davis.

We are also indebted to the members of an advisory symposium in San Francisco whose interdisciplinary focus pointed us in the direction of this book: Jessie Bernard, writer and sociologist; Ruth Glick, Director, National Study of Women's Correctional Programs; Helen Kelley, President, Immaculate Heart College; Marjorie Knowles; Jessie Kobayashi, Board of Directors, Institute for Educational Leadership; James O. Lewis, Human Relations Executive, California Teachers' Association; Madeline Mixer, Director, Western Regional Office of Women's Bureau, U.S. Department of Labor; Robert Seidenberg, psychiatrist; Alice J. Vandermeulen, Economics Department, U.C.L.A.; John Vasconcellos, Assemblyman, 24th District, California; Lenore Weitzman; Joan Hoff Wilson, History Department, California State University at Sacramento; and Peter Wood.

We are indeed grateful to the attorneys whose learned discussions have evidenced an understanding of the legal whole as well as of the interrelationship of its parts: Diane Blank, Janice Goodman, and Jemera Rone of

Bellamy, Blank, Goodman, Kelly and Stanley, New York; Rhonda Cope-
lon, Liz Schneider, and Nancy Stearns of The Center for Constitutional
Rights, New York; Nancy L. Davis and Joan Messing Graff of Equal Rights
Advocates, San Francisco; Ellen B. Ewing, Kentucky Commission on
Human Rights; Brenda Feigen Fasteau, Fasteau and Feigen, New York;
Margaret Gates, Co-Director, Center for Women's Policy Studies; Nancy
Gertner, Silvergate, Shapiro and Gertner, Boston; Ruth Bader Ginsburg,
Professor of law, Columbia University; Isabella Grant, Chairperson, Com-
mittee on Equal Rights, California Bar Association; Cynthia Holcomb Hall,
judge, U.S. Tax Court; Sarah T. Hughes, judge, Federal District Court,
Dallas; Gladys Kessler, Berlin, Roisman and Kessler, Washington, D.C.;
Jean L. King, Ann Arbor, Michigan; Sybil H. Landan, Hofstra Law School,
Long Island; Sylvia Law, New York University School of Law; Judith
Lonnquist, Jacobs, Fore, Burns and Sugarman; Carlyn McCaffrey, Assis-
tant Professor, New York University School of Law; Judy Mears, American
Civil Liberties Union, New York; Virginia B. Nordby, University of
Michigan School of Law; Kathleen Peratis, Women's Rights Project,
American Civil Liberties Union, New York; Elizabeth Rindskoph, Execu-
tive Director, New Haven Legal Assistance Association; Sheribel Rothen-
berg, Assistant Regional Attorney, U.S. Equal Employment Opportunity
Commission, Chicago; Barbara Shack, New York Civil Liberties Union;
Paula Smith, Salmanson and Smith, Austin, Texas; Nadine Taub, Rutger's
Law School; Sarah Weddington, member, Texas House of Representatives;
Ruth Weigand, Associate General Counsel, International Union of Electri-
cal Radio and Machine Workers, AFL-CIO; and Mary Wenig, Professor of
law, St. John's University Law School and Chairperson of the Equal Rights
Committee, American Bar Association, Section of Real Property, Probate
and Trust Law.

We would also like to take this opportunity to thank the Rockefeller
Foundation for providing the funding necessary to research and produce this
project. However, the views expressed in this book are entirely those of the
Commission on the Status of Women, Equal Rights Amendment Project.

We would especially like to thank and acknowledge the dedicated effort
of Harriet Shepler, our typist, whose clerical expertise and personal serenity
in the face of continual crisis made the timely publication of this work
possible.

Finally, special acknowledgment must go to Hazel Greenberg whose
eclectic imagination and consummate literacy are largely responsible for
whatever successes this book may ultimately achieve. In editing this
material, Dr. Greenberg not only served as guiding force for many of these

ideas but also demonstrated near genius for translating massive data into coherent, cogent prose. We recognize that without the brilliant, dedicated effort of Dr. Greenberg this book should never have been realized.

Anita Miller
Chairperson, California Commission on the Status of Women
Director, Equal Rights Amendment Project

Introduction

Tradition enshrines the status quo. What has been valued as "classic" and "enlightened" is inevitably aligned with a "rationalism" expressed in part by Alexander Pope's dictum that "whatever is, is right." These classical and 18th century values persist in our age of supposedly "objective" science. Our contemporary social scientific view of society's institutions, especially of marriage and the family, assumes that the present way of organizing our society is the right way, merely because it is the traditional way, merely because it exists and persists. And this is rationalistic, therefore true. This "functional" analysis of society makes two presumptions: the endurance of an institution proves its validity, and since social equilibrium is the proper goal for society, the other criterion of validity is how well an institution contributes to that balance. The concept of functionality, then, is inextricably bound to tradition and stability, permitting no room for change or development. What is "good" is what fits into the present system. Sex role divisions, persistent over time and nicely convenient for the controlling class, are "functional." Except that they are not. And these assumptions are untrue. They ignore the facts. The fact is that institutions arise as solutions to one set of circumstances and become inappropriate or unnecessary when these circumstances change, e.g., physical strength in a primitive and nontechnological world is no longer the criterion for superiority—man is no longer "the hunter." Moreover, even the original institutional response to a social need might have been the product of unfair power plays and incorrect notions based on undeserved privilege and prejudice about which we can later become truly "enlightened," e.g., granted the social need for cheap and abundant labor in the South, why create the institution of slavery, and why choose blacks to serve that institution?

The extent to which *myths* are necessary in our society to make *reality* palatable for all members of the social hierarchy testifies to the devastating nature of that reality. The myths of equal justice, equal opportunity, egalitarian marriage, the myths of motherhood, "woman's place," and woman's power in America in the face of obvious victimization, discrimination, and inequality serve to keep everyone in his/her place, to allow the social machinery to grind on despite the confusion created by the disparity

1

between the ideal and the real. They provide us with symbols of identification which dramatize our "proper" roles to us, mask reality, and prevent change.

Carried to the extreme, unexamined support of traditional institutions would prevent constitutional amendment altogether. Yet, even the founders of our Republic and the creators of the Constitution had sufficient foresight to know that their very power of foresight was limited. They knew they could predict neither the problems that would arise because of or in spite of what they had written nor how changes in society, institutions, and individuals would require reciprocal change in what they had written. Wisely they wrote into the Constitution the very sanction for its growth and adaptation. By doing so they recognized the inevitablity of change and, implicitly, the relativity of truth, both practical and theoretical, as well as the need for the Constitution to respond to changing social reality.

This book is about change, constitutional and societal. It assumes that fear of power loss plus fear of the unknown add up to fear of change and the acceptance of the status quo no matter how unhappy the consequences for those who suffer under it. It tries to define that unknown in order to make it less frightening.

For half a century women have struggled within the system for the Equal Rights Amendment; if it is ratified, we will spend the next half century trying to change that system by making it conform to the ERA. The enormity of the task of achieving practical conformance to the theoretical principle of equal rights is testimony itself to the magnitude of the need. The ERA is both a symbolic recognition of that need and a mandate for change; it is both psychological and legal in effect. It is, perhaps, the culmination of the "women's rights" segment of the Movement, which works for normative changes in society through legal and institutional means, but goes beyond this, at least in theory, to the "liberation" issue, for in denying that sex is a valid legal classification of persons, it implicitly denies societal values based on biological differences between the sexes and recognizes that social roles are learned and, therefore, relative. It is, then, a legal validation of a value-oriented, as well as normative, social movement.

Even as ERA changes laws, anticipation of its impact must recognize the gap between laws and mores, between structural and cultural changes, between normative and value changes. Behavior can be legislated; emotions and attitudes cannot. Reluctance to change, whether arising from fear or from misconception of that change, will provide severe obstacles to the full implementation of the ERA. In each area of impact that we consider, political, economic, social, and psychological, we have taken account of those barriers to the ERA's impact and to the consequent problems it will cause for society even before it provides solutions. These problems must not, however, make us neglect the long view, must not frighten us into accepting a status quo which is, in fact, dysfunctional to the operation of our society, contrary to social scientific fantasy.

A recognition of the dysfunctional nature of our social institutions with regard to sex stereotyping is a prerequisite for the perception of the benefits that will follow the institutionalization of equality, benefits to both women and men, because the costs of inequality are to both women and men. The utopian vision of the future in some of these essays is premised on past and present signs of the *need* for change as much as on abundant evidence of the *demand* for change.

Those signs are revealed in an honest assessment of present sociological reality. The fact of demand tells us not only that structural change is mandated, but that some cultural change has already taken place; the fact of widespread unhappiness in present institutional modes of living, whether it is consciously traced to sexism or not, tells us that structural change is necessary. Legal change is necessary not only to initiate and institutionalize changes in mores but to *recognize* progressive change in mores. This other side of the coin is, then, that the law must catch up to and acknowledge social change; it must fulfill a need. Those who foresee the destruction of marriage and family life as a result of the ERA must consider the very real demand for either changes in those institutions or alternatives to them, as well as the costs to those who are as yet unaware of the destructive nature of those institutions. The winds of change originate from within a system; they are not imposed from without. Fear of the ERA as destructive to our institutions is unfounded; rather, ERA will accommodate new institutional necessities, and with the grace of acceptance, will effect constructive adaptation rather than destruction.

But the grace of acceptance from those who are as yet unaware of the costs is not easily won; yet, even without it initially, there is hope. It is the psychological nature of human beings to resolve cognitive dissonance; that is, people cannot long behave in a way which is antithetical to their beliefs and emotions without mentally adjusting them to one another. Changes in behavior to conform to the law will eventually involve concomitant emotional changes in belief. This sequence is yet another dimension of the relationship between laws and mores. While there is an inevitable cultural lag between them, the long view will see that immediate balking must eventually give way to psychological conformance.

Rest assured, though, that the accommodation will not be merely psychological rationalization. Changes in the economic and political rights of women will give them the opportunity to change traditional opinion about their abilities and their "place." Sexism is a self-fulfilling prophecy: women don't achieve because they think they can't, because they are told that they can't, and because they are not allowed to, yet the fact that they don't is taken as proof that they can't. New role models can change this cyclical lie; once they have the right and opportunity to prove their worth they will be accepted as worthy. In this way, egalitarian ideology in the private sector may develop from changes in the public sector, and this *can* be handled through the legal process. Normative changes can lead to value changes, and the movements for women's rights and women's liberation may come together as they should.

ERA is more than a mandate for changing laws and a defense weapon or legal recourse. It is a symbol which, by dramatizing a need for equality, legitimizes that need. The very act of emancipation defines one's slavery. Legal recognition of freedom makes one sensitive to violations of one's freedom previously ignored or fearfully suppressed. The ERA will unite women, raise their consciousness, and increase their perception of themselves as an oppressed group at the very moment of their (theoretical) liberation. Liberation itself, as Herbert Marcuse has said, depends upon the consciousness of servitude. And Kirsten Amundsen has defined the preconditions for any liberation struggle as awareness, self-respect, and determination.[1] The ERA provides all three: it creates awareness of discrimination, justifies self-respect, and initiates determination by making legal recourse a realistic solution. Helen Mayer Hacker, in her famous application of the minority group model to women, emphasizes that the definition of a minority group includes both the fact of discrimination and the awareness of discrimination. Those who don't know they are being discriminated against on a group basis and those who accept such discrimination as valid lack the minority group consciousness.[2] By creating awareness of discrimination and militating against the acceptance of socialized inferiority, ERA brings more women into that "minority" group and serves as a prelude to group action.

Women often fail to internalize this group identification because of an important differentiating factor in their socialization: while most minority group members are socialized within their group, women's conceptions of themselves derive as much from their relationship to men as to women because of the proximity in which they co-exist; consequently, they internalize male attitudes toward them. In fact, self-hatred is a frequent reaction of minority group members, and the closer one gets to outsiders, the greater the temptation to deny that group affiliation. Even those women who have crossed class lines and "made it" in the man's world feel they must deny their feminine affiliation in order to maintain respect and to avoid self-hatred. The ERA's psychological impact on such career women will attenuate self-hatred by symbolically sanctioning self-respect; it will eliminate the anxiety and guilt resulting from the discrepancy between what they are and what they "ought" to be. They will be legitimately entitled to their high positions *as* women, and if the world is anybody's oyster, then men as a "class" are no longer "superior." Moreover, if there is no superior there can be no inferior class. Furthermore, on those women who presently conform to the stereotype, the ERA's psychological effect will symbolically undercut the self-fulfilling prophecy which renders them unfit to be anything but passive and dependent; by providing them with opportunities for growth, they will begin to grow into them.

We are living at a time when old and new values for both men and women exist simultaneously, when socialization is not clear-cut, when one set of ideals conflicts with another. This creates role conflict for women in that it becomes more difficult for them to achieve identity and self-esteem because they are not sure what the terms of "success" are for them. Female conditioning combined with the manifestly egalitarian principles of equal opportunity in education and work produce confusion for women with intellectual abilities and aspirations and a poor self-image and little self-respect for women who cannot rise above the traditional stereotype.[3] Both career women and homemakers are anxious about their femininity, so they take refuge in the psychological defense mechanism of reaction formation, in an exaggerated conformity to the sex role in some or all of its aspects.[4] Certainly this phenomenon, along with the self-hatred mentioned earlier, has contributed to female opposition to the ERA. And yet, the ERA as a legal standard can only help to clarify new norms and create more flexible roles, personalities, and behaviors. It will make manifest what are presently only latent ideals and thereby affect the socialization process indirectly. By sanctioning either set of norms as success criteria, ERA will make role freedom an opportunity rather than a burden. As Margaret Adams comments: "Today's fragmented and disintegrating world makes it essential for every individual and group of individuals to have an *easily defined, clearly perceived, and socially reinforced role,* which will preserve a sense of real identity and counteract the climate of futility and the relentless assault of status-conscious, competitive individualism."[5] (emphasis added) The ERA performs this defining and reinforcing function by expanding rather than limiting the acceptable roles for women; by increasing the rights and self-respect of both homemakers and professionals; by transforming role ambiguity into role choice.

Men, too, have found the presence of conflicting ideals a burden. Stress is created for men when sex role definitions are not clear-cut. Mirra

Komarovsky has found that the absence of strain usually indicates that a complete change in role definition has taken place, for example, the replacement of the normative expectation of male intellectual superiority with the ideal of intellectual companionship between equals. But where emotional allegiance to the traditional pattern is still strong despite ideological commitment to sex role redefinition, as in attitudes toward working wives (where the stake, in practical consequences, is much higher), men show considerable psychological conflict.[6] The clear delineation of social expectation by the ERA's legal change will, in the long run, reduce this stressful situation for men as well as women. Clarity and uniformity of definition must be pursued in order to alleviate confusion, and legal change to sanction new mores and create new ideals and expectations is an absolute necessity in achieving this goal.

There are, basically, two kinds of opposition to the ERA: there are those categorically against equality, who complacently accept the "comfortable" status quo and who fear the unknown and the unfamiliar; and there are those who argue that a constitutional amendment is not the proper method of achieving equality. These people prefer the methods of state legislative reform, legal challenge in the lower courts, or appeal to the Supreme Court under the Fifth and Fourteenth Amendments. What should be noted about all these methods is that they are individual tests allowing latitude of interpretation and application of both the laws and amendments about what actually constitutes "discrimination." Only the potential for equality exists within the Constitution in the Fifth and Fourteenth Amendments, but as it is totally dependent upon Supreme Court interpretation, equality is far from being guaranteed (not that ERA won't be subject to Court interpretation, but the standard of review will be much stricter and will give the Court much less leeway). In other words, such opponents argue that each law should be tested individually to determine whether it is, in fact, "discriminatory," or really "protective," or perhaps a "bona fide qualification," or can otherwise be rationally justified as a valid classification (e.g., one Court decision under Title VII allowed motherhood as a bona fide reason for an employer not to hire a woman).

The ERA is a necessary clarification of the equal protection clause of the Fourteenth Amendment. While the Fourteenth Amendment has been interpreted to define race as a "suspect" (i.e., illegal) classification, the same has not been done for sex. Sex is, in fact, the only "class" not covered explicitly by the Constitution as illegal; "equal protection" has been explicitly extended to all other groups, to blacks, aliens, even corporations, but sexual equality remains implicit, and therefore, debatable. What this means is that a law or practice involving race discrimination is "suspect" and must be subjected to "strict scrutiny" by the Court in order to be upheld. Since the burden is on the discriminator to prove a serious necessity for the classification, this has generally meant that it is almost never upheld. On the other hand, when a classification (e.g., sex) is not "suspect," the standards of review under the Fourteenth Amendment are far more lenient, and "compelling state interest" or "rational relationship" tests can be used far more easily to uphold the classification. In this case, the burden is on the victim of discrimination to prove the law or practice illegal. Since it is not *assumed* to be illegal, as in the case of race, this has meant a very uneven treatment by the Court. The ERA, by defining sex as an equally "suspect" classification, requires "strict scrutiny" and makes it far more difficult for the Court to use the "compelling state interest" or "rational relationship" tests to uphold the law or practice. In cases where a law or practice is neutral on its face (i.e., seemingly not based on a sex classification), a disproportionately discriminatory impact upon one sex can be used to invalidate it under ERA. While hardly absolute in its practical, if not theoretical, meaning, the significance of ERA is that it provides a universal legal definition of female equality, outlawing distinctions between people on the basis of sex as a violation of constitutional rights.[7] And this is the most serious sanction in our legal system.

The more conservative method, which still permits sex to remain a legal classification under certain circumstances (e.g., labor laws, family laws, draft laws) is not only slow and difficult, it is also selfish—an attempt to use the law for one's own ends rather than for the benefit of all. It is easier to keep one's protections without being required to make sacrifices if definitions remain hazy. The ERA is an almost absolute clarification and, for that reason, is fearful and "radical."

It is not difficult to see that, however sugar-coated the tacticians' pill, any acquiescence to differences in treatment on the basis of sex, for whatever reason, is philosophically based on at least a latent belief in "biological differences" as a valid determiner of sex roles. The issue here is whether the biological difference between the sexes is responsible for their present social roles and functions or whether these roles are socially learned, are culture-bound, and have little relevance to physiology. In a broad philosophical sense, any law or principle promulgating equal rights for both sexes assumes, if not a minimum of biological differentiation, then certainly a maximum of social malleability despite the differences. This is why we believe that ERA goes straight to the heart of the "liberation" issue in intent, even if it remains a "rights" issue in effect. If ERA reform were merely a "women's rights" movement, there wouldn't be so much opposition to it, for all but the staunchest male chauvinist agrees (or says he does) to "equal pay for equal work" and an end to occupational and economic discrimination against women. No, the ERA touches deeper nerves, if not in fact, then in symbol.

We inevitably return to the kind of opposition which fears equality no matter how it is achieved because its ramifications are unknown. A child's fear of the dark is cured by entering it in order to learn that there is no reason for fear. Immersion in the dark is the only way to lighten it; avoiding it perpetuates the fear. The purpose of this book is to lighten the darkness (and hence, the fear) surrounding the ERA through an immersion in that unknown and a realistic depiction of an ERA future. We have invited these writers to define both the legal and social limitations to, as well as the possibilities for, substantial societal change via the Equal Rights Amendment. Their speculation on an ERA future has revealed two things: firstly, that the impact of the ERA is not as far-reaching and dramatic as its opponents have depicted it to be; and secondly, that wherever its impact will be to effectively institutionalize equality, it can only benefit the entire society, both men and women. In both cases, fear of the future is unwarranted, and public education about these facts of ERA life is the first step toward transforming the ugly toad of today into the beautiful prince of tomorrow.

Male opposition to the ERA is multidimensional but is generally based on two assumptions. One is the belief in "woman's place," although individuals may differ slightly as to the parameters of that enclosure, and this is premised on the biological differences argument (i.e., motherhood is her natural and only role). The other is the belief that power implies hierarchy,[8] that, as Eva Figes so aptly put it, "male dominance must be maintained at all costs, because the person who dominates cannot conceive of any alternative but to be dominated in turn."[9] But power need not imply hierarchy; power can be shared, and ERA advocates desire female equality not superiority.

We are talking about rights, not power, and there will be benefits and losses on both sides. In fact, many of the discriminatory laws which the ERA would invalidate are disadvantageous to males precisely because men are considered responsible adults in charge of taking care of women, who are considered almost as legal "minors" or children. Of course, the invalidation of such laws creates female waffling about the ERA. To give some examples, only men can be drafted (when there is a draft); statutory rape, as the law defines it, can only be committed by a male and only a woman can be its victim; welfare benefits are often denied a family if the man, though unemployed, is present or, under some plans, less money is provided for a family with an unemployed male; most states allow females to marry at a younger age than males; males have far less labor protection than women do; males are not granted some kinds of jury exemptions or work leaves for family responsibilities that women are; many laws make it illegal for men to use vulgar language in the presence of children and women; a man may be sentenced to prison for the same crime for which a woman may be sentenced to reformatory (although such a sentence is likely to be longer for the woman); a husband is solely responsible for any criminal conspiracy between him and his wife even if she has committed the crime but did it in his presence; alimony and child support laws (supposedly) favor women; and, of course, the man is assigned the sole economic responsibility for the family.[10] It should be obvious even from this meagre list that men will benefit from the ERA as much as women will.

Consequently, even the most valiant attempt at equality on the private level is prevented by laws which reinforce sex roles. Family laws requiring the man to support the family and the woman to be homemaker restrict their lives. By defining the wife only in terms of her husband, in effect negating her identity, the law creates the cultural stereotype of the dependent female. So it is that the legal costs to men and women are not the only costs of sexism. There are psychological costs; and a conscious assessment of them is necessary in order to show that they are far more expensive than the costs of equality. The exclusive focus on the latter builds barriers to ERA's implementation and limits its impact (witness our sections on ERA's limitations). Consequently, although ERA will not directly affect the psychological costs of sexism, these costs must be brought to awareness in order to more effectively implement ERA on an individual attitudinal level. And without change on this level, ERA will be meaningless. A brief suggestion of them is therefore warranted in this context.

Studies have shown that in terms of their traditional sex roles, female discomfort results from what women *can't* do, from the passivity arbitrarily imposed upon them; male discomfort results from what men *must* do, from the activity arbitrarily assigned to them.[11] Conformity to the feminine role makes women less capable of functioning in roles other than the domestic; it extracts mental costs which result in the medical, behavioral, and psychological problems documented so well by Phyllis Chesler;[12] its almost exclusive involvement with and orientation toward children has increased the chance for mental breakdown or depression when the children finally leave home; it has often made suicide and crime appealing methods of gaining male attention and of establishing some identity. Analagous to the female syndrome caused by the loss of women's only role when children leave home are the mental problems common in males around age 65 or during times of unemployment when their only important functional role is taken away. The pressures on men to achieve have resulted in their shorter life expectancy and higher mortality rate, both of which are aggravated by the cultural prohibition of emotional expression. The psychological costs of establishing a male identity begin in childhood when males outnumber females in mental institutions two to one, when boys create much more severe delinquency problems than girls, and when boys encounter far more difficult discipline and learning problems in school due to the discrepancy between masculine and student role requirements. Moreover, when people conform to their assigned sex roles, the male-female relationship is often less than truly rewarding, almost *by definition*. While it is a rarity for both husband and wife to adhere precisely to their stereotypes, the more they do, the less likely is intimate and intense communication between them for two reasons: the male role does not allow for openness and sincere emotion and further, power relationships are not generally conducive to intimacy.[13] Generally, as Janet Saltzman Chafetz concludes, "It would appear that where femininity exacts a high price in the realm of functioning in instrumental roles outside the context of the home, masculinity exacts its greatest toll in the development of rewarding interpersonal relationships within and outside of the family."[14] These then are only a few of the costs of conformity.

When people do *not* conform to the social myths because the myths do not account for reality but merely serve to glorify the convenient in order to keep everyone "happily" in her/his place, the psychological and practical costs are also great. People suffer guilt and anxiety when they find they cannot live up to myths in which society has taught them to believe. The myths of romantic love, of sacred motherhood, of working wives have no basis in fact; they leave those who conform to them dissatisfied and those who do not conform to them uncomfortable. The myths created to maintain social order have become dysfunctional instead. And fears of the ERA are founded precisely on these myths and a concomitant unawareness of the benefits to be gained by equality. Thus, while a recognition of the relativity of sex roles leads to the possibility of change, a recognition of social reality leads to the desirability of change.

That America has nourished the contradictory ideal of egalitarian marriage in and of itself presumes its worth. It then becomes all the more outrageous that our society does not act more quickly to redeem itself once confronted with reality. And empirical evidence does prove that marriages which *are* based on equality of husband and wife in all aspects of life are the happiest and the most fulfilling. Constantina Safilios-Rothschild found that career women have far more egalitarian and "companionate" marriages and that companionate marriage is incompatible with sex inequality.[15] It is ironic indeed that our highest ideals are stunted both by present reality and by continual opposition to good faith attempts to realize them, the ERA pointedly among them.

The ERA makes a choice of myths based on its clarification of the present discrepancy between the ideal and the real, between the functional and the dysfunctional. The ERA will not destroy marriage.[16] To the extent that traditional marriage is in danger, it is due to social roles and social reality, which make relationships premised on erroneous myths either impossible (when people can't conform to them), and therefore disappointing, or empty (when people try to conform to them), and therefore meaningless. If marriage should become obsolete, it will be because alternatives are perceived as less costly, not because of the relatively limited legal changes mandated by the ERA. For those who fear the demise of marriage, isn't it better to accommodate the institution to changing needs than to eliminate it as a viable choice by a merely defensive rigidity? Flexibility is healthier than rigidity in institutions; one sows the seeds of evolution, the other of revolution. ERA reform is certainly the way of adaptation rather than elimination or destruction.

The irony is that in an age when women's liberation is accused of contributing to the higher divorce rate, both the rates of marriage and remarriage have increased. Socialization and the indoctrination of myths preserve the institution despite the widespread unhappiness it has been found to nurture. Or can some of the practical advantages of marriage in a sexist world be responsible? Bonnie Kreps notes that economic discrimination against the working woman causes her to see marriage as an escape from financially unrewarding drudgery.[17] And divorce is not presently in the best interests of *women*: they have fewer legal grounds to demand it and less preparation to cope with it, plus the fact that alimony is very irregularly enforced. No, it is men who press for divorce. Efforts to liberate women are not responsible for the divorce rate. But the implication of these attitudes is that women are clinging to marriage as an escape, as the lesser of two evils. Is marriage to be preserved as a prison? Or shall our society risk an honest choice, without loading the dice for marriage?

Another irony of the situation is that society often unwittingly loads the dice *against* marriage, making it an impossible choice for women with other ambitions as well. A few examples will serve to clarify the irony. A direct correlation has been found between female socioeconomic status and single-hood: that is, the greater the economic independence of females, the greater the likelihood that they will be single. This trend is evidence of the desire to reject the traditional female sex role of dependence.[18] But to reject that role, despite socialization, women must also reject marriage itself because society defines no way to accommodate their aspirations with marriage. Unless the institution of marriage changes, it will not incorporate this present demand, and independent women will be forced to choose between two incompatible alternatives. The same relationship exists between education and marriage: the pressure of and strain between the two roles of student and wife make divorce common in student marriages.[19] Further, marriage has been shown to be distinctly disadvantageous for the woman academic, who tends to be single anyway for the reasons already mentioned. While marital and parental status have not been found to hamper female productivity in academia, married women are paid less, get fewer honors, and are taken less seriously than single women.[20] Given the sociological reality of female aspiration, is not rampant discrimination against married women doing far more than the ERA to destroy marriage?

Because human paradox can only be sustained for so long, there must eventually be attempts to resolve the contradictions just described. Thus, marriage is already beginning to accommodate egalitarian relationships in an attempt to remain viable in the face of those loaded dice, not to mention the correlation between marital happiness and equality. As women participate more in the work world, as they are no longer barred from equality by a world in which physical strength determines superiority, as they are liberated from unplanned childbearing by contraception and from housework by technology, cultural pressure is brought to bear from within the institution itself. But the cultural lag which prevents recognition of these changes and continues to define woman and her function traditionally, results in role conflict and dysfunctionality for women, as already discussed. These roles are no longer necessary for survival or even structural convenience. They are merely "time-honored." The ERA provides the recognition necessary to bridge that cultural gap by acknowledging cultural change and catching the law up to social demand.

In tracing the problems of institutions like marriage to sexism, we attempt to make people conscious of the source of their unhappiness. Ordinarily, they see their failure and discontent as individual, blaming themselves not institutions or sex roles. Those who complacently accept the status quo do not think about the source of their problems.[21] The basic American principles of individualism and freedom of opportunity blur institutionalized injustice and make many unwilling to admit that collective political action is a prerequisite for improving their own lives. By pointing to a few successful women, the unconscious sexist adopts the existential attitude that any woman with ability and enough determination can also achieve success, thus locating whatever might be wrong in the individual and assigning responsibility for change to the individual. The fallacy in this argument is perhaps already too obvious at this point in the movement for human liberation, but it is worth emphasis. Whether or not individual women have overcome the system, the injustice which makes them merely exceptions to the rule amounts to a determinism that circumscribes from birth not only their life chances but their very aspirations. It is only through faulty internalization of their prescribed inferiority that some women do succeed. But whether a woman believes what she has been taught about herself, whether she aspires beyond that ascribed status and fails, whether she fails at marriage, school, or work, she is still unaware of where the real guilt often lies, given the lip service America pays to individualism, liberty, equality, and opportunity. There is nothing wrong with these ideals in and of themselves; they are only harmful when they are false, when people accept guilt and responsibility for failure which is not theirs but which is built into a system which does not realize its ideals. Sexism is a major roadblock to the realization of those ideals for both men and women.

In fact, the cost of the ethic of individualism, undermined as it is by sexism, is perhaps more to men, for while women are at least programmed for failure, men are programmed for success, and there is none but individual responsibility for failure. There are several factors militating against men's consciousness of their owm victimization by sexism. Clarice Stasz Stoll mentions several of them. For one thing, while many activist groups work for men, gender-related problems are not dealt with as particularly *men's* problems. "The system is at face value one where men succeed, therefore how could problems exist as a result of being male?" Further, men have more resources for expressing grievances and so get more accomplished that women, and it is, after all, frustration which initiates group consciousness and pinpoints the nature of oppression. Finally, the nature of all-male groups reinforces attitudes of masculinity which hinder any perception of themselves as oppressed. "Better" and "superior" are the only labels to which they respond. For all of these reasons individual guilt and anxiety over failure strike men even harder than women. And further, to the extent that the ideals of freedom and opportunity *are* realized for men, despite the sexist roadblock, at least the responsibility is properly and logically assigned.

But the fact is that if a woman can be discriminated against on the basis of sex, so can a man; and men need legal protections *as* men as much as women do, whether they want to admit it or not. We have seen briefly how the ERA's institutional and legal changes will benefit men as well as women, how sexism limits even male freedom and opportunity. In cases such as striking down good protective labor laws for women rather than extending them to men, men and women must work together to interpret the ERA for the benefit of humanity rather than oppose ERA out of male pride or female selfishness. Women who fear the ERA because they will lose "protections" and privileges must realize that protections, like the chivalry which pretends to exalt women but in fact distances and dehumanizes them, are often false and serve as a way of keeping women down and limiting their access to male spheres. This is true legally, and it is true psychologically and socially. Until *all* people can benefit from legal "protections," they should not be selfishly accepted or sought by anyone.

Men thus pay for the mask of invulnerability by exchanging necessary protection for pride. Women pay for the mask of vulnerability by exchanging social responsibility for unique protection. But whether women's opposition to the ERA is due to real contentment with their social irresponsibility or whether they are trapped by that role, it is laziness and fear which allow them to object to the expansion of that role for other women who are not willing to make the trade. While manifestly based on fear for our sacred institutions or of biological disruption, female opposition is latently based on the fear of both the implicit devaluation of their own lives by the expansion of the feminine sex role and the challenge of taking responsibility for their own destiny with its possibility of failure. As Chafetz says, "To ask people who have been trained to be dependent and of whom little has been expected to make the real effort to be independent and competent is to ask a lot; to ask this when it also entails the obvious costs of nonconformity seems almost ridiculous."[23] We have seen how women (and men, too) feel responsibility for failures that are not even really their own, failures that can instead be traced to sexism; perhaps because they know the pain of such self-inflicted blame, women fear the further responsibility that would require and be integrally related to their own deliberate action, like that men have had to a far greater extent than women, like that represented by ERA.

Real freedom and opportunity *are* frightening. Men have known such existential paralysis for centuries. And suffering falls justly upon those who fail when these ideals are effectively realized. Responsibility is an awesome burden and gift when one really *is* in control and can honestly accept blame or credit for one's own failure or success. But while ERA is an attempt to make freedom and opportunity real for both women and men by eliminating the roadblock of sexism, it is a right, not a proscription nor an obligation; it is opportunity, not demand. It doesn't devaluate; it values all lives equally and makes it possible for a man to aspire to homemaker if that's what his personality requires as well as giving a woman the right to aspire to the presidency if she has the ability. The women who oppose ERA want freedom *from* responsibility; ERA advocates want freedom *for* responsibility. The former see the imposition of new obligations rather than the acquisition of new rights. It is a matter of perspective. And by their opposition these women consciously or unconsciously seek the approval of their threatened male protectors. Proponents, of course, see domination, restriction, and enslavement where opponents see protection. In this spirit Bonnie Kreps accuses: "In accepting the traditional view of herself as secondary and inferior, woman has provided justification for the charge of inferiority."[24]

As for the "womanly virtues," they will not be lost, but merely individualized. As Vivian Gornick and Barbara Moran say, "These virtues are too important to our happiness and our survival to be the sole responsibility of a powerless underclass."[25] If they are so important to preserve, then the fact that they might be extended should be welcomed by those who fear their loss. The anticipation of uniformity and boredom in an ERA future testifies to imaginative impoverishment. Simone de Beauvoir counters: "I fail to see that this present world is free from boredom or that liberty ever creates uniformity."[26] Emancipation will increase diversity, will expand the relations of women beyond those involving men, not eliminate those relations. Women will be better companions and worthier human beings.

The articles in this book deal with the political, economic, social, and psychological impact of the ERA and the conformance of laws to it. In order to distill the truth about ERA and thereby dispel the opposition, we must analyze two complementary perspectives on its effectiveness: the limitations to and the possibilities for its impact on society. In each area of impact our writers assess both perspectives, sometimes within the same article, sometimes adopting one or the other perspective.

Each section dealing with limitations details some of the barriers to the effective implementation of the ERA, the ways in which ERA can do nothing without a cooperative effort of every individual to make it a reality. The fact is not that ERA will have little impact but that legal change alone can neither destroy existing institutions nor create better forms without commensurate social and psychological change. The necessarily reciprocal relationship between law and cultural mores is assurance that revolutionary and "disintegrative" change cannot be the impact of ERA. Even legally, ERA is only a mandate for change, a potential to be realized only by sincere and dedicated effort on the part of individuals within the legal system. Nor is legal conformance on the books the final solution to the implementation problem, for it is people who enforce and obey those laws. Anti-ERA forces, fearful of the egalitarian ethic itself and naïvely assuming an ideal world unaffected by political and psychological realities, have overstated ERA's ramifications in order to create a monster worthy of attack.

On the other hand, the principle of ERA must be taken seriously. And the possibilities it contains must be implemented. In each section dealing with possibilities our writers assess the actual and potential impact of ERA to show both the ways in which present reality is detrimental to everyone's best interests and the ways in which we will all benefit from the complete institutionalization of equality. Not only can we live peaceably and comfortably with the limited potential ERA provides, but we can live richly with the possibilities we might use it to actualize. ERA cannot do anything society does not want it to do, does not *make* it do; but used wisely, it can be an incomparable tool for constructive social growth.

Beyond its original intention, this book has become more than a treatise on the Equal Rights Amendment; basically, it is about the nature and possibility of social change and its relationship to specifically legal change and political reality.

We have tried to account for both the problems and solutions of ERA, to recognize the realities while anticipating utopia. We hope in this way to have approached the unknown in the spirit of sincerity and truth, for we recognize the validity of Carolyn G. Heilbrun's statement:

> Thinking about profound social change, conservatives always expect disaster, while revolutionaries confidently anticipate utopia. Both are wrong. But in the end, I am convinced, the future lies with those who believe salvation likelier to spring from the imagination of possibility than from the delineation of the historical.[27]

The ERA is no more and no less than *possibility*, and this book attempts to delineate the inadequacies of the historical legacy and to imagine possibilities of a better future. Let ERA symbolize and effect a new era of humanhood.

Footnotes

1. *The Silenced Majority* (Englewood Clifs, N.J.: Prentice-Hall, Spectrum Books, 1971), p. 170.
2. "Women as a Minority Group," in *Masculine/Feminine: Readings in Sexual Mythology and the Liberation of Women,* ed. Betty Roszak and Theodore Roszak (New York: Harper and Row, Colophon Books, 1969), pp. 130-48.
3. Amundsen, p. 120.
4. For a discussion of this pheonomenon see Judith M. Bardwick and Elizabeth Douvan, "Ambivalence: The Socialization of Women," in *Woman in Sexist Society: Studies in Power*

and Powerlessness, ed. Vivian Gornick and Barbara K. Moran (New York: New American Library, Signet Books, 1971), pp. 238-39.

5. "The Compassion Trap," in *Woman in Sexist Society,* p. 561.

6. "Cultural Contradictions and Sex Roles: The Masculine Case," in *Changing Women in a Changing Society,* ed. Joan Huber (Chicago and London: University of Chicago Press, 1973), pp. 111-22.

7. For an excellent overview of the arguments for and against ERA see Judith Hole and Ellen Levine, *Rebirth of Feminism* (New York: Quadrangle Books/New York Times Co., 1971), pp. 54-77.

8. For a discussion of sociological concepts of power relative to this point see Clarice Stasz Stoll, *Female and Male: Socialization, Social Roles, and Social Structure* (Dubuque, Iowa: Wm. C. Brown, 1974), pp. 204-207.

9. *Patriarchal Attitudes* (Greenwich, Conn.: Fawcett, Premier Books, 1970), pp. 47-48.

10. For more information on legal discrimination see Leo Kanowitz, *Women and the Law: The Unfinished Revolution* (Albuquerque, N.M.: University of New Mexico Press, 1969).

11. Janet Saltzman Chafetz, *Masculine/Feminine or Human?: An Overview of the Sociology of Sex Roles* (Itasca, Ill.: F. E. Peacock, 1974), p. 59. For an extended discussion of the costs of sex roles see pp. 54-56.

12. *Women and Madness* (New York: Avon, 1972).

13. See Chafetz, pp. 165-72, for an excellent discussion of the implications of only partially internalized sex roles in marriage.

14. P. 195.

15. "Companionate Marriages and Sexual Inequality: Are They Compatible?," in *Toward a Sociology of Women,* ed. Constantina Safilios-Rothschild (Lexington, Mass.: Xerox, 1972), pp. 63-70.

16. In terms of breaking up families, let us not ignorantly accuse the ERA while blinding ourselves to certain present discriminatory laws like welfare, which embody the man-provider, woman-homemaker-mother fantasy of male legislators, assigning roles and benefits accordingly. Even discounting the actual discrimination involved, the effect of such laws has often been to drive the unemployed father from the home, since only his absence, not his mere unemployment, is assumed to necessitate support. While the AFDC law was extended in 1961 to provide federal support for *intact* families with a temporarily unemployed parent (later amended to preclude the mother from qualification), fewer that half of the states have adopted this program. Here is a concrete example of the way in which equality will preserve the family, not destroy it.

17. "Radical Feminism 1," in *Radical Feminism,* ed. Anne Koedt, Ellen Levine, and Anita Rapone (New York: Quadrangle/The New Times Book Co., 1973), p. 235.

18. Elizabeth M. Havens, "Women, Work, and Wedlock: A Note on Female Marital Patterns in the United States," in *Changing Women in a Changing Society,* pp. 213-19.

19. Saul D. Feldman, "Impediment or Stimulant? Marital Status and Graduate Education," in *Changing Women in a Changing Society,* pp. 220-32.

20. Marianne A. Ferber and Jane W. Loeb, "Performance, Rewards, and Perceptions of Sex Discrimination among Male and Female Faculty," in *Changing Women in a Changing Society,* pp. 233-40.

21. Stasz Stoll, p. 181.

22. Ibid., p. 191.

23. P. 222.

24. P. 234.

25. Introduction to *Woman in Sexist Society,* p. xxx.

26. *The Second Sex,* tr. and ed. H. M. Parshley (New York: Bantam Books, 1961), p. 688.

27. *Toward a Recognition of Androgyny* (New York: Harper and Row, Colophon Books, 1974), p. x.

POLITICAL IMPACT

Introduction to Political Impact

Our analysis of the political impact of the ERA has two dimensions: first, the degree of its efficacy in the political arena, and second, the nature of its projected effect on the political system itself. Its political limitations, the obstacles to its implementation, threaten to negate the possibilities of ERA impact in any arena. Implementation in the political sphere is not a matter of adjustment; it is a matter of *affirmative* action, without which the ERA will remain merely an unrealized mandate for change. In other words, this section assesses the ERA as a political instrument for legal change, recognizing that it is only a tool, not the finely chiseled new world.

There are, generally, three levels of governmental legal procedure: constitutional amendments, laws, and the regulations and guidelines which enforce the laws. Implementation is problematic at all levels. On the first level, the ERA provides legal recourse for the challenge of discriminatory laws and practices in the courts; on the second level, it requires discriminattory laws to be rewritten. These are, then, the two major sources of constitutional amendment implementation: congressional legislation and judicial interpretation and enforcement. ERA impact is limited or made possible by the degree of cooperation of these two branches of government.

On the third level of implementation we are dealing not with changes in the law to conform to the ERA but with the implementation of the laws themselves. There are already antidiscrimination laws on the books, e.g., Equal Pay Act, Title VII of the Civil Rights Act, Title IX of the Education Acts Amendment, Executive Order 11246, yet that is where they have largely remained—on the books. They have not effectively realized equality because they have not been properly implemented. Either proper regulations and guidelines have not been formulated by administrators of the laws or, once formulated, they have not been enforced. Consequently, the disobedience of the regulated group may not be effectively censured or altered, either through lack of appropriate power or lack of will on the part of the administrators of the laws. Without effective implementation, the best intentioned laws remain merely tokens; moreover, without the intense efforts of those outside the legislative and administrative process to realize full implementation, those tokens will become icons of tradition and,

19

ironically, virtual impediments to progress.

Mary C. Dunlap takes up the judicial component of ERA implementation. She considers the projections for and anticipates the obstacles posed by judicial ERA interpretation. While the ERA is a supposedly definitive constitutional statement, the human relativity involved in judicial enforcement and its dependence on attitudinal socialization and psychological resistance or openness boggles the imagination. ERA is hardly as clear-cut as it appears on the surface and as proponents of equality would like it to be; even as opponents insist that it is.

Dale Rogers Marshall and Janell Anderson deal with the political realities of ERA implementation on the level of legislation. They show how the political structure as well as individual circumvention strategies militate against proper implementation and, therefore, impact. Their emphasis is on what can be done to minimize these effects by people outside of the political process itself.

With these two articles, then, we have a double-barreled assessment of the legislative and judicial limitations of the ERA as an instrument to rewrite laws, to create new ones, and to challenge old laws and behaviors in the courts. The political road to actually implementing equality is a long one. The struggle will merely begin with ratification. But perhaps the ERA is only "limited" in the context of unnecessarily high expectations. A realistic appraisal of the ERA's potential efficacy should not produce disappointment and resignation but stimulate creativity in forging it as a weapon for legal and social change.

Jo Freeman really combines both perspectives (reservation and expectation) as she defines the resources of the present political context which can accomplish effective implementation of the ERA. Like Marshall and Anderson, she emphasizes the gap between the written commitment and political-behavioral enforcement, recognizing the need for outside pressure to make the word act. She goes on to speculate about the effect that the ERA struggle has had on women's political expertise and its implications for their political future once ratification insures their fuller participation in the system. Further, Dr. Freeman anticipates the possible effects of this equal participation on the political system itself, the second dimension of the ERA's political impact, made possible only by the minimization of its limitations.

Given the political limitations of the ERA, it is unrealistic for its opponents to fear revolutionary change, but if it is used effectively, ERA will produce beneficial change for society and improve the very political system of which it is the product. Reciprocity of impact is perhaps the keynote of our theme. And it is for this reason that fear of ERA change is incongruous with its possible but limited impact thoughtfully delineated by our authors.

We look forward to a political system in which a woman's vote, as one echo of her political voice, will no longer be meaningless, in which Sandra and Daryl Bem's comment will no longer be true, to wit, that

> the society that has spent twenty years carefully marking the woman's ballot for her has nothing to lose in that twenty-first year by pretending to let her cast it for the alternative of her choice. Society has controlled not her alternatives, but her motivation to choose any but the one of those alternatives.[1]

Yet, it is obvious from the very terms in which this statement is cast that ERA alone cannot alter this political misfortune; it is one weapon in an arsenal to be used with and controlled by social approval, and that includes society at large as well as its army of legislators, judges, and administrators.

Footnotes

1. "Training the Woman to Know Her Place: The Power of a Nonconscious Ideology," in *Roles Women Play: Readings Toward Women's Liberation,* ed. Michele Hoffnung Garskof (Belmont, Ca.: Brooks/Cole Pub. Co., 1971), pp. 88-89.

The Equal Rights Amendment and the Courts

Mary C. Dunlap

INTRODUCTION

In our constitutional system, law is not retrievable from a series of stone tablets containing unambiguous formulae by which every dispute is to be resolved and all conduct governed. This misconception about law pulses throughout many angry disputes concerning the Equal Rights Amendment; numerous arguments about the Amendment assume that, once written upon the Constitution, the principle of "equality of rights" without regard to sex will have a fixed, certain, and virtually immutable definition, to be applied to the variegated forms of our future.

Oppositely, interpretation of that principle promises to be a process at least as complex and difficult as any process by which other fundamental constitutional changes have been wrought, in the interaction between law and society. How long any stage of this particular process may take cannot be readily gauged. The processes of change accompanying other significant constitutional amendments (e.g., First Amendment freedoms of speech, press, and religion, Fourteenth Amendment due process and equal protection) remain unfinished today. Also, the idea of "completing" a guarantee of basic rights, for all time, cannot be reconciled with the essence of human life—invention, creativity, and struggle (or, put simply, motion).

Close to the erroneous proposition that the Equal Rights Amendment will soon acquire a clear, concrete meaning in our legal system is the deeply naïve assumption that "equality" is a status which can be successfully and justly bestowed upon persons, or upon rights of persons. Yet this notion of "magic wand equality" poses great dangers; those who wish for rapid, easy eradication of sex-based discrimination share, with those who do not care

22

about the problem, a susceptibility to the facile view that the Equal Rights Amendment will operate automatically.

Along with the attributions of certainty and automatic effectiveness to the principle of equality of rights of men and women goes the attribution of uniform judicial treatment of the Amendment. When it is considered that our judicial system has never been and is not today in agreement about the meaning of "equality," and when we recognize that the system affords a continuous tug-of-war among courts, within courts, and over time, it becomes obvious that the Equal Rights Amendment will yield tentative, experimental and sometimes self-contradictory results long before it can yield hard-and-fast solutions. This is not to say that some cases will not be rather promptly decided concerning the Amendment's meaning; neither is this to say that a large measure of seeming certainty will not be contributed to the meaning of the Amendment by initial Supreme Court decisions. Rather, it is only necessary to remain aware, in any analysis of the Amendment in relation to the courts, that conflicts within the judicial system about "equality" must necessarily lead to setbacks and stalemates in the processes of giving life to the Equal Rights Amendment.

At the center of the relationship between our courts and the Equal Rights Amendment lies a paradox: American judges and lawyers, having been a major cause of sex-based discrimination under law, will hold a major share in the power to decide whether, and by what means, the Equal Rights Amendment will guide us through the eradication of a sex discriminatory legal system and through the creation of a nondiscriminatory one. The proposition that American judges and lawyers have been primary in the development of a dual arrangement of law regarding male and female is not meant to recriminate, but to describe: court decisions, postures of advocacy, and applications of law that have drawn or accepted arbitrary, ignorant, and nonindividualized distinctions between male and female have contributed directly to the growth and perpetuation of a sex-differential legal process. It is these self-same steps of advocacy and judicial decision making that will serve, in the interpretation of the Equal Rights Amendment, either to preserve or to overturn the basic duality through which women and men are viewed and treated under law.

This article is premised upon the idea that attempts to predict and to affect judicial handling of the Equal Rights Amendment will become more effective and reliable once a working understanding is gained of the stimuli toward and inhibitions against equality of the sexes that currently (and historically) shape our judicial system. This article seeks to contribute to that working understanding.

I. THE U.S. SUPREME COURT AND THE
EQUAL RIGHTS AMENDMENT

A. Overview: Supreme Court Decision Making as the Law of the Land

This constitution and the laws of the United States which shall be made
in pursuance thereof; and all treaties . . . *shall be the supreme law of the
land;* and the judges in every state shall be bound thereby, any thing in
the constitution or laws of any state to the contrary notwithstanding.
(emphasis added)

U.S. Const. Art. VI.

The Equal Rights Amendment places the principle that "equality of rights
under law shall not be denied or abridged. . . on account of sex" in the
highest and most powerful form available in our system of laws. As an
amendment to the Constitution, that principle is proposed to be located at the
top of the hierarchy, in the company of other principles which, in theory,
guide or control the entire operation of law in the United States.

At the top of the human hierarchy that corresponds with the supremacy
doctrine sit the nine decision makers of the United States Supreme Court:
these are the final arbiters of federal constitutional controversies.[1] In this
theoretical sense it can be fairly asserted that the Supreme Court will
constitute the single most important interpreter of the Equal Rights Amendment.

However, awareness of the primacy of the Supreme Court's interpreter
role in relation to the Equal Rights Amendment must be tempered by
realization of the procedural, political, and psychological limitations upon
that role. The Supreme Court hears and decides only a fraction of the cases
in which its complete review is sought. The length, contents, and emphases
of the Court's docket are mightily affected by these procedural, political,
and psychological limitations upon Supreme Court review.

To illustrate the significance of this operational truth in predicting the
course of the Equal Rights Amendment, let us imagine that cases involving
the Amendment, in which the Supreme Court's review is sought, are darts
thrown at a target. The target is ringed by procedural restrictions (e.g., the
Court will not hear most cases), political inhibitions (e.g., the Court will
avoid handling certain "hot potatoes") and psychological constraints (e.g.,
the Court will resist hearing particular matters which frighten, anger, or bore
it). Of course, the metaphor of a single target with distinct rings is
oversimple. Procedural limitations are sometimes infused with political and
psychological ones (e.g., the recent case of *DeFunis v. Odegaard,*[2] which
raised the question of the constitutionality of affirmative action styled law

school admissions policy, was found inappropriate for review because it was deemed "moot"). Also, the Court is frequently divided within itself as to appropriate limitations upon its docket. Finally, the procedural, political and psychological barriers to Supreme Court review are subject to change. In these ways, the Supreme Court's standards for selection of cases are enshrouded in a kind of irresolvable and continuous mystery.

Thus, trying to predict whether a particular case will "activate" the interpretive powers of the Supreme Court is not unlike attempting to decide whether a single dart will hit the center of nine moving targets. In situations where the targets tend to take up positions upon a discoverable straight line, prediction is facilitated; otherwise, the level of guesswork in estimating the polarities and priorities of the Court is extreme.

There are very few senses in which the present Supreme Court is in substantial internal agreement. From the newly flourishing practice of dissenting opinions taken from refusals to hear cases,[3] it is fair to say that the Court is severely divided within itself as to the occasions and issues which should afford its review. At least one of the Justices, namely William H. Rehnquist, has declared openly[4] that he views the need of the Supreme Court to limit its jurisdiction as a pressing priority. Of course, the dispute concerning the volume of the Court's caseload has a lengthy history. Justice William O. Douglas has written upon the question several times over the years, and historians will quickly recollect that the ostensible basis of Franklin D. Roosevelt's "court-packing" strategy lay in the declared need to increase Supreme Court personnel to meet the growing caseload of the '30s.

The future outcomes of this dispute concerning the availability of Supreme Court review in constitutional cases may have a critical bearing upon the course of the Equal Rights Amendment. To the extent that the Supreme Court resolves to impose further limitations upon the cases that it will hear, it is possible that Equal Rights Amendment cases will receive short shrift in the process of priority setting.

It has been widely observed that, in the 1970s, and under the influence of former President Nixon's Supreme Court nominees in particular, a period of conservatism and retrenchment in the Court has begun. Some observers go further, describing the Burger Court as actively engaged in the dismantling of personal rights and governmental and institutional responsibilities which were established or illuminated in Warren Court decisions. Under either view, the probability is greatly diminished that the Burger Court will engage in vigorous, demanding articulation of the principle embodied in the Equal Rights Amendment, at least to the degree that such articulation requires so-called judicial activism.

On the other hand, the Supreme Court since 1971 has heard and decided a considerable number of constitutional challenges to sex-differential laws and actions;[5] the proportion of Supreme Court time spent upon these questions in the 1970s appears substantially greater than the proportion of such time spent by earlier courts. While this change is probably better explained by reference to factors other than that of judicial activism focused upon sex discrimination (i.e., legal strategies of the Women's Movement, increasing numbers of women in the legal profession, elevated and simultaneously reactionary social consciousness about the wrongfulness of a dual system of laws), the indication that the Supreme Court today is far readier to hear and decide certain sex discrimination cases cannot be ignored.

Needless to say, this quantitative and structural perspective upon the Supreme Court misses much. Without examination of the reasoning and the results of Supreme Court decisions, the possible directions of the Court concerning the Equal Rights Amendment cannot be sketched. At the same time, in the process of examining the contents of relevant decisions for trends and leanings, an eye must be left open to the bearing of the operational politics of the Supreme Court, as a bureaucracy, upon the demands of the Equal Rights Amendment. Matters such as the number of cases the Court can and will hear and the degree of accessibility of the Court generally will influence the contents and consequences of Supreme Court decision making about the Equal Rights Amendment over time.

B. An Historical Perspective: The Equal Rights Amendment in Constitutional Context

1. Felix Frankfurter as an Example

> Lawyers, with rare exceptions, have failed to lay bare that the law of the Supreme Court is enmeshed in the country's history; historians no less have seemed to miss the fact that the country's history is enmeshed in the law of the Supreme Court.

> The history of the Supreme Court is not the history of an abstraction, but the analysis of individuals acting as a Court who make decisions and lay down doctrines, and of other individuals, their successors, who refine, modify and sometimes even overrule the decisions of their predecessors, reinterpreting and transmuting their doctrines.
>
>   Felix Frankfurter,
>   Law and Politics

It is nothing but profoundly ironic that the words of the late and eminent jurist Felix Frankfurter should open this section. Perhaps, of all men who ever served on the U.S. Supreme Court Justice Frankfurter worked hardest to demystify and to give popular, progressive consciousness to and about the Supreme Court; and, of all the men who have ever served on the U.S. Supreme Court, Justice Frankfurter wrote and acted in the most reactionary and philosophically incongruous way concerning the legal status of women.

A brief analysis of Frankfurter's views is offered here as a demonstrative example of the falsity of the common notion that liberalism necessarily correlates positively with respect for the ideal of equality of rights. Exposure of the untruth of this notion is crucial to an understanding of the possible irrelevance of the patent nonliberalism of the Burger Court's majority to the initial fate of the Equal Rights Amendment.

Throughout the hardest fought battles of Mr. Justice Frankfurter's career runs a strong theme—dedication to the ideals of economic fairness and active governmental regulation of the greedy, the landed gentry, and the corrupt. Within this theme come many subthemes, including zealous safeguarding and articulation of the need for labor unions, dedicated spokesmanship for social welfare activism, and a continuing insistence upon making law comprehensible to the People.

At the same time that Felix Frankfurter gave incomparable zeal and energy to writing about the plight of such victims as Sacco and Vanzetti and the Scottsboro Boys and to vindicating social welfare interests of the People, Felix Frankfurter called himself "a parochial Harvard man."[6] That description denies too much and too little. The parochial influence of Harvard upon Frankfurter barely shows in many domains of his life and action; on the question of women's rights, the influence is obtrusive. Like Harvard itself, a pinnacle of American elitism and a center of American genius and creativity, Frankfurter himself, in 1948, declared that "(the States may) draw . . . a sharp line between the sexes"[7] and, further, that

> the Constitution does not require legislatures to reflect sociological insight, or shifting social standards, any more than it requires them to keep abreast of the latest scientific standards,[8]

thus deciding that Michigan could constitutionally prohibit women from being bartenders.

The opinion of Justice Frankfurter in *Goesaert v. Cleary*[9] has frequently been cited and discussed as a point upon the linear tradition of a separate legal and constitutional place for women.[10] Yet this decision is perhaps far more significant than a mere point on the line for purposes of assessing the potential relationship of the Constitution as a whole to the Equal Rights Amendment.

At stake in virtually every constitutional case is a multitude of conflicting political interests. Judicial decisions vary with regard to the quantum of

candor with which judges call these conflicting interests by their proper, or
at least recognizable, names. In *Goesaert v. Cleary*,[11] a record had been
made below the Supreme Court, showing the motive beneath the anti-
female-bartender legislation; an all male labor union, seeking to get and to
keep jobs for its members, had lobbied for the legislation. Mr. Justice
Frankfurter took note of this aspect of the record, saying:

> [W]e cannot give ear to the suggestion that the real impulse behind this
> legislation was an unchivalrous desire of male bartenders to try to
> monopolize the calling.

Unchivalrous for whom, indeed? Surely the Court itself was being "unchivalrous" to the women in Michigan seeking bartending jobs in a postwar
labor market swamped by returning veterans. But let us not pick nits.

What is most strikingly germane to the present discourse was Mr.
Frankfurter's willingness to discard evidence of economic greed and high-
handedness in deciding the case of *Goesaert*. This action, or affirmative
inaction, runs firmly contrary to the position of a man who had often
criticized Taft[12] and Coolidge[13] for their blindness and praised Brandeis[14]
and Holmes[15] for their vision in bringing facts, underlying socioeconomic
realities, and pure, frank sensitivity to *life* into judicial processes.

To go deeper, the crux of Mr. Justice Frankfurter's resolution of competing interests in *Goesaert* lay in his lack of dedication to the ideal of equality
of rights, insofar as women are concerned. As a result, the power of unions
and state government to squeeze women out of jobs was (tacitly)
strengthened by law, and the right of women to equal employment opportunity was left constitutionally defenseless. It should be remembered at this
point that it was Mr. Justice Frankfurter who had actively rebuked the
Supreme Court for its decision of 1936 refusing to uphold a state minimum
wage law "for women workers obviously incapable of economic
self-protection."[16]

In light of Frankfurter's own conduct in the *Goesaert*[17] decision, the
conclusion is justified that his criticism of the 1936 decision of the Supreme
Court did not spring from a mighty dedication to the cause of equalizing the
economic power of women. Indeed, Mr. Justice Frankfurter had either never
believed that such an end was possible or worthwhile, or he had *lost* this
spirit at some point. When Frankfurter wrote of the philosophical, political,
and ethical world, he spoke in terms of "men"; when he wrote of workers,
he often used the words "men and women." Perhaps one might find an
explanation for Frankfurter's *Goesaert* decision in his long-standing preoccupation with the need for unions. But where, as of *Goesaert,* did Mr.

Justice Frankfurter's priorities lead? The *Goesaert* opinion should be read as a whole; its tone of mocking women, whose interests Mr. Frankfurter professed to deserve "special" protection, rings loud inside the mind.

As mentioned at the outset, Felix Frankfurter's views have been used here to illuminate the grave distortion involved in assuming a connection between liberalism and concern for human equality. The Aesop's moral of this story, no part of which should be read as an attack upon the person or greatness of Frankfurter himself (for that would be both silly and useless), is this: the Equal Rights Amendment cannot be assumed to have a safer, happier fate in the hands of liberals than in the hands of any other politically identifiable group.

As long as the fundamental priorities of the Supreme Court—whether led by conservatives, liberals or otherwise—do not change to include a strong and self-critical attempt to overcome the basic ambivalence with which women are viewed in the law ("we must protect women; we must protect ourselves from women; but women deserve equality"), the fate of the principle of equal rights will be shallow and, possibly, tragic.

2. The Equal Rights Amendment within the Constitution as a Whole

At a given time, some parts of the Constitution are substantially more ambiguous, controversial, lucid, or insignificant than others. Moreover, a clause may be interpreted by the Supreme Court to mean something quite different than it meant earlier or will mean later. The late Chief Justice Earl Warren was asked, in 1971, why the Court decided *Brown v. Board of Education of Topeka* as it did; he looked up, almost alarmed at the simplicity of the question as he saw it, and answered, "Why, because of the Fourteenth Amendment—because of equal protection of the laws." The equal protection clause, whose meaning in the present century has seen dramatic shifts and counter-shifts in and through the interpretative processes of the Supreme Court, hardly seems so self-explanatory; nevertheless, there was a look of pure inspiration and confidence on the Chief Justice's face when he gave his answer.

In reference to individual or personal rights, the term "equal" occurs only once[18] in the Constitution. The Fourteenth Amendment (section 1) reads in pertinent part:

> No State shall . . . deny to any person within its jurisdiction the *equal* protection of the laws. (emphasis added)

It would be an understatement to observe that current Supreme Court definitions of what constitutes a denial of equal protection are confusing and internally contradictory. The business of projecting the course of today's Supreme Court as to equal protection appears to be a logical never-never land. Chaotic or not, the past, present, and future scope and limits of equal protection will have profound effects upon interpretation of the Equal Rights Amendment. This is because the equal protection experiences of America represent an ultimate and central struggle in our system between person and government, between subgroup and government, and between individual and legal category. Also, political and judicial clashes concerning equal protection have formed precedents, shaped approaches, and revealed biases and beliefs about equality that ratification of the Equal Rights Amendment, by itself, can neither dissolve nor reconcile.

The pulsebeat of equal protection history pounds audibly in the debate that has accompanied the Equal Rights Amendment across the states. One person's call to freedom is another's cry of fear; the threat of endangered family, womanhood and manhood here is the promise of human renascence there. At the same time, the Equal Rights Amendment represents a frontal assault upon equal protection history and its consequences. The women of all colors who organized to pass the Fourteenth Amendment, in and before 1868, walked away voteless, and the U.S. Supreme Court found no force in the claims of equal protection denied—on behalf of women—until 1971. Thus, support for the Equal Rights Amendment on the basis that equal protection will not otherwise be afforded to all persons regardless of sex has become a common theme of legalist proponents.

Yet the provocative realization that the historic and continuing anomalies, promises, and dangers of equal protection are bound to affect judicial interpretation of "equality of rights" pursuant to the Twenty-seventh Amendment should not overshadow other sources of constitutional insight upon the principle.

The Nineteenth Amendment reads:

> The right of citizens of the United States to vote shall not be denied or abridged by the United States or by any State on account of sex.

Whether the Supreme Court will draw guidance in its task from the Nineteenth Amendment, the working clauses of which are identical to the Equal Rights Amendment, remains to be discovered. In a logical world, the conclusion that the Nineteenth Amendment should bear strongly upon interpretation of the Twenty-seventh would be irresistible, for the principle is logically inescapable that the parts of the Constitution must be read to work as an harmonious whole. But, like equal protection, if the Nineteenth Amendment serves as a legal touchstone to the Supreme Court, it too may serve as a political one. Early hyperliteral readings of female suffrage kept women out of office and out of the courts.[19] If you do not believe that "equality of rights under law" leaves room for such politically inspired tunnel vision as that by which the Nineteenth Amendment was first read, then please look again.

C. A Psychological View: The Supreme Court and "Women"

When we examine U.S. Supreme Court decisions concerning "women," we frequently see the Court in its most societally reflective position. At least to the extent that American culture is ambivalent toward the "female," the U.S. Supreme Court has often behaved likewise. But perhaps the Court has gone further. The conflicting state of constitutional law concerning women has now reached a stage of virtual irresolvability which will continue until and unless the Equal Rights Amendment is ratified and is interpreted by the Court to guide impartial and rigorous reexamination of the current legal images of "male" and "female."

In 1971, for the first time since 1868 when the Fourteenth Amendment was ratified, the Court found within the equal protection clause a limited prohibition of discrimination by state government against women in *Reed v. Reed.*[20] *Reed* held that a state law preferring males over females as administrators of estates was inconsistent with the guarantee of equal protection. The *Reed* decision was widely heralded as a step upon the long road toward legal equality of persons regardless of sex.

Yet the seeds of the current jungle, now grown up in the form of Supreme Court decisions since *Reed* concerning constitutional rights of men and women, were beginning to sprout in the reasoning of the *Reed* Court. In another view the jungle preexisted *Reed,* and the Supreme Court's few scythelike strokes in *Reed* could not cut back the confusion in any lasting way.

After the *Reed* decision, the standard for measuring a deprivation of equal protection based upon sex remained ambiguous: the test requiring only that government should show an *acceptable* reason for its sex-based line-drawing was left standing alongside the "new" test that government should show a *substantial connection* between sex-based line-drawing in a law and the end to be accomplished by that law. Needless to say, this confusion as to the proper standard for equal protection of the sexes has permitted havoc in the "harder" cases decided by the Court since *Reed.*

Tacit in the Supreme Court's decision of *Reed v. Reed* was an awareness within the Court that the standard used to measure equal protection vis-à-vis women was neither a potentially strong standard nor a new one. In the decision of *Frontiero v. Richardson,*[21] this tacit awareness became an overt dispute. The majority in *Frontiero* held that the armed services' presumption of the economic dependency of wives, for purposes of greater allowances to married service*men*, denied equal protection to service*women*, whose spouses were not presumed dependent. But there was no majority of the Court in *Frontiero* as to the proper standard for measuring denials of equal protection to persons on account of sex.

Justices Brennan, Douglas, White, and Marshall took the position that sex, like race, alienage, and national origin, amounts to a suspect category which, when used in legal line-drawing, gives rise to classifications that the courts must scrutinize strictly; or, put a bit more simply, that legal lines based upon sex are justifiable by government only if it can show that a *compelling* governmental interest is served and can only, or best, be served by the drawing of a sex-based line.

In *Frontiero,* Justice Stewart simply did not agree to this standard, but he agreed that the result was necessitated by the logic of *Reed.* Justice Rehnquist alone disagreed with the result, determining that the military benefits scheme did not deny equal protection.

The concurring opinion of Chief Justice Burger and Justices Powell and Blackmun took the position that: (1) the decision in *Reed* "abundantly supports"[22] the judgment that the military benefits scheme denied equal protection, and (2) the position of Douglas, Marshall, Brennan, and White, declaring "sex" a legally suspect category, improperly preempted the state legislatures' political consideration of the Equal Rights Amendment. The latter suggestion of this concurring opinion is informative indeed, for it indicates that three members of the Court view the issue of the Equal Rights Amendment as follows: in considering the Equal Rights Amendment, the states will be deciding whether sex, like race, alienage, and national origin, *must* be viewed as a suspect category when used in the law to draw a line. For Chief Justice Burger and Justices Powell and Blackmun, there is no escape from the proposition that "hard" cases questioning sex discrimination by law cannot be decided without "political interference" by the Court until 1979.[23]

Several cases raising or containing questions about the constitutionality of sex-based line-drawing have been decided by the Court since *Frontiero.*[24] It is unnecessary to discuss them all in order to grasp the tangled mess in which issues of assuring equal protection to the sexes are now located. One decision since *Frontiero* deserves particular attention in the search for psychological clues as to the current leanings of the Supreme Court where "women" are concerned.

In the case of *Kahn v. Shevin,*[25] a Florida law granting an annual $500 tax exemption to widows was upheld by the Court against the challenge that it denied equal protection to widowers, who received no such exemption. Justice Douglas' opinion in *Kahn* shows the vitality of the theme, running throughout Supreme Court decisions of this century, that women must be specially protected in economic terms because of their relative economic weakness *as a class*. The decision in *Kahn* cites the 1908 decision of *Muller v. Oregon*[26] in support of the proposition that "(g)ender has never been rejected as an impermissible classification in all instances."[27] The decision of *Muller* was greeted by many in its time as a highly progressive, sensitive decision which took cognizance of physical and social data depicting the economic weakness of women (through a famous Brandeis brief) in order to uphold protective laws limiting the work hours of females.

By its decision in *Kahn*,[28] the majority of the Court indicated its continuing disposition to afford women *special* protection suited to their class-wide, generalized need for legally created economic "cushions." The trade-off for these "cushions" has tended to be the inability (and the expectation of inability) of masses of women to provide for themselves in economic terms—or, put simply, economic dependency of women upon men and economic vulnerability to sex-based discrimination. In psychological terms, *Kahn* reinforces a notion that "women" can properly and justly be viewed as a separate, special class under law, provided that the law in question can somehow be interpreted to "benefit" women. The resulting standard of "equal protection" as to women is age-old in Supreme Court terms: if government can convince at least five Supreme Court Justices that its sex-based lines "benefit" women, as the government did in *Bradwell*,[29] *Muller*,[30] *Goesaert*,[31] *Hoyt*,[32] *Kahn*,[33] and *Ballard*,[34] the sex-based lines in question will be held valid for equal protection purposes.

The recency and authorship of *Kahn*, written in 1974 by William O. Douglas, a Justice who has been particularly vigilant in some cases involving sex-based discrimination,[35] indicate the depth of the Supreme Court's psychological ambivalence concerning "women" and, in particular, the struggle between advocates of full equality and advocates of the natural or immutable specialness of women. What the Court's opinion in *Kahn* says, in the face of this struggle, is that equal protection of the laws may or may not be found to be denied in a given situation involving differential rights of men and women depending upon whether the purpose and/or effect of a particular sex-based line is considered by the judicial majority to be "good" for women.

The dangers of this standard are as dual as the legal system that it has perpetuated. First, what may be considered "good" for women as a weaker class may actually operate to condone and perpetuate that class-wide proneness to weakness by judicial sanction. Second, what may be considered "good" for women as a class may, like the Florida tax exemption scheme, give actual benefits only to women who are wealthy enough to acquire them, while having no actual benefits for poor women, and having detrimental effects upon the positions and attitudes of men, rich and poor alike.

Kahn cannot safely be viewed as a residual, insignificant glance backward at the Supreme Court's fading tintype of the "little woman." *Kahn* and other decisions of the Court from *Bradwell*[36] on must be exhaustively analyzed for their political, psychological, and legal portents concerning Supreme Court readings of the Equal Rights Amendment. If the process of interpreting the Amendment is affected whatsoever by the psychology of the Court concerning "women," then these ancient, current pictures of wives, widows, pregnant women, and soldiers must be regarded just as cautiously as the images of equality hypothetically traced on the brains of the Court by the abstract pen of a constitutional amendment.

II. FEDERAL-STATE JUDICIAL RELATIONSHIPS

A. "States' Rights" Controversies Affecting the Equal Rights Amendment

One considerable source of ideological resistance to the Equal Rights Amendment, in ratification debates particularly, has gathered within the circle of opposition to the federalization of power. As one opponent put the matter, "I don't want to see the federal government enforcing a view that I may be adamantly opposed to."[37]

At present, the Equal Rights Amendment has been attacked with a vehemence bordering upon panicky hatred by a number of reactionary[38] and radical[39] organizations alike for its purported potential for federal invasions of privacy, freedom of religion, states' rights to control marriage, divorce, homosexuality, recreation, and other subjects of state police power. Howsoever lightly these attributions of threatened federal power-grabbing are taken by the cool observer, the repetition of this theme in state-level Equal Rights Amendment debates foretells certain problems that await lawsuits based upon the Amendment, once these reach the federal judicial system.

As with the Supreme Court, the question of what federal trial and appellate courts will do in the interpretation of the Equal Rights Amendment must be preceded by the question, *what suits based upon the Equal Rights Amendment will federal district courts elect to hear?* It is quite possible that some federal district courts will await specific Congressional action concerning their jurisdiction (translate: power) to hear Equal Rights Amendment-based suits before they take on the managerial, political, and legal rigors of these actions. It is also quite possible that, by reference to doctrines such as abstention, federal district courts will elect to duck "hard" cases, whether or not Congress sets up orderly procedures for the federal judicial disposition of Equal Rights Amendment-based disputes.

In front of federal judges who find the "abstention" position persuasive, believing that the state courts should rule first upon the constitutionality of state laws called into question under the Amendment, the process of federal judicial decision making upon the Amendment may be surprisingly slow. In this manner, it is predictable that some quite significant litigation will be swallowed up by the time-consuming, expensive process of state-level litigation.

The point of all of these predictions is simple: to the extent that there is resistance in the federal courts to making room for the hearing of Equal Rights Amendment cases, whether such resistance arises from political biases, financial and managerial considerations of the federal courts, or other sources, the business of getting federal courts to hear and decide Equal Rights Amendment-related cases promises to be an uphill battle.

An unavoidable political observation must accompany this prediction about bureaucratic resistance of the federal courts, as institutions, to the increased workload promised by ratification of the Equal Rights Amendment. The Amendment states in section 2:

> The Congress shall have the power to enforce, by appropriate legislation, the provisions of this article.

Congress' action will be prerequisite to the realization of federal judicial enforcement and elaboration of the Equal Rights Amendment's principle. If Congressional legislation providing money, resources, and explicit declarations of judicial power to the federal courts is not forthcoming upon ratification of the Amendment, it is highly probable that the role of the federal courts in giving meaning to the Equal Rights Amendment will fall very short of its potential, to the apparent glee of the John Birch Society and the Communist Party alike.[40]

B. Pinpointing Regional Resistances to Equal Rights Amendment Implementation: The Patchwork Quilt of the Sexist Tradition

In the phenomenally controversial ratification process, a kind of patchwork quilt of anti-Amendment regions has emerged. These regions hardly compose a geographic "North and South" of sexism, but their emergence nonetheless suggests areas in which resistance to the Equal Rights Amendment will prove resilient upon and after its ratification. Once the Amendment is ratified, every state as well as the federal government has been given a two-year period in which to clean sexism out of its legal house, front yard and backyard alike.

In terms of the depth and pervasiveness of various legal forms of denial and abridgment of equal rights to men and women, even if the measure of these forms is Congress' limited accounts,[41] it is indisputable that two years will prove too short a time for thoughtful, deep-reaching implementation of the Amendment. More broadly, because legally created and protected forms of sex discrimination are not all to be caught in the "he" and "she" of the codes, and because the denial and abridgment of equal rights occurs as readily at the levels of official discretion, written regulations, county ordinances, and individual conduct by government officials as it does at the level of black-and-white state law, the two-year period subsequent to ratification cannot sanely be viewed as the main stage of Equal Rights Amendment implementation. For states now refusing to ratify the Amendment, the two-year period may be spent in continuing tactics of opposition.

Ideally, the federal courts are free of the regionalism that defines states; in practice, the degree to which federal courts avoid regionalism turns powerfully upon the political and personal independence of the federal judiciary and the people that work with it—lawyers, court reporters, clerks, marshals, and others. However, the fact remains that there are whole states in this country where competent federal civil rights lawyers are virtually impossible to find and where the judiciary, howsoever independent, sometimes suffers accordingly.

If the U.S. Department of Justice, state attorney generals' offices, and public interest attorneys consider Equal Rights Amendment litigation as anything less than a necessity on the path to human freedom, it is hardly arguable that judges, with rare exceptions, will tend to do likewise. In regions where the cause of the Equal Rights Amendment has proved particularly unpopular, the need will be extreme for informed lawyers and open-minded judges to give their efforts to the process of making the Amendment meaningful.

III. PREDICTIVE SKETCHES OF
JUDICIAL INTERPRETATION OF THE EQUAL RIGHTS AMENDMENT

A. The Courts as Refined Political Animals

What should "equality of rights" mean? Equality has been a prime subject for major philosophical works throughout the centuries, and the matter of equality of the sexes has often been an articulate part of this theme.[42]

At the outset, it is worth noting that the focus of the Amendment is upon equality of rights under law and *not* upon equality of persons nor upon the equality of men and women. This feature of the Amendment makes the "vive la difference" school of opponents, with its emphasis upon the biological identifiability of the sexes as a form of "proof" that equality is impracticable, seem ridiculously illogical. For if it is legal rights that are to be afforded equally and *not* "different" persons who are to be made unexceptionally equal in the law, then opposition to the Amendment founded in "la difference" is nonresponsive, unless "la difference" explains why *rights* should not be afforded equally. Thus, it becomes plain that the "vive la difference" perspective carries some hidden meanings which should be unraveled before one decides to join them.

One of the subtle implications of the "la difference" position appears to be that every person can and must be defined, or at least identified, sexually; the flip side of this implication is that whenever the rules for sexual identification do not find clear-cut "males" and "females," society is endangered. Listening to the undercurrent of the argument that the Equal Rights Amendment threatens the American family, one hears this: the American family is dependent upon the inequality of rights afforded by law to men and women.

While this entire exploration of the "biological antiequality" school might at first perusal appear to be off the subject of the courts and the Amendment, it is assuredly not so. Some courts have already shown strong reactionary potentials relative to the Women's Movement, and it is predictable that readings of the Equal Rights Amendment may draw from those potentials. The "biological" school is itself founded upon this adversity, sprung from the notion that the Women's Movement and Equal Rights Amendment proponents are inseparable co-conspirators in a vast plan to castrate men, dump on housewives, steal babies to fill government day care centers, draft teenage girls, outlaw heterosexual marriage, and make everyone wear the same kind of underwear.[43] The most serious problem posed by this wild collection of reactions is that it distracts energy and attention from the work of discovering what the real hazards of the Equal

Rights Amendment process may be and reducing these risks as fully as possible. To the degree that courts are vulnerable to distraction by political extremism, whether centered upon the Women's Movement or the Amendment itself, the loss of judicial resources in the resolution of false controversies about the equality of "male" and "female" may be considerable.

As mentioned in the introduction, perhaps the most palpable hazard of Equal Rights Amendment implementation lies in the theory of "magic wand equality" that can be mistakenly read into the Amendment. This theory erroneously focuses upon equality as a *status* conferrable by law upon persons rather than as a positive *value* in the distribution and exercise of rights. By this theory, once the Amendment is ratified, the magic wand of equality will be waved over women and men once and for all. Then a hypothetical judge will be free to say, and indeed will be required to say: "Okay, you're equal now, so go out and get a job, and take over the world, since it is yours now, too."

Under this misreading of "equality," courts must resign their powers to ascertain the conditions of *individuals,* relying instead upon the assumption that the status of equality has been conferred by law upon everyone who comes before them. The "magic wand" theory of equality obviously holds an enormous potential for political backlash-style decisions. Whether it is adopted by courts that have shown a dispositional capacity for political backlash will depend upon many factors, including the initial readings of the Amendment by the Supreme Court and the style and operating definitions of equality adopted in legislation passed to implement the Amendment. The main factors, however, in the day-to-day operations of trial courts will probably be the attitudes of judges toward equality of rights, the Women's Movement, civil rights activities generally, and toward their own powers to do justice.

Flexibility is the living membrane of judicial interpretation; it is at once the source of fair results, arbitrary ones, and all that come between. To draft a law upon any subject and expect it to have only a single, reasonable meaning in all cases ignores the necessity of courts as well as their humanness.

If it is correct that the "inequality of rights" upon which the Amendment is focused has resulted from judicial processes as well as legislative ones, then to place the onus of Equal Rights Amendment implementation solely upon the legislative branch will prove markedly ineffective in the disassembling of a sex-divided legal system. The removal of inequality-producing assumptions about women and men from the legal process simply cannot be accomplished by legislative red pencils in codified law working alone.

The Courts are basic to the achievement of a legal system that does not deny or abridge rights on account of sex, not only in terms of the technical definitions of the Equal Rights Amendment that will evolve through case precedents but in terms of the operating politics of the judiciary insofar as questions of sex-based discrimination are concerned. Legislatures can act to implement the fullest and soundest theory of the Amendment in the living law, but only judges can breathe the spirit of equality into the law in the daily operation of our courts.

B. The Present as Prologue: Treatment of Sex Discrimination under Title VII of the Civil Rights Act of 1964

Certainly the most recent and widespread experience of federal courts in defining "sex discrimination" has arisen in the hearing of cases charging sex-based discrimination in employment under Title VII. Through these cases, the federal judiciary has begun to develop standards, tests, and measures for the phenomenon of unequal employment opportunities as it affects female workers in particular. The experience of federal courts handling Title VII sex discrimination cases is likely to bear in several ways upon federal judicial interpretation of the Equal Rights Amendment.

As amended in 1972,[44] Title VII prohibits employers, including private employers of 15 or more persons,[45] labor organizations, and government at all[46] levels, from following employment policies or practices which, by design or by effect,[47] discriminate against one or more employees on account of race, national origin, color, religion, or sex. Literally hundreds of cases involving allegations of sex discrimination in employment have been decided by the courts between 1965 and the present. The most important question that this litigation raises in relation to the process of Equal Rights Amendment interpretation is this: What will be the effects of the Title VII experience of the judiciary upon interpretation of the Equal Rights Amendment? A related question of great significance raised by the Title VII experience is this: Have courts deciding sex discrimination cases under Title VII developed standards and predispositions about the meaning of "equality of rights" as applied to women and men? This article cannot answer these questions in a full way; instead a brief discussion of a few facets of these questions is attempted.

For purposes of this discussion, a relatively limited sample of published opinions[48] concerning cases of discrimination under Title VII has been reviewed. This sample of opinions by no means represents the "State of Title VII Law" insofar as sex discrimination in employment is concerned for the following reasons: (1) many opinions and decisions on the subject are unpublished; (2) cases that are settled in early stages of litigation do not usually engender judicial opinions; and (3) an exhaustive look at the "State of Title VII Law" in sex discrimination cases would require thoroughgoing study of the actual conduct of employers and unions, including patterns of adaptation and defensiveness, in relation to Title VII.

Also, judicial opinions range widely in the degree to which the underlying facts of a case may be gleaned from them. Thus, any discussion of the themes of case law on a given subject requires a certain amount of reading between the lines. This mode of analysis is necessarily risky because the political and psychological motivations of a case and its results may be buried far beneath the level of articulation required in judicial opinion writing.

1. Judicial Attitudes toward Aggressive Women under Title VII

In the case of *Newman v. Avco Corp.*,[49] the trial court determined that Defendant maintained racially discriminatory promotion and seniority systems which discriminated against blacks by relying upon subjective supervisorial evaluations and by not rehiring blacks after a plant closure, and determined that prior to 1965 the only blacks employed by Defendant were janitors and charwomen. The court also found that the company's firing of one black employee named Mr. Dennis was retaliatory, due to the employer's anger with Dennis because of his "aggressive but proper representation of black employees."[50]

Not a single case in Volume 7[51] shows a court finding that the firing of a female was improperly due to her "aggressive but proper representation of female employees." Indeed, several cases suggest that a quite different standard has been applied to defensive showings in Title VII cases of activism, militancy, and aggressive civil rights-oriented conduct on the part of women.

In *East v. Romine, Inc.*[52] the trier upheld the defenses of the Defendant employer, who was charged by Plaintiff, a female, with refusing to hire her as a welder because of her sex. The court's opinion took notice of Plaintiff's other Title VII complaints and/or charges against Defendant *as a proper reason* for the refusal to hire her. Of course, that conclusion is precisely contrary to Title VII which prohibits the refusal to afford equal employment opportunity to a person in retaliation for his/her participation in or filing of charges.[53] But, more important to the issue at hand, the standard for an employee's conduct in *East v. Romine, Inc.* is completely opposite to the standard of *Newman v. Avco Corp.*; in *East*, the court expressly concludes that the female Plaintiff's *legally protected* steps to challenge discrimination are a proper reason for the refusal to hire her.

Juxtaposing *East* and *Newman,* one might suspect that the difference in standards arises from the fact that *East* is a sex discrimination case while *Newman* concerns race discrimination. Or one might simply dismiss the significance of the difference by reference to the fact that two different courts and two different judges were involved.

Assuredly the characteristics of courts and judges have demonstrable effects upon results in discrimination cases as in all other kinds. But the difference between standards in *Newman* and *East* cannot be adequately explained solely by reference to the differences between types of cases or courts. The sex of the Plaintiff seems relevant when other cases utilizing *East* type reasoning are collected.

Plaintiff, a black female, in *Goodloe v. Martin-Marietta Corp.,*[54] charged Defendant employer with using a racially discriminatory college degree requirement for computer jobs. The court in *Goodloe* failed to require the Defendant to show that the college degree was job-related. It disavowed the testimony of Plaintiff's witnesses on the ground that these witnesses themselves had filed complaints of discrimination against the company and must therefore be biased. Finally, the court took notice of Plaintiff female's "litigious nature,"[55] based upon her filing of a discrimination case at the state level, and thus decided that the company's purported reason for discharging Plaintiff, *to wit,* that she had used provocative obscenity in argument with another employee, was a valid and non-discriminatory reason for firing her. In *Goodloe,* as in *East,* the Plaintiff was sanctioned because of her "litigiousness," that is, the Plaintiff's case of discrimination was decided to be without merit because she had filed suit(s) or charge(s) concerning discrimination. Again, in contrast, the court in *Newman* looked beneath the employer's defense that Mr. Dennis had misbehaved in the course of his civil rights activism, and the court concluded that this "reason" for firing Dennis was a *pretext* for unlawful retaliation against Mr. Dennis. It must be recalled that Title VII expressly prohibits the actions of an employer taken against an employee because of his/her filing of charges, complaints, or testimony in opposition to discrimination.

Under the standard of *Goodloe* and *East,* a female Plaintiff, regardless of race, is "damned if she does and damned if she doesn't" oppose discrimination. The strong implication of *Goodloe, East,* and decisions of this ilk is that if women intend to sustain cases of discrimination, they would be best advised to be quiet, self-concerned and—above all—"ladylike," mannerly, and nonaggressive. The standard is circular to the extent that a modicum of aggressiveness is a prerequisite to survival in the context of filing discrimination charges and of litigation.

Lying a level deeper in these cases is the implication that, whereas activism and even militance on the part of ethnic minority males are at least permitted if not rewarded by *some* courts, activism and militance on the part of women, of whatever race, are sometimes viewed as proper reasons for employers to discharge such employees, the law to the contrary notwithstanding. The relevance of this emergent double standard for the process of judicial interpretation of the Equal Rights Amendment is clear: courts that have already shown the propensity to develop or apply a double standard for proper conduct of men and women in employment discrimination cases will be particularly susceptible to spreading that double standard into Equal Rights Amendment cases, because of backlash motives or simply because of unconsciousness or disbelief that discrimination against women of every color is as great an evil in our system as is discrimination against ethnic minority men.

2. Quota Hiring and Promotion Policies: Sex-Differential Availability of Court Ordered Affirmative Action in Employment

Among the decisions reported in Volume 7 of the C.C.H.'s *Employment Practices Decisions*[56] are numerous opinions in which courts have ordered Defendants to employ, hire, promote, and/or train particular percentages of the discriminated-against group(s) bringing suit. A perusal of these decisions indicates that court-ordered hiring and promotion of certain percentages of ethnic minorities to remedy racial discrimination is far more common than court-ordered hiring and promotion of females to remedy sex discrimination. Less than ten decisions in Volume 7 contain orders or indications of judicial intent to order goal-based hiring of women. Furthermore, while hiring proportionate to the numbers of a minority group in the relevant local work force is a common formula for minority hiring goals, rarely have Defendants been ordered to hire women—of all races —proportionate to their local work force ratios.

Employer seniority systems have been successfully challenged on many occasions under Title VII for their racially discriminatory effects.[57] Yet very few cases can be found where a court has ordered a Defendant to redefine seniority to eliminate past practices of sex discrimination.[58] Indeed, courts have sometimes found that the greater seniority of men in employment to which women have been refused access in the past justifies a higher rate of compensation to those men.[59]

The apparent timidity of some courts to order quota hiring and promotion of females and to overturn sex discriminatory seniority systems in cases where the wrongs of sex discrimination can be best remedied by such means indicates an unwillingness on the part of those courts to implement the sex discrimination prohibitions of Title VII with the same measure of vigor and seriousness shown in cases of race-based employment discrimination. This judicial resistance against using thoroughgoing means to eradicate sex discrimination in the domain of employment will be likely to penetrate judicial behavior in other areas addressed by the Equal Rights Amendment.

3. An Afterword: On the Bright Side of Title VII

The perspectives upon Title VII given so far have emphasized the negative side of case precedents concerning sex discrimination in employment in order to illustrate existing judicial inhibitions to the implementation of full equality of rights without regard to sex. However, this vein of pessimism, or realism, should be read in context. On the bright side, some courts have begun to gain an exposure to the phenomenon of sex discrimination in employment, and some courts have answered the challenge of applying consistent Title VII principles to *all* prohibited forms of discrimination with energetic, relentless examination of evidence and theory, whether plaintiffs are males or females, activists or not, and whether the case involves racial or sex discrimination. If these courts take the lead in Equal Rights Amendment cases, drawing from their experience in locating and uprooting the very subtlest forms of sex-based inequality in employment, then interpretation of the Amendment along the no-nonsense lines of the most careful and best reasoned Title VII cases is still possible.

Footnotes

1. U.S. Const. Art. III. §§ 1, 2, *Marbury v. Madison*.
2. 40. L. Ed. 2d 164 (1974).
3. See the 1973-75 *U.S. Reports, passim*.
4. Article in American Bar Association Journal (1974).
5. See I. C. of this article, *infra*.
6. Frankfurter, *Law and Politics* (Capricorn Press, 1962), p. 289.
7. *Goesaert v. Cleary*, 335 U.S. 464, 69 S. Ct. 198, 93 L. Ed. 163 (1948).
8. Ibid.
9. Ibid.

10. See, e.g., L. Kanowitz, *Women and the Law: The Unfinished Revolution* (Albuquerque: University of New Mexico Press, 1969), pp. 33, 172.

11. Citation at fn 7, *supra*.

12. Frankfurter, pp. 37-40.

13. Ibid., pp. 10-15.

14. Ibid., pp. 39, 110, 116.

15. Ibid., pp. 72-77.

16. Ibid., p. 73.

17. Citation at fn 7, *supra*. I.B.2.

18. The term "equal" is used elsewhere, in various quantitative references to the Senate, House, and electoral college. Art. I, §3; Art. II, §1; Art. V; XXIIIrd Amendment.

19. Babcock, et al., eds., *Sex Discrimination and the Law: Causes and Remedies* (Little, Brown Co., 1975), pp. 58-70.

20. 404 U.S. 71, 92 S. Ct. 251, 30 L. Ed. 2d 225 (1971).

21. 411 U.S. 677, 93 S. Ct. 1764, 36 L. Ed. 2d 583 (1973).

22. Ibid.

23. 1979 is the year by which the Equal Rights Amendment will either be ratified or die, temporarily or otherwise.

23. *Roe v. Wade*, 410 U.S. 113, 93 S. Ct. 756, 35 L. Ed. 2d 147 (1973); *Doe v. Bolton*, 410 U.S. 179, 93 S. Ct. 739, 35 L. Ed. 2d 201 (1973) (declaring Texas' and Georgia's antiabortion statutes unconstitutionally denied due process of law); *Cohen v. Chesterfield County School Board* and *Cleveland Board of Education v. LaFleur*, 414 U.S. 632, 94 S. Ct. 791 (1974) (determining that mandatory maternity leave policies denied due process of law); *Geduldig v. Aiello*, 42 U.S.L.W. 4905 (1974) (deciding that employee-paid scheme of disability insurance run by California that excluded "normal" pregnancy from sources of paid disabilities did not deny equal protection to women); *Kahn v. Shevin* (see article, *infra*); *Taylor v. Louisiana*, 43 U.S.L.W. 4167 (1975) (determining that state scheme which resulted in a general exclusion of women from juries violated Sixth Amendment); *Ballard v. Schlesinger*, 43 U.S.L.W. 4158 (1975) (determining that armed forces' policy of retaining nonpromoted female officers did not deny equal protection to men).

25. 42 U.S.L.W. 4591 (1974).

26. 208 U.S. 412, 28 S. Ct. 324, 52 L. Ed. 551 (1908).

27. 42 U.S.L.W. 4591.

28. Justices Brennan, Marshall, and White dissented in *Kahn*, citing both *Reed* and *Frontiero*.

29. *Bradwell v. Illinois*, 83 U.S. (16 Wall.) 132, 21 L. Ed. 442 (1873), held that the state could constitutionally prohibit women from becoming lawyers.

30. Citation at fn 26, *supra*.

31. Citation at fn 7, *supra*.

32. *Hoyt v. Florida*, 368 U.S. 57, 82 S. Ct. 159, 7 L. Ed. 2d 118 (1961), disapproved in *Taylor v. Louisiana*. Refer to fn 24, *supra*.

33. Citation at fn 25, *supra*.

34. Citation at fn 24, *supra*.

35. For examples, Mr. Justice Douglas dissented in both *Goesaert v. Cleary* (fn 7, *supra*) and *Geduldig v. Aiello* (fn 24, *supra*).

36. Citation at fn 29, *supra*.

37. Quotation from *ERA and The American Way* (film produced by Mollie Gregory, for the Nevada League of Women Voters, 1974).

38. The best example is probably the HOTDOGS of the John Birch Society, who have accused ERA supporting governors' commissions of a Communist influence. Babcock, et al., see fn 19, *supra*, p. 184.

39. The best example is probably the American Communist Party, whose opposition to the ERA is based on an inference of federalized tyranny beneath the Amendment.

40. See fns 38 and 39, *supra*.

41. The record of Senate debates, containing reference to some forms of legal inequality of the sexes, is contained in 118 *Congressional Record* S4247-4272 (March 20, 1972); 118 *Congressional Record* S4372-4430 (March 21, 1972); 118 *Congressional Record* S4531-4613 (March 22, 1972).

42. See, for example, XVI of Plato's *Republic* on the "Equality of Women."

43. See, for example, the writings of Phyllis Schlafly, in the *Phyllis Schlafly Reports* (1972-).

44. 42 U.S. Code §2000e et seq.

45. 42 U.S. Code §2000e.

46. 42 U.S. Code §§2000e (f)—(h); §2000e-16.

47. See, *Griggs v. Duke Power Co.*, 401 U.S. 424 (1971).

48. For this analysis, the decisions contained in Volume 7 of C.C.H.'s *Employment Practices Decisions* were surveyed. This analysis does not purport to represent that Volume 7 is special but only that it is fairly representative of the diverse patterns and problems of judicial decision making under Title VII.

49. 7 E.P.D. §9117 (M.D. Tenn. 1973).

50. Ibid.

51. See fn 48, *supra*.

52. 7 E.P.D. §9356 (S.D. Ga.).

53. 42 U.S. Code §2000e-3.

54. 7 E.P.D. §9197 (D. Colo. 1972).

55. Ibid.

56. See fn 48, *supra*.

57. See, e.g., *U.S. v. Georgia Power Co.*, 7 E.P.D. §9167 (N.D. Ga. 1974); *Pettway v. American Cast Iron Pipe Co.*, 7 E.P.D. §9291 (5th Cir. 1974).

58. See, e.g., *Meadows v. Ford Motor Co.*, 7 E.P.D. §9103 (W.D. Ky. 1973).

59. See, e.g., *Brennan v. Victoria Bank & Trust Co.*, 7 E.P.D. §9358 (5th Cir. 1974).

Implementation and the
Equal Rights Amendment

Dale Rogers Marshall and Janell Anderson

When the Equal Rights Amendment (ERA) to the United States Constitution is ratified, NOTHING WILL HAPPEN. Groups which have been concentrating all their attention on achieving ratification may be shocked by that statement. But the truth is that ratification is meaningless without implementation.

The purpose of this paper is to discuss some of the realities of the implementation of public policy so that people with an interest in ERA can work to increase its significance. First, we discuss the fact that implementation is problematic not automatic and its effectiveness depends upon the patterns of political mobilization. Secondly, the sources of distortion in implementation will be discussed. Finally, ways of minimizing the distortions will be covered. The paper emphasizes the importance of participating in the implementation of public policy such as the ERA. The result of ERA will be shaped by the sum of the efforts of the participants—the efforts of the well-wishers minus the efforts of the detractors. Our desire is to make the net result benefit all Americans.

I. The Problem of Implementation

A constitutional amendment is like a hatrack. It provides a framework on which to hang judicial interpretations of other rules, laws, and statutes. It is a rule which can guide future decisions. It authorizes changes in laws and institutions but does not automatically activate those changes. A constitutional amendment, like government, is "not something which just happens." It has to be "laid on" by somebody.[1]

The ERA will establish a requirement that all statutes, both state and national, provide equal treatment for women. It is patterned after the 15th and 19th Amendments, which required equal voting rights for Negroes and women, respectively. These Amendments did not automatically render all contradictory voting laws unconstitutional. Neither will the ERA automatically strike down all discriminatory sex-biased law. Someone must perceive a law to be sex-biased and convince legislatures to pass corrective legislation in order to overcome the inequities of old laws. In theory the ERA can have a variety of consequences. For example, the effect of the Amendment could be to strike the words of sex identification from law rather than render the entire law unconstitutional. Thus, rights under the law would be extended to both sexes. Or, in other cases, rights could be removed from one sex so that neither sex would have them. But if a law serves only to restrict, deny, or limit the freedoms or rights of one sex, such restrictions might not be extended to both sexes; instead the law could be declared unconstitutional.

But while in theory the ERA will no doubt make it more difficult for the political system to deny the equal protection of the law to women, it does nothing in and of itself. Without implementation, any amendment or piece of legislation is simply a rule for a game which is not being played by anybody. An amendment must be followed by court and legislative action designed to put the rule into effect. How the ERA is actually applied will depend upon the political mobilization patterns which are created by the issue of women's rights.[2]

Several generalizations can be made about political mobilization in our policy process. First, the policy process typically involves a multiplicity of groups. It is likely that the implementing legislation and court action introduced on behalf of women's rights will call forth a multiplicity of interest groups, all perceiving a stake in the change. Some of these groups will favor the change, some will oppose the change altogether, and some will desire a change that differs slightly from the one proposed.

Second, the groups which are involved in any issue have varying amounts of resources and they expend them according to the intensity of each issue. This goes for friends as well as enemies. Each group has its own set of priorities and finite resources. Many, however, will have greater resources than most women's groups and will not have to make much of an expenditure to oppose them because delay and circumvention are less costly than positively pursued objectives.

Third, the game strategies of the groups will also vary. Again, the strategies for opposition are easier than the strategies for programmatic change. This means that women's groups will need to develop a strategy for themselves which is more than simply a reaction to the turbulence around them. They must cope with the political system in order to achieve positive results. This depends upon their understanding of the political situation in which they must operate and their relative position as well as other groups' interests in contention.

Women's groups face what economists call the "freerider" problem. This means that the benefits which will accrue to any one member of the group as a result of group action is so slight that motivation for participation may be low. This is due to the fact that women's groups work for changes which will be beneficial to all women or all members of that group. These changes are public in that the benefits which accrue as a result cannot be withheld from any member of that group or class of persons, i.e., women. It is, therefore, difficult to get women to participate in the organized pressure system which provides the public goods. And women's groups need to develop strategies to deal with this situation.

The fourth characteristic of political mobilization patterns is that the policy outcome will be the result of negotiation. This means that the players will not get everything they ask for nor will changes be fundamental or sweeping in nature. Changes will be incremental and gradual.[3]

In sum, implementation of policy does not happen automatically. The actual results of a policy will be shaped by which groups with what resources and strategies become active in negotiating the incremental changes typical of our policy process.

II. SOURCES OF DISTORTION IN IMPLEMENTATION

Attempts to apply the ERA must take into account the problematic nature of implementation in our decentralized political system with a multiplicity of competing groups. There are many potential hurdles which can distort the intended objectives. However, others have faced and overcome these hurdles and so can women. Their position has much in common with that of consumer and environmental groups. They began with defensive legal strategies and moved on to positive legislative strategies which instituted programmatic change. This must happen in the case of the ERA as well.

The difficulty is that the political system is unabashedly skewed in favor of delay and deadlock, circumvention and the status quo. This bias occurs because the American system values individual rights and the federal system over effective policy implementation. This means that all implementation involves extensive participation by multiple agencies, jurisdictions, non-governmental organizations, and individuals. Thus, the road to policy achievement is tortuous and difficult. This quote from Bailey and Mosher concerning the administration of the Elementary and Secondary Education Act (ESEA) illustrates the problem well.

> When a law, unprecedented in scope, has to be administered through State and local instrumentalities, on an impossible time schedule, by an understaffed agency in structural turmoil, beset by a deluge of complaints and demands for clarification of the legislation at hand, as well as cognate legislation already on the books; the wonder is not that mistakes are made—the wonder is that the law is implemented at all.[4]

Nevertheless, the distortions which occur, if known, can be managed. The hurdles can become well known footpaths.[5] Let us indicate some of the major sources of distortion.

Illusive Goals and Agreements

First, illusive goals and agreements are a constant problem. Goals of an amendment or piece of legislation are never clear, and there are often contradictory goals embodied in a given policy. Thus, groups trying to implement the policy inevitably exercise a lot of discretion which results in conflicting interpretations and activities. Similarly, even though implementing groups may agree on general goals, disagreements on procedures quickly surface. An example in which there was apparent agreement on objectives initially and where disagreement surfaced to block the program is provided in Martha Derthick's study of the implementation of the "new towns in-town" legislation.

Late in the summer of 1967, the Johnson administration started a program to build model new communities on surplus federally owned land in metropolitan areas. During the next year, the White House and the Department of Housing and Urban Development (HUD) announced seven projects. But nearly three years later, the program had clearly failed. Three of the projects were dead, and the rest were in serious trouble. Almost no construction had been initiated.[6] Although initial agreement was perceived by federal officials to be widespread, disagreements rapidly surfaced. Several local groups strongly opposed low cost housing; local officials preferred kinds of development that would yield more tax revenue; and conservationists were opposed to plans for construction. As apparent agreement rapidly yielded to pervasive disagreement, the program ground to a halt.

Another example of the way in which illusive agreements contribute to policy distortion is provided in a study of the Economic Development

Administration (EDA) in Oakland.[7] Here the conflicts were covert and became evident only after some time had passed. The interests and organizations involved thought they wanted to do something, but experience taught them that they had been mistaken. As events unfolded, latent conflicts became manifest, the original agreements had to be renegotiated, and a new and even more antagonistic situation emerged. For example, the federal agency involved discovered that funding recipients were interpreting the agreements in ways that conflicted with federal interpretations. An agency that appeared to be a single organization with a single will turned out to be several suborganizations with different wills. The apparent solidity of original aims and understandings gave way as people, organizations, and circumstances changed.

Pressman and Wildavsky show that the seemingly simple and straightforward is really complex and convoluted. The initial surprise comes if one does not appreciate the number of steps involved, the number of participants whose preferences have to be taken into account, the number of separate decisions that are part of what we think of as a single one, and the geometric growth of interdependencies over time where each negotiation involves large numbers of participants and decisions. It is important to be aware of these sources of distortion, to realize that goals and agreements are illusive, and to expect the process of implementing the ERA to be long and complex.

Leadership Strategies

A second major source of distortion in implementation is a result of leadership strategies, a result of what the government officials choose to emphasize and the techniques they use to achieve their ends. Political agendas are made not born. Government officials, legislators, administrators, and governors try to control the agenda of issues being considered. They have their own rationale for doing what they do, and it may be a source of pain or pleasure to you. However, what needs to be said is that all officials have strategies to accomplish certain objectives considered unnecessary. It is the latter problem which concerns us here.

Nondecisions: The first and most difficult strategy to deal with is nondecision, in other words, the lack of attention to specific issues and policy problems which are of interest to women. For example, certain bodies may simply fail to raise questions which activate the implementation of the ERA.[8]

Diversions: This is a strategy you will instantly recognize from Monday night football. The quarterback seems to pick up the ball and run toward the goal but somehow ends up handing it off to another ball carrier who may or may not know where the goal is. If the strategy is truly diversionary, you can rest assured that the hand-off will be to someone who knows that the "real" goal is not implementation of the ERA. Resulting activity will be purely cosmetic.[9]

Pats-on-the-head: This strategy is the one where the governor's person-in-charge-of-women's-things comes to you and says, "You are doing a wonderful job; keep up the good work; no, we do not plan to increase your budget for the next fiscal year." This is a "nice doggy" attempt to keep you from preempting other priorities. It is understandable but nevertheless results in very little material progress.

Marginal changes: This strategy is one which you can hope for and do the most with. It is a strategy which will allow the accomplishment of pro-grammatic goals on a regular basis over time. This is the way the system works when it works at all. Marginal change is a humanly possible goal which can be accomplished within a fiscal year, legislative session, or what have you. The political allocation of time, as much as anything else, permits marginal rather than fundamental/ revolutionary/overnight change.

Science and technology or "expert-expert who's got the expert?": California is a culture which is very hip to science and technology. That is why expert witnesses, reams of factual data, and so forth are important in hearings on problems and policy change. What officials, as well as others, do is to get experts and facts to reinforce their own positions. The game is at its most sophisticated when Rand testifies for one position and the Stanford Research Institute testifies for another. The proposals are different and the game is called "whose-expert-witness-do-you-believe-the-most?"[10] As you probably recognize by now, this game is used both by and against you. It is expensive. It is sometimes necessary. Save a little money in the budget and/or court the favors of those who can serve as experts in support of women's issues. This game is taken very seriously by most governments.

II. SOURCES OF CORRECTION:
WAYS OF MINIMIZING DISTORTION IN IMPLEMENTATION

There are many ways in which groups interested in implementing policy can compensate for the kinds of distortion we have been describing. We have already mentioned the importance of being realistic about the time and complexity of the implementation process. This includes letting officials know that you are "wise to" the delaying strategies that they are using and will not be deterred by them. In addition, attention should be given to the following ways of minimizing distortion: "self-correcting" devices in legislation; mobilization of groups via coalition building; mobilization of groups via education of members and the community; and mobilization of individuals. Each of these strategies is important and needs further elaboration.

"Self-Correcting" Legislation

One of the best ways to prevent distortion is to provide for "self-correcting" devices in all legislation designed to implement ERA. These are important because even after an amendment is implemented by legislation, the legislation may not have the intended results. Laws get distorted by regulations and guidelines, by the compromises involved in implementation, and these can make the laws ineffective. Thus, protections against failures should be incorporated into the legislation. Protective devices include grievance procedures and requirements for periodic evaluation of programs and agencies. These serve to hold policy makers accountable for the results of legislation. Although some might not recognize the need for these devices, they are proven necessities. Some of the best known checks on policy execution are ombudspersons, legislative oversight, judicial review, citizen participation in bureaucratic decision making, and the publicizing of bureaucratic operations. Legislation designed to implement ERA should include provisions for these corrective devices so that modifications in the legislation can be made to increase its effectiveness.

Coalition Building

If the political world is as intricate and interdependent as we have described it, then group mobilization is an essential part of implementation.[11] Individuals are least likely to have the necessary resources to define appropriate issues and mobilize sufficient support to achieve favorable decisions. Organized action is a must. Clearly, allies or coalition partners are needed, but this need raises many questions. For instance, how many allies should be sought? Who shall they be (providing there is a choice)? How can an alliance be maintained? What follows are some guidelines concerning these questions. Ultimately, however, it is political "savvy" that will guide action in this sphere.

First, more is not necessarily better. This means that the more allies one has the more groups there are to share in the winnings, however limited. Costs must also be considered. The more groups involved, the harder it is to maintain policy consistency and to appease the most intensely concerned. Soliciting supporters consumes time, energy, money, and skill which could be spent on alternative opportunities or uses. Only judgment can help decide when additional support brings no further net gain.

In politics there is so much uncertainty that it is not possible to calculate a minimal winning combination. Politicians typically search for as many allies as they can muster. If they get too many, they may incur additional costs and reduce individual or group shares; but at least they have won. Without wide support, they risk losing all, perhaps by a single vote. Understandably, the politicians attempt to overcome uncertainty by going all out for victory. When they know they can win, as do candidates from safe districts, they seldom attempt to maximize support or wage an expensive campaign. There is little to gain and much to lose.

Who should be chosen as potential allies? Who will make the best partners, assuming that one has some choice in the matter. Frequently one finds oneself allied with either strangers or persons or groups whom one might not typically have invited. In these cases the coalition is produced by necessity, but the "necessity" is in recognizing that more is to be gained by acceptance than by rejection of an "unholy alliance."

If there is a choice, one alternative worth considering is to select a partner who is sufficiently powerful to assist in winning but is unlikely to dominate the coalition and one's organization in particular. Powerful partners extract prices for their participation, and it is this presence which makes victory possible, but the price is apt to be higher. Selecting less important partners who do not pose threats of domination can still be expensive in terms of the share of the winnings they claim. The greater the number of lesser partners, the greater the interdependence and the higher the bargaining costs. Just how costly is impossible to say, since all the relevant variables have not been identified, but common sense clearly suggests that the more people or groups one must coordinate the more resources will be consumed.

One final crucial element to be considered is the interests and values of potential partners. A coalition is probably most easily formed among those who have either similar values or complementary interests. When political battle lines are drawn, it is relatively simple for political partners who share basic preferences of ways to live and what to live for to identify their friends and enemies. However, it is not necessary to share basic values in order to form coalitions; indeed, most coalitions are based upon complementary interests which develop in particular situations caused by certain types of political issues.

If antagonistic groups ally, the reason is that they perceive themselves to have complementary interests that can be either protected or advanced by coordinated actions. Complementary interests, then, are different goals which can be mutually advanced by concerted efforts. What is of note is that the interests are different but not incompatible in particular situations, even though the basic values of the partners may be fundamentally incompatible. Neither partner is much concerned about the other's interests, but cooperates in order to achieve one's own objectives. Because coalitions of complementary interests are particular and situational, they tend to be unstable and last only as long as the interests remain complementary. Coalitions that are based upon shared values are apt to be more enduring because values are more stable than interests. Rational political behavior requires attention to the changing interests of others and sufficient flexibility and imagination to find or make interests complementary. On occasion one may even have to identify another's interests and convince them of their importance.

Coalitions are not likely to maintain themselves unless expected gains remain positive. This need not mean that once the original goals have been achieved a coalition will immediately cease to operate, because other complementary interests may be found, including the psychic benefits to be derived from continued mutual association. In national politics such tentatively satisfying gains may not be as important as continued material payoffs. The long-standing congressional coalition of Northern Republicans and Southern Democrats is a product of reciprocal gains on crucial legislation; it will cease only when these are not forthcoming. This was true for the coalition of John L. Lewis's United Mine Workers and the coal operators and the railroad management and unions. Each benefited from a healthy coal market and was disadvantaged by competing fuels and means of transportation. Finally, of course, changing technology and competing coalitions defeated the Lewis group. But for thirty years it was successful in maintaining itself and providing considerable benefits to the partners. A rational coalition builder does not build coalitions on sentiment alone, and she or he does not always expect them to continue after their specific objectives are achieved.

Education of Group Members and the Community

There are several things that organized women's groups should do to mobilize their members and facilitate the implementation of ERA. First, there should be special conferences devoted to the issue of ERA implementation. This includes the formulation of new as well as reform of existing legislation. These conferences could be held in all regions of all states. Annual conferences could also be utilized as a forum for such an activity. Action packets should be developed to serve as the basis for these conferences on ERA implementation. They should outline the issues, possible actions, and available resources, including speakers and written materials.

Groups should form their own task forces for aiding the implementation of the ERA, and the task forces should develop coalitions. This means better and broader participation.

Commissions on the Status of Women should strengthen their roles as coordinators and facilitators of information for women's groups. Women's groups, like other groups, often act in isolation from one another and do not have any idea of what is happening outside their particular area of expertise and interest.

Local communities must become involved in helping the ERA make a difference for women. The education of the community will help alleviate tensions and fears that the women's movement is a threat to traditional institutions and more. Especially vital will be panels where men and women have been effective in liberating women's minds and energies. Now women and men need to work together for objectives which are perceived as beneficial to both sexes.

Certainly, visits must be made to legislators and administrators in order to educate them as to what is going right and wrong with the ERA. Lobbying activities are most effective when legislators and administrators can look upon them as learning experiences which aid them in their work. Be especially attentive to committee members who get assigned to women's issues. Take drafts of legislation to them. The work of legislators is time-consuming. Don't wait for them to formulate new laws or think up issues for themselves. Be assertive in suggesting, demanding if necessary, that the ERA be actively implemented. Get administrators to suggest these things as well. A great many laws and reforms get enacted because the administrators pressed for it.

Finally, men and women from the community who are supporting the goal of "equal rights" for women can be used by women's groups as ambassadors for implementing the ERA. These persons are especially good to use when intransigent cases must be treated or sensitive areas penetrated. They should be highly respected and well known to most people in the community. Commissions on the Status of Women can identify such persons for women's groups and suggest participation to those who may not have participated in women's issues before.

Mobilization of Individuals

Even though group mobilization is essential to the implementation of ERA, women can also do some things as individuals which will facilitate the implementation of the ERA. First, women should run for office and take leadership positions in agencies and the courts. In other words, they must "infiltrate" the ranks and work for the advantage of other women as well as themselves. They can also work actively in campaigns of other women and men, and if their candidates win, their influence can increase. Second, those with money and/or time should use it as a means of influencing (properly, of course) ERA's implementation. This is the way men do it, so why shouldn't women? Money and time can be put to work for candidates and legislation supportive of ERA. Women have unfortunately been hesitant to exercise their political rights, thinking that they are "not qualified." But women's political participation is essential to the success of ERA. Women are beginning to be aware that they have underestimated their qualifications and that participation is the best way to utilize and increase their qualifications.

There are no guarantees about the outcomes of these strategies for improving the implementation of ERA. The results are necessarily problematic. But history suggests that active concern by interested citizens is essential to success. We look back and admire what the suffragettes accomplished. We are clearly at another turning point, and this time *we* have a chance to make a difference and earn the respect of future generations.

Footnotes

1. T.D. Weldon, *States and Morals* (New York: McGraw-Hill, 1947), p. 47.
2. See especially Theodore Lowi, "American Business, Public Policy, Case-Studies, and Political Theory," *World Politics* 16 (July 1964): 677-715, for an especially illuminating exposition on the patterns of political mobilization which occur with differing types of public policies.
3. See C. E. Lindbloom, *The Policy Making Process* (Englewood Cliffs, N.J.: Prentice-Hall, 1973) for an account of man's limited capacities as well as the limits of the political process.
4. Stephen K. Bailey and Edith K. Mosher, *ESEA: The Office of Education Administers a Law* (Syracuse: Syracuse University Press, 1968), p. 99.
5. See "Environmental Lobby Suffers Second Year of Defeat for Its Major Proposals," *California Journal,* November 1971, pp. 296-301, 309-311, for an excellent account of the environmentalists in achieving policy legislation. It is also an excellent account of how a group with freerider problems can overcome the barriers to success.
6. See Martha Derthick, *New Towns In-Town* (Washington, D.C.: Urban Institute, 1972), p. xiv.
7. Jeffrey Pressman and Aaron B. Wildavsky, *Implementation* (Berkeley: University of California Press, 1973), p. 91.
8. The classical exposition is Peter Bachrach and Morton Baratz, "Two Faces of Power," *American Political Science Review,* December 1962, pp. 947-52.

9. Murray Edelman, *The Symbolic Uses of Politics* (Urbana: University of Illinois Press, 1964).

10. "Three Reports, Two Views: PUC, Rand, and SRI Studies," *California Journal,* June 1973, pp. 192-93.

11. Anthony Downs, *An Economic Theory of Democracy* (New York: Harper and Row, 1957); also William Mitchell and Joyce Mitchell, *Politics: Problems and Outcomes* (Chicago: Rand McNally, 1971), ch. 7.

The Political Impact of the ERA

Jo Freeman

Political power is both an end and means of social change. The acquisition of it allows one to use the resources of the government to pursue one's goals, and the capability of instigating changes in society can create political influence. This chicken-and-egg phenomenon means it is often hard to distinguish the way in which a new source of power represents a gain in and of itself from the way in which it is merely a tool for further changes. American history is replete with instances in which the latter is mistaken for the former. Prominent among these is the major goal of the 19th century Women's Movement—the vote. In a political system based on the principle of majority rule, the vote is the *sine qua non* of effective citizenship. Yet suffrage leaders' assumptions that women would use the vote to improve their condition were not borne out.[1] Feminist activists found the fruits of victory not nearly so exciting as the fight to gain them and turned their energies to other pressing causes of the day, while women willing to participate in the regular party process found themselves "swallowed up . . . and carefully shut out of the decision-making process."[2]

The failure of the 19th Amendment to result in any real participation by women in political institutions illustrates the always acknowledged but often ignored fact that political rights are not the same as political power. Rights are a necessary but not sufficient condition for gaining power. As long as any social movement stops with the attainment of political rights, not only can it not bring about changes in social conditions, but it often cannot even protect its rights.[3]

Political rights, like law in general, can be a significant contributor to social change but only if their limitations and the context in which they operate are properly understood. Law is at best "a catalyst of change rather than a singular effector of change."[4] It is when we expect law to do too much that it does too little.

Ideally, the necessary conditions for social change to occur via the political system would encompass the following:

1) A public commitment to change stated through statutory law and judicial interpretation that specify the means and directions of changes as thoroughly as possible. Laws which are vague and ambivalent are hard to enforce and easy to circumvent. When the meaning of a policy is left to be worked out in the courts or the administrative agencies, it becomes subject to bargaining—a process in which the most powerful interest and/or the status quo frequently has the edge.[5]

2) Energetic administrative enforcement and implementation coupled with a sympathetic understanding of the ramifications of the beneficiary's problems. It is not uncommon for a definitive policy to be hamstrung at the administrative level. This can be done by a simple lack of an enforcement agency, a lack of funding, a lack of experienced personnel, a lack of support from superiors, or too close a relationship with, and thus too much sympathy for, a regulated group. Those who enforce policy and those for whom policy is enforced do not always share the same perspective.[6]

3) Active, organized effort by the beneficiaries to encourage and facilitate their members' taking advantage of special programs as well as making demands on the system to improve these programs. The structure of our government is such that it requires a great deal of outside pressure and even outside help for it to implement many of its policies. This is especially true of those policies which have as their goal major social changes. Unfortunately, those policies most in need of an outside push are those intended to benefit the most disadvantaged classes, i.e., those with the least resources to pressure the government.

Optimally, these three conditions must take place within a context of crisis to impart the sense of urgency necessary for their execution. The numerous checks and vetoes within our governmental structure assure the necessity for a high degree of consensus among many groups before any changes can be instituted. Such consensus is only possible when desired changes are perceived as minor ones or when the feeling that "something must be done" is acute. Obviously, these necessary conditions and their facilitating context are rarely if ever obtained. The value in posing them is to provide a heuristic device, a standard by which to measure efforts for change and their potential for success.

By placing the ERA within this ideal framework, one can see what other ingredients are necessary for it to have the greatest impact and how limited its impact might very well be if nothing further were done. Ratification of the ERA will symbolize a public commitment to equal rights for women, but it will not by itself accomplish any of the major goals which supporters of equal rights seek for women. The ERA can be a tool for change, but it is a tool that must be properly used.

Ratification of the ERA will have both tangible and symbolic effects— neither of which can be entirely predicted. There has been a good deal of debate on the legal effects of the ERA with very little agreement. What is clear, however, is that:

> The Amendment would restrict only governmental action, and would not apply to purely private action. What constitutes "State action" would be the same as under the 14th Amendment and as developed in 14th Amendment litigation on other subjects.[7]

Therefore, what would likely be declared unconstitutional are: 1) a plethora of state laws restricting the rights of married women, 2) the common law assumptions that wives and husbands have different legal responsibilities to and different inheritance rights from each other, 3) divorce and custody laws which differentiate on the basis of sex, 4) restrictive work laws applying to women only, and 5) federal and state laws which differentially subject men and women to jury and military service.[8]

These tangible effects, the specifics of which laws are likely to be affected in that way, are not matters of popular debate. It is only among lawyers and in the legislatures that there is much discussion of possible court interpretations of the meaning of the ERA. Even the Amendment's strongest opponents must distort and magnify its possible legal implications out of all semblance to reasonableness and reality in order to create an ogre worthy of attack. The real impact of the ERA, the reason it has attracted so much public support and such heated, if not extensive opposition, is not the way in which it might change laws on the books but the effect it might have in the minds of people.

The Equal Rights Amendment is symbolic of a reorientation of public attitudes and public policy toward women that has been sought for many years. As indicated by repeated polls, support for "efforts to strengthen or change women's status in society"[9] has been growing steadily. However, this support is not so much for a set of specific policies as it is for the general idea that women and men should more equally share the responsibilities and privileges of this society. Because support for change is diffuse and unfocused, the ERA provides an excellent rallying point. It is simple, straightforward, consonant with traditional American values, relatively untainted by partisan associations, and easy to interpret in any way one wishes. It serves the function of most symbols in that it is an "invaluable means of communicating a common set of meanings at an elementary level."[10]

The fact that the ERA is so basic, so general, and so broad is both its main asset and its defect. It provides a rallying point for supporters of change but only the vaguest guide as to what direction those changes should take. There are two possible, politically relevant, symbolic impacts the ERA might have, two ways in which the American people might interpret its ratification. One is as a symbol of victory, and the other is as a mandate for action.

Because the ERA utilizes one central concept of the Women's Liberation Movement, and one which is also a fundamental value of American society—equality—it is easy to confuse the attainment of equal rights with equality itself. Such a confusion could lead to the belief that the ERA alone is powerful enough to effect equality without further concerted action. Like the vote, what is only a partial means to an end could come to be seen as an end in itself. And like the postsuffrage era, the post-ERA era could see a failure of women to take the responsibility of organizing to pressure for more tangible changes. If ratification of the Equal Rights Amendment is viewed as the major victory of the Movement, then it could well lead to false expectations. It could lead people to believe that change will come easily and be done largely by the government. Yet, as is clear from the heuristic model outlined above, the government is only one factor in political change, and as other situations have shown, even the best-willed government cannot bring about change by itself. If reliance on the government as the instrument of change is the primary consequence of attaining the ERA, then the victory will have been a pyrrhic one.

The other interpretation of the ERA is one that leads to action instead of complacency. It is a more informed perspective that understands the limitations of any law, including a constitutional amendment. This alternative perspective realizes that a public commitment to change is at best only one of many ingredients necessary to bring it about and perceives the ERA's ratification as a signal for further mobilization.

The appropriate impact of the ERA should be as a symbol that women are to be taken seriously as full citizens for the first time in American history. Since such full participation is a fundamental goal of the Women's Liberation Movement, and the ERA has been perceived by many as a product of that Movement, its ratification should also legitimate feminism in general as well as many of its other goals. Certainly this "halo" effect is portended by the ERA's opposition, which sees its ratification as the forerunner of a feminist onslaught. Such a legitimation of feminist goals would not only facilitate their discussion and attainment but create expectations that certain changes will and should occur.

Such expectations, if thwarted, often lead to disaffection, anger, and further organization to bring them about. This is exactly what happened when "sex" was added to Title VII of the 1964 Civil Rights Act, prohibiting discrimination in employment against women for the first time on a national level. Although few women were even aware of the prohibition's existence, those who were became increasingly disgusted at the indifferent attitude of the Equal Employment Opportunity Commission, set up to enforce the Act. Consequently, it was people within the EEOC who first conceived the idea that the "sex" provision would be taken more seriously if there were "some sort of NAACP for women." While they couldn't organize such a pressure group, they spoke to many who could, and this action eventually resulted in the formation of the National Organization for Women in 1966.

This organization is one of several that contribute to the fulfillment of condition three of the model. These groups have not only been invaluable in getting the ERA out of Congress but have pressured the EEOC to enforce the "sex" provision of Title VII and aided passage and implementation of many other policies aimed at improving the opportunities and status of women.[11] The fact that these groups exist and have some of the resources necessary both to pressure and help the government develop and implement policies to benefit women greatly enhances the prospects of the ERA. It is these groups that carry the responsibility of seeing that the ERA is interpreted as a mandate for action; they are the ones that will have to function as watchdogs over the Amendment's implementation and guide the Movement of which it is a part.

While no one can prescribe exactly what functions these groups must perform, there are several obvious ones which should not be neglected. The means to carry out some of these needs already exist; others must be created. They include:

1) Funding and staffing a litigating body to pursue a strategy of selected legal cases which will lead to good judicial interpretations of the ERA. There is nothing preordained or absolute about court decisions. Judges are human just like legislators, and while they are subject to fewer pressures, their decisions can be influenced by the timing and nature of the cases they must decide. *Brown v. Board of Education of Topeka*[12] was not a lucky accident. It was the final move in efforts by the NAACP Legal Defense and Education Fund to narrow down the meaning of "separate but equal" until it became a *reductio ad absurdum*.[13] It is agreed by proponents and opponents alike that the ERA will result in a good deal of litigation before its specific meaning can be known. Whether this litigation is haphazard or planned will be a great determinant of what that meaning will be.

2) Mass education about what the ERA will and will not do and about other laws necessary to create a basis for real political change. In many ways the effort necessary to achieve ratification has been more beneficial than the Amendment itself. Debate over ratification has provided a forum in which to discuss the problems of women and the means necessary to alleviate them. Women's status has been subject to questioning in ways it never had been before. Neither the public nor the legislatures should be allowed to believe that ratification of the ERA means that vocal women will shut up. It would be very easy for the men who dominate policy making to argue that the Amendment is victory enough for the time being, that women should be quiet until time and the courts have determined just what impact it will have. Women's groups should make it clear that both the symbolic and tangible impacts are equally important and that the ERA's signal as a mandate for action should not be ignored.

3) Work with any government agencies concerned with enforcing or interpreting any policies on women so that they will be administered in women's interests. Women's organizations represent only one expression of an enforcement agency's clientele. Clientele are those "groups whose interests [are] strongly affected by an agency's activities [and provide] the principle sources of political support and opposition."[14] They include both those who are regulated and those in whose interest regulation occurs. As a general rule, the former are much better organized and more powerful than the latter. Thus, it is often the case that enforcement agency administrators are in contact with and come to identify with the regulated clientele and to adopt their perspective, even though contrary to the original intention of the policy. However, this general rule is not a hard-and-fast one. Women's organizations are quite capable of "capturing" an agency and influencing its implementation efforts—especially if sympathetic women can be instituted as the agency's principle administrators.

4) Mobilization of masses of people to demonstrate support as needed. Of the many resources organizations can use to influence policy, membership commitment is the most available to women's organizations. People must be stimulated to write letters to Congress and administrators, vote for sympathetic candidates, file and finance law suits and other complaints, lobby, march, and protest when necessary. Again, the effort to ratify the ERA is proving beneficial in this regard as the state debates provide an opportunity to reach potential new supporters with pro-equal rights arguments as well as to expose people to the often ridiculous positions of opponents. This momentum must not be lost with ratification. While the courts are determining the fine points of ERA implementation, women should turn their energies to other relevant areas, especially the elimination of all forms of

private discrimination, affirmative action, and the creation of institutions which will meet women's needs. The political education about how to organize supporters and how to influence legislatures still has many uses to which it can be put.

If the federal and state governments are highly resistant to developing and instituting policy to improve the status of women, organizational efforts by women's groups will have minimal impact on them. In the more likely case of governmental indifference, such pressures are the key to any success. The old adage of greasing the wheel that squeaks loudest is truer of government than almost anything else. Government agencies are subject to a sufficient number of demands to effectively prevent them from looking for any problems they don't already have. Putting laws on the books or adding amendments to the Constitution will not by themselves induce positive responses from a male-dominated government. A classic example of this lack of interest in women's problems occurred in the fall of 1969 in an interview the President's Task Force on the Status of Women had with one official of the Civil Rights Division. Why, they wanted to know, had not the Justice Department filed a single sex discrimination suit since the 1964 act was passed?[15] "We respond to social turmoil," the official told them. "The fact that women have not gone into the streets is indicative that they do not take employment discrimination too seriously." [16]

The ultimate solution, of course, is not merely legitimating equal rights under the Constitution but achieving equal participation in politics and society. That is the only way to make the Justice Department official's statement truly meaningless. However, this is a goal not likely to be reached in the near future, perhaps not in our lifetimes. But one can speculate on some of the many steps that may be taken on the way and their spin-off effects.

The initial impact of the ERA on the political system is already being experienced both by women and by the system itself. Two years of female time and energy went into getting the ERA out of Congress once Martha Griffiths submitted her discharge petition on June 11, 1970. During those years, the National Organization for Women, the Women's Equity Action League, the Business and Professional Women, and many other organizations and individuals oriented themselves to Congress as they had seen no need to before. The experience gained by those involved in this effort has not been lost. The Women's Lobby emerged out of the Ad Hoc Committee for the ERA, and both NOW and WEAL have turned their hard won expertise toward lobbying Congress on other issues of interest to women. The results have been impressive. More legislation on the status of women was passed by the Ninety-second Congress than had been passed by all previous Congresses put together. While the record of the Ninety-third Congress left something to be desired (most probably due to time spent on Watergate), the Ninety-fourth has resumed the momentum of the Ninety-second.

This new concern of Congress for women's issues is obviously not due solely to lobbying efforts. But most of it can be attributed to other beneficial side effects of the ERA fight. Primary among them was the climate it created in Congress of the presence of serious constituent interest in women's rights. The ERA, of all the legislative issues, was probably the most generative of voter response from a wide cross section of the population. As there was yet little organized opposition to women's rights legislation in general, this mail created the impression that there was strong constituent support for the whole policy area. And both the mail and the numerous respectable organizations which backed the ERA helped to dispel the negative impression of the Women's Liberation Movement created by the press. As Rep. Martha Griffiths (D-Mich. retired) expressed it, "The ERA created a moral climate for reform. Once it was put through, everything else became logical."[17]

The other major side effect was the establishment of liaisons by feminist organizations with Congressional staff and other established women's and liberal organizations. The ERA lobbying effort provided an excellent excuse to establish working relationships with and to educate staff and to seek support from nonfeminist organizations. The incipient network this created made it easier to know who to approach for what kind of support and/or information for other bills.

These effects are being at least partially replicated in the states, although with tremendous variety depending on the state. But there have been other effects as well, effects which are likely to have much longer-range impact on the political system because they increase women's feelings of political efficacy and change their self-image.

As *The American Voter* pointed out a decade ago:

> It is the sense of political efficacy that, with factors like education, age, and region controlled, differs most sharply and consistently between men and women. . . . Moralistic values about citizen participation in democratic government have been bred in women as in men; what has been less adequately transmitted to the women is a sense of political competence vis-à-vis the political world.[18]

An immediate impact of the ERA has been to increase the sense of political efficacy of those women involved in the fight. One result of their experience has been to make activity within the traditional political realm appear more possible and more appealing than it was before. To many, politics no longer seems too remote nor so irrelevant. A logical consequence of these feelings is not only to lobby for more legislation but to put oneself in a position to vote for more legislation, i.e., to run for office. This is initially most likely on the state level but should eventually be felt on the national as well. Women with political aspirations have traditionally been more likely to express them in running for state or local office than national office. Too, the lack of direct financial and career benefits available to state legislators compared to national ones means that the competition from qualified men is less. This movement has already begun. Between 1969 and 1974, women doubled their representation in the state legislatures.

Needless to say, the acquisition of elective office is only a first step. The next one is the acquisition of influence within the legislatures and the administrations. Women currently, and for a long time to come, must face resistance by male political leaders to both their running for and being in the legislature. However, the difficulties they encounter, while not inhibiting them, do bias the ways in which they acquire influence. According to Jeane Kirkpatrick, women legislators, more than men, are likely to carve a place for themselves on the basis of their dedication, hard work, and expertise rather than their personal friendships and symbiotic relationships with other legislators. The barriers which currently restrict their power are serious only when women attempt to move out of the ranks into positions of public leadership.[19]

Ironically, these barriers and the traditional sex roles which mold the life experience of most women representatives contribute to their high quality as legislators by protecting them from many of the temptations associated with holding public office. The freedom of many from the necessity of earning a living and the lack of realistic hopes for higher office insulate them from the pressures men experience to further their careers at the expense of the public interest.[20] As these restrictions cease, it is likely that new women entering the legislature will be less like their predecessors and more like their male peers.

As women increase their numbers in state legislatures, it would not be unreasonable to assume that an increasing amount of legislation relevant to women would be passed. This legislation will not come as a result of numbers alone, however. It is only with the advent of the Women's Liberation Movement that any but a few women representatives have taken interest in women's problems. Thus, one can infer that the continuation of this Movement as an active pressure group would be necessary for improvements to continue. Nonetheless, an increase in the number of women legislators is likely to increase the heterogeneity of those women elected and thus lead to an increase in sensitivity to the different problems women experience as a result of their traditional role. For example, currently only well-off and/or single women can easily escape the burden of family tasks and related female obligations. It was considered newsworthy when Rep. Yvonne Braithwaite Burke (D-Ca.) asked for a leave from House duties to have a baby, and when State Sen. Susan Catania (R-Ill.) nursed hers in the newly constructed women's room off the Senate floor. Although a public official who equally shares her household tasks with her husband has not been reported, such an event would probably be treated with similar surprise and shock. As these events become more commonplace, legislation to make such tasks easier on all women is a logical result. And, hopefully, those practices which cannot be changed by legislation—such as sharing housework—can be induced by a change of public opinion and increased private pressure. Such changes, however, will not necessarily extend to the problems of women whose needs are not reflected in the legislature. This would include women in the lower and SES brackets and other groups whose men are also underrepresented.

More women legislators are likely to lead to more women administrators as well, both elected and appointed. As women, in legislatures and out of them, learn how to use their vote to demand more benefits and more power, male political leaders will compete for this vote by recruiting more women to hold office. These developments in turn will both have an impact on and be a result of changes in the female population at large.

Much of women's poor sense of political efficacy comes from their traditional sex role training in passivity. This reinforced by the educational system which discourages girls from showing independence, exercising leadership, or pursuing nontraditional interests and occupations. Women who have not already learned the lesson of submission by the time they graduate learn it soon after as they confront the limited employment opportunities and limited pay available to them compared to men. Even if a woman has not been raised to believe that her only role and only fulfillment is as a wife and mother—a dependent of men—she discovers that it is probably the most remunerative option currently available to her.

Legislation prohibiting discrimination in education and employment—if successfully implemented—will create many more opportunities for women. The provision of day care centers and reproductive freedom will alleviate many of the uncertainties and burdens of family obligations. This should lead to greater economic independence and thus to greater freedom of action. With greater economic independence comes an increased sense of personal competence in general and with this an increased sense of political competence. [21] Both will be reinforced by the existence of many female role models in politics and in other authoritative positions.

What is less certain is the impact greater female political participation will have on public policies not directly relevant to women's condition. The evidence, though scanty, indicates there will be little. Many studies of voters have shown sex differences in the answers to various questions about political matters. However, most of the differences are small, and they are usually not consistent. Women are either more conservative or more liberal than men depending upon how one defines the terms. Thus, efforts to stereotype men's and women's attitudes lack statistical validity. Instead, factors such as age, race, socioeconomic status, and education play a far more important role in determining one's stands on political issues than does gender.[22] While one might postulate a continuation of the minor differences that will exist as long as men's and women's roles and social positions remain different, it is likely that the greater female participation necessary for these differences to have a policy effect would also be instrumental in wiping them out. As Kirkpatrick points out, "The same traditional roles which make women legislators more public spirited discourage them from becoming legislators at all."[23] In fact, the only way one could reasonably postulate serious sex differences in policy perspectives would be if one advocated not equality but female predominance. This is not a likely consequence of the ERA.

However, the fact that serious sex differences in policy making are not likely does not mean that political equality will have no effects on policy at all. Such a fundamental change in the distribution of power that political equality would entail is bound to have a major effect on society and eventually on policy. But the change will come as a consequence of the redistribution itself not because women occupy more policy-making roles.

Speculating about the effects of a major power redistribution is obviously conjectural. The multitude of ramifications could not even be guessed. But for the sake of argument, let us speculate upon one possible consequence. If, as asserted earlier, political participation would increase with economic independence, and vice versa, political equality would imply that economic opportunities were also equally distributed among men and women. Bergmann has calculated that if the current number of employed hours were equally distributed by sex, everyone would work a 31-hour week.[24] Whatever other effects such a redistribution would have, it would certainly lead to more leisure time for both men and women. What people do with their leisure time is always open to debate, but given the particular values of our society, it would not be at all surprising if a major consequence were more time spent getting a formal—and perhaps informal—education. Such a potential increase in the general level of education is of great significance to the political system for education has been shown to affect one's opinions on political and social issues more than virtually any other factor. In particular, the possession of a college education is associated with a cluster of attitudes and values commonly designated "liberal."

Work redistribution would also provide more time to be active politically, and it is the politically active who influence policy. A major critique of our political system is that most people don't have the resources to influence policy, and time is certainly an important resource. Time coupled with education could well lead to more active involvement in politics by more people, thus bringing us closer to our democratic ideals. Whether such greater involvement would lead to better public policy, one cannot say. But, if it were to occur, political involvement would provide the opportunity to overcome some of the alienation created by our vast, technological society.

Footnotes

1. The 1972 and 1974 elections indicate women may be starting to use the vote to elect preferred candidates.

2. William O'Neill, *Everyone Was Brave* (Chicago: Quadrangle, 1969), p. 267.

3. The classic example of this is the loss of *de facto* voting rights by blacks in the South after the Civil War.

4. James P. Levine, "Methodological Concerns in Studying Supreme Court Efficacy," *Law and Society*, 4 May 1970, p. 592.

5. See Harrell R. Rodgers, Jr. and Charles S. Bullock, III, *Law and Social Change* (New York: McGraw-Hill, 1972), pp. 198-99; Theodore J. Lowi, *The End of Liberalism* (New York: W. W. Norton, 1969), ch. 5.

6. Harmon Zeigler, *Interest Groups in American Society* (Englewood Cliffs, N.J.: Prentice-Hall, 1964), pp. 292-93; Philip Selznick, *TVA and the Grass Roots* (Berkeley: University of California Press, 1949); Marver Bernstein, *Regulating Business by Independent Commission* (Princeton, N.J.: Princeton University Press, 1955).

7. "The Proposed Equal Rights Amendment to the United States Constitution," a Memorandum of the Citizens' Advisory Council on the Status of Women, Washington, D.C., March 1970, pp. 10-11. Originally introduced into Congress in 1923, for the first twenty years the ERA was worded to read: "Men and women shall have equal rights throughout the United States and every place subject to its jurisdiction." This wording would likely have prohibited private action that violated the principle of equal rights, but the wording recommended to the Senate on May 23, 1943, which was eventually passed in 1972, was altered to read, "Equality of rights under the law shall not be denied or abridged by the United States or by any State on account of sex."

8. Ibid., p. 11. The authors based their assessments on Congressional Committee reports on the ERA since these reports "are regarded by the courts as the most persuasive evidence of the intended meaning of a provision." (p. 10)

9. Virginia Slims Corp. has sponsored "American Women's Opinion Polls" in 1970, 1972, and 1974 which asked this and other questions. The first two were done by Louis Harris and the third by the Roper Organization.

10. Sheldon W. Wolin, *Politics and Vision* (Boston: Little, Brown and Co., 1960), p. 76.

11. See Jo Freeman, *The Politics of Women's Liberation* (New York: McKay, 1975), chs. 3 and 6.

12. 349 U.S. 294 (1955).

13. For a brief description of this strategy, see Thomas R. Dye, *The Politics of Equality* (Indianapolis: Bobbs-Merrill, 1971), pp. 29-34.

14. Herbert A. Simon, Donald W. Smithburg, and Victor A. Thompson, *Public Administration* (New York: Alfred A. Knopf, 1950), pp. 29-34.

15. At that time Justice was the only government agency that could go to court. The EEOC was not given this power until the Civil Rights Act was amended in 1972.

16. Interview with Benjamin Mintz, Office of Civil Rights, Justice Department, October 1969.

17. Interview of February 1973.

18. Angus Campbell, Philip E. Converse, Warren E. Miller, and Donald E. Stokes, *The American Voter* (New York: Wiley and Sons, 1964), pp. 485-87.

19. Jeane J. Kirkpatrick, *Political Woman* (New York: Basic Books, 1975), ch. 6. This book is based on indepth interviews of 50 women state legislators with records of effectiveness who attended a conference by the Center for the American Woman and Politics at the Eagleton Institute of Politics, at Rutgers, N.J. in May 1972.

20. Ibid., chs. 7 and 8. Almost all of Kirkpatrick's interviewees were wives and mothers, accepted most traditional female roles and interests, and embodied the traditional role expectations—except for their strong interest in politics. Their feelings of political efficacy derived from being raised in socially conscious families who stressed community activity, including political participation, regardless of sex.

21. One study of data from the 1956, 1960, and 1964 Presidential elections concluded: "When working women and [housewives] were compared at each education level, it was found that women who engaged in work were more politically involved and participated more in the political process than those who stayed at home; and further, that they had a higher sense of political efficacy and a higher sense of citizen obligation." [Morris Levitt, "The Political Role of American Women," *Journal of Human Relations* 15 (1967): 32.]

22. See Jane Jacquette's Introduction to *Women in Politics* (New York: John Wiley and Sons, 1974) for a good review of the literature. The Virginia Slims Polls (1974) also conclude that "gender appears to be among the weakest influences on attitudes and opinions." (p. 120)

23. Kirkpatrick, p. 214. Although many of her interviewees felt women were "more realistic, more moral, more humane, more grandiose, less corruptible, less pompous, less sentimental" (p. 162), they did not relate these differences to observable policy or party differences. Instead they were attributed to freedom from the need to earn a living. I do not know of any study which shows that sex will predict any voting differences (except on women's rights issues) by legislators.

24. Barbara R. Bergmann, "The Economics of Women's Liberation," Project on the Economics of Discrimination, University of Maryland, 1972, p. 8.

ECONOMIC IMPACT

Introduction to Economic Impact

Establishing equality in the workplace is not an easy task at a time of economic crisis. When unemployment runs rampant, many people consider feminist objectives for equal economic participation selfish, and those objectives are difficult to implement when hiring is at a minimum anyway and layoffs go by the "last hired, first fired" rule. 51% of nothing equals nothing, and progress comes to a shuttering halt. Carolyn Shaw Bell assesses these economic realities in terms of the extent to which they impede the implementation of the ERA. What can we realistically expect to be the impact of the ERA in a depressed U.S. economy? However, Dr. Bell does not find the picture totally bleak; rather, she finds that certain positive factors about economic crisis itself aid rather than hinder the realization of the ERA.

Further, the failure of affirmative action programs to date provides a concrete analogy to other kinds of implementation problems which the ERA will face in materializing equality in the workplace. Enacted by Executive Orders, Affirmative Action hasn't the force of law, but it has the perhaps more powerful force of financial sanction. Even so, it has been ineffectively implemented, as have other antidiscrimination laws. It is an excellent example of the way in which amendments and laws stagnate in the face of both active individual opposition and inertia, as treated in our articles on political impact. Anne Miner brings her practical firsthand knowledge to bear not only on these limitations to the ERA's economic impact but also on the ways in which the ERA can be used to flex the muscles of employers toward true affirmative action.

ERA economics groans beneath the weight of the statistical disproportion between women and men, both professionals and laborers. The touchstone of ERA commitment is the comfort with which one can envision a totally 50-50 sharing of every occupation and the extent to which one welcomes it. The probability that this is a comfortable expectation to only militant feminists defines the burden of the ERA.

But statistics are only the tip of the iceberg. We have become conscious of the fact that occupational sex role division is culture-bound, that is, in one culture a job considered masculine may be considered feminine in another.

71

But what is not often mentioned is that the status or prestige of the culturally feminine occupations is almost universally lower in every case. Where a man does the same job as a woman, even within the same society, that job has a fancier label, more prestige, and higher financial rewards, e.g., physicians in Russia are predominantly women, but the profession has low status; the swankiest restaurants have waiters, not waitresses; men are "chefs" in important establishments, not "cooks" in the home, college "professors," not elementary school "teachers," and on and on. Even when women enter the male-dominated professions, they are given the unrewarding detail work often identified as more "feminine." In the face of such discrimination women are forced to lower their career expectations and then are accused of being more "naturally" suited to and fulfilled by familial responsibilities, which in turn militate against their professional participation even further. The wheel of fortune goes round and round, and only the ERA can stop its vicious circle and give women an equal chance at its economic rewards and responsibilities. Cynthia Fuchs Epstein discusses the opportunities the ERA will provide for professional women as well as the consequences of equal opportunity for other spheres of life.

The full economic implementation of the ERA would have an enormous impact on society. Full and equal participation of women in the work force at all levels is only the beginning of its ramifications. The future holds possibilities for both a redefinition of work itself and an economic restructuring of society, currently organized around male assumptions and male convenience, which are only relative and which make female participation difficult. Dual-career family needs will entail the reorganization of work role and domestic role relationships as well as environmental change.

As work becomes more important to women, it will become less important to men, since men will no longer be the only ones to define themselves in achievement and economic terms. A different value will be set on work itself for both sexes as family, community, and play activities become more integral parts of our lives through the sharing of both work burdens and work rewards. It may, in fact, be true that work as "self-fulfilling achievement" has been overvalued by feminists. Fulfilling work depends upon socioeconomic status, prestige, and challenge. How many men, let alone women, have jobs which rank high in these variables? What is needed is a de-emphasis on work itself as the *only* useful and fulfilling way of expressing oneself. This means, for one thing, channeling men into the learning experience of the very real gratifications as well as frustrations of family life and responsibility. Janet Saltzman Chafetz explores some of the ways in which a fully implemented ERA might possibly redefine the role of work in our lives and, concomitantly, reorganize work and family life. A more viable and efficient relationship between the family and the economy is both a possible outcome of and a necessity for the realization of the ERA.

The economic reorganization of family life is not only important to the world of work outside the family but is important in and of itself, that is, within the family structure. Anne K. Bingaman considers the economic inequities in marriage and divorce. With emphasis on sex discrimination in marital property rights and credit, she focuses on the possibilities for ERA impact, a much more tangible one than any the ERA will have on the social or psychological inequalities of the marital relationship. In terms of ERA theory, this article illustrates well the potential use of the ERA to reform those laws which are sex neutral in their language but which have a discriminatory impact upon one sex because of present social reality—a crucial area of the ERA's legal jurisdiction.

There are many other specific individual economic rights, outside marriage and the world of work proper, that will be affected by the ERA: government benefits like social security, insurance premiums and payments, differential treatment in employment and disability coverage due to pregnancy, to name only a few. We have chosen insurance ratings as a financial problem of individual rights to point up a very subtle issue in the application of the ERA. We are, in fact, using the issue to tell as much about ERA theory as about insurance. The matter of sex differentials in insurance ratings is a particularly crucial problem because such classifications seem to be based on biological differences between the sexes; that is, it is widely assumed that biological factors are responsible for life expectancy differences between women and men. Moreover, when the sacred cow of biology is involved, people generally assume any "discrimination" to be legitimate, necessary, or at best, unavoidable. Thus it doesn't appear immediately that ERA can or should have any impact.

In the course of extending ERA theory even into the domain of apparent biological sex differences, Ann Freedman and Barbara Brown go far beyond the matter of insurance rates *per se* to show exactly how the ERA will or potentially can operate in the legal process and what possibilities its application holds for the replacement of sex classifications with sex neutral rules (classifications which cross sex lines). They do this even by allowing for the possibility that characteristics unique to one sex will be exempted under the ERA and considered a legal basis for classification under certain conditions. While this is by no means a foregone conclusion, theirs is the very kind of reasoning which must be marshalled against the possibility of such court interpretation, for we cannot ignore the ERA's limitations.

For this reason, it would be well to assume that the definition of legal equality under the ERA will not be absolute but problematic. The ERA goes a long way toward clarifying sex as a "suspect" classification, which the Fourteenth Amendment does not do (see introduction to this volume). But in practice we have a continuum of discrimination, ranging from very obvious situations in which women's rights are abridged as a result of social roles assigned or denied them for no rational or factual reason to those shady areas in which biology seems to provide the rationale for legal (or constitutional) discrimination. When learned, and therefore relative, social behavior can be faulted for the discrimination, the ERA is likely to be interpreted by clear-cut standards of review: that is, "strict scrutiny" of a particular law or practice based on a sex classification would require a very serious reason indeed to justify it as a valid exception. When apparently biological behavior is responsible for the discriminatory law or practice, it may very well be difficult to get the Court to refrain from exempting the classifications from the ERA. Our discussion of the use of biology as a rationale for discrimination is directed toward this projected Court mentality and is in the way of preparation for it. Should proponents of equality be successful in securing a narrow interpretation from the courts of the biological mandate for discrimination, the ERA is likely to have a very far-reaching effect in the more social areas, and a powerful impact would be assured.

Hopefully, the discussion of biological discrimination will point up two things: first, the legal significance of ERA and its limitations and possibilities for legal impact; and second, the need for a rational assessment of the role of biology in specific cases. If biology is to be considered in any way an adequate rationale for differential treatment, at the very least it must be proved, rather than assumed, that physiological sex differences both cause and necessitate a particular legal sex classification. If women are to attain full economic equality through the ERA, they will have to marshal their greatest resources of legal logic and scientific research. Again, as we must often emphasize, ERA is a tool that can be used or left idle or interpreted so narrowly as to make it meaningless. We have used the economic realm to demonstrate the legal potential of ERA because that is where present litigation has centered and where the issues are likely to be most critical.

Economic Realities Anticipated

Carolyn Shaw Bell

The economic impact of ERA will depend on the particular economic climate that exists at the time implementation is called for. Whether changes necessitated by ERA itself, or by the altered social climate that it represents, will be easily accepted can be predicted only in terms of a specific time-frame. Over the long run quite different goals, strategies, and problems will be relevant to ERA than appear in the short run. It is never easy to draw a firm distinction between the immediate and the eventual, and it is particularly difficult in the case of social change or innovations like ERA whose consequences, almost by definition, cannot be exhaustively catalogued. Economists, however, have labored over the problem of distinguishing short and long term in a variety of circumstances, and their approach may prove useful in this case.

In dealing with market phenomena, economists analyze changes that occur from a realignment of existing elements over varying periods of time. For example, the currently existing supply of labor consists of those people who are at present working plus those actively seeking work. This supply can vary, over the short run, by several millions of people and by a larger number of labor-hours. It is possible to lengthen or shorten work-time, so that everyone employed puts in fifty or twenty hours a week, or it is possible to vary the amount of vacation and/or leave. People can retire early or late, young people can find a change in the relative attractiveness of school, or the legal school-leaving age can be altered. It is possible to find jobs for those not in the labor force—including drop-outs, those with home responsibilities, or the disabled—or conversely, to persuade people to give up their jobs and leave the labor force. All such changes would be *short-term* variations in the supply of labor, and most of them can be effected by changing the price offered for working, e.g., market wages relative to the costs of going to school or taking care of one's home or retiring. These changes in wages need not be great and they can also occur fairly rapidly.

On the other hand, within this country the potential labor supply clearly has finite limits. The number of people living here in 1975 cannot be readily expanded or contracted beyond the natural rates of births, deaths, immigration, and emigration which affect the existing population. One can envisage, however, policies to encourage (or discourage) childbearing, efforts to prolong life, and barriers to the movement of people between countries. But all these changes would take time to affect the supply of *labor*: a rise in the birth rate does not immediately increase the number of available workers. Furthermore, while such shifts in human behavior may be induced by changes in wages, or prospective wages, relative to other prices, other inducements must, in all likelihood, also exist. The customs of people, their ways of living and bringing up children, their ideas of what is conventional in or appropriate to our society, all the surrounding framework of human behavior would also be forced to change. Such alterations in the social climate—involving political, ethical, and institutional shifts—take years and perhaps generations to be accomplished. The economist must recognize such *long-term* trends, even as they involve noneconomic or at least nonmarket phenomena.

It is also possible to distinguish categories of change which, although occurring primarily in response to economic stimuli, take longer to work out than the short-term shifts of the existing population described earlier. To continue with the example of labor supply, the number of physicians giving health services can be fairly rapidly expanded by wage changes or other economic incentives. Those with medical training who do research or administrative work, who have retired, or who devote their time to home responsibilities can be coaxed or prodded into active service in the health care delivery system. The supply of medical services is somewhat elastic, to use the economist's adjective. However, at the moment there exists only a finite number of people with sufficient medical *training* to yield such an expansion of the supply; to get more services would mean training more people to become physicians. But medical training itself takes time. And the resources used to educate doctors and develop their specialized skills may themselves be limited, so that the number of potential physicians is not readily enlarged. Given enough time, however, such limitations can be overcome.

Such time-period analysis can be usefully applied to the economic impact of ERA. In the short run, the immediate economic climate and the existing structure of prices and wages may provide either obstacles to or encouragement for the implementation of the Amendment. In the long run, the legislation may bring about economic changes inducing shifts in the social climate. (Of course, the legislation may itself encourage such long-run shifts directly.) This paper will focus chiefly on the first of these, with some attention given to the second. Because the economy can vary sharply in the short run, distinguishing different types of economic conditions will be more helpful than attempting to predict the economic climate for a given date. An economy emerging from a decade of stagnant growth will provide quite a different atmosphere for ERA than one entering a period of sharp decline in production and employment.

THE ECONOMIC CLIMATE FOR SOCIAL CHANGE

It has been argued that the process of *innovation* achieves success most frequently during periods of economic advance: recovery if not booming prosperity, steady development if not accelerating growth. What are the implications of this reasoning for acceptance and implementation of ERA?

The argument has two major sources. Most analysts of income distribution agree that cutting more equal shares out of a steadily growing pie is far easier than changing the distribution of an existing or shrinking volume of material goods and services. And, in fact, the only significant reductions of poverty, either recently or historically, have taken place when the general populace has enjoyed rising levels of economic well-being. Second, the analysis of technological change seems to show beneficial results from an expanding economy. Technical innovations generally require optimistic expectations on the part of entrepreneurs and somewhat ebullient acquiescence on the part of those consumers or workers or buyers or bankers whose functioning changes as a result of the innovation. Both these moods are associated with "good times," when people find their own economic prospects and the general outlook not only satisfactory but positively encouraging. But neither example speaks directly to the economic climate needed to assure the success of innovations like ERA which comprise not only economic but social change. Both, however, contain suggestive ideas.

As of mid-1975, the most common fear was that a period of economic depression would impede the acceptance of implementation of ERA. Learning how to deal with major new legislation would impose costs on firms already saddled with rising costs. Integrating the laws making women's rights and responsibilities no less or more than those of men into the social fabric would create more problems and rising costs for governments and organizations at every level. Making the rights and responsibilities of women no less or more than those of men constitutes, in a very real sense, a massive redistribution not only of income but of status and of social and cultural wealth. Both assets and liabilities are involved: women will become liable for new forms of debt or responsibilities and men will acquire new rights in property or claims to property. These are very powerful arguments for hoping that ERA can be achieved at a time when economically, at least, everyone is becoming better off.

On the other hand, impending economic emergency or a threat of economic catastrophe can also mobilize people to accept different patterns of action. Certainly the experience of World War II offers a clear case of the acceptance of rapid and profound upsets in social attitudes and behavior. Not only did women penetrate, easily and with general approval, barriers to occupations and conditions of employment, but they were encouraged to adopt life styles which asserted their independence and capability rather than cautioned to accept the usual role of submissive helplessness. When women's contributions as workers in fields and factories were deemed socially useful, it was easy to change institutional arrangements providing child care facilities, training courses, and new modes of sharing in transportation and living surroundings. Nor does the irony that all these circumstances reverted with equal rapidity once the war was over negate the fact that an economic emergency did facilitate social change. One could even argue that, if ERA came into being which the country faced severe depression or serious readjustments, the existence of such economic problems could facilitate the implementation of the new legislation.

During the years since the end of World War II, the composition of the labor force has changed significantly, with particular implications for equal rights to work and wages for men and women. This thirty-year period has also encompassed several economic cycles, with the longest period of prosperity (and the sharpest coincidence of inflation with depression) known to recent economic history. Throughout, the trend of increasing participation in the labor force by women has not slowed. It follows that the economic contributions of women have become more firmly embedded in national production, income, and employment than ever before. Oddly, however, these contributions have not yet been fully recognized. One immediate result of ERA may be to finally force public recognition of the existing situation.

WOMEN AS WORKERS: THE RIGHT TO UNEMPLOYMENT AS WELL AS TO JOBS

In 1947 about 32% of all women over 16 were in the labor force (including the armed forces) compared to 87% of the men. Comparable figures for 1973 show 45% of the women and about 80% of the men participating in the work force. It follows that the total working population today includes a far higher proportion of women than it did in the years immediately after World War II. One simple, but rarely cited, conclusion is that women were responsible for much of the growth in output which occurred over the same period when gross national product in real terms more than doubled. The volume of goods and services available to people during these years would have been far smaller without the labor services of women. Of course, the employment of women has not yet achieved the levels of output that are potentially available when women have equal access to all jobs and all types of occupations. The occupational segregation which characterizes employment has prevented productivity gains by preventing women from using all their abilities and skills. But to a considerable extent the great productive engine of the U.S. economy has become dependent on womanpower.

What has been noticed is the effect on unemployment rates, as presently calculated, of this change in the composition of the labor force. In each of the postwar recessions unemployment has reached successively higher rates, and in each of the subsequent recoveries the rate has failed to drop completely back. As a result, policy makers have revised the so-called full employment target rate from 4% unemployment to 5 or 5 1/2%, with the bald explanation that the presence of large numbers of women and teenagers make it impossible to attain the lower figure. It is taken for granted that unemployment among women will be higher than among men. In fact, this assumption needs to be carefully examined.

First, the accepted notion that women have higher rates of unemployment than men has not been true among nonwhites, for example, until recently—almost half the women have been in the labor force for many years, and unemployment among men exceeded that among women until about 1963. Second, among part-time workers the rate of joblessness for men exceeds that for women—women outnumber men in the voluntary part-time labor force by about two to one. Further, the steady increase in the number of women and the proportion of white women who have joined the labor force has tended to erode these differences, so that unemployment rates for men and women have tended to converge. Moreover, the classification of unemployment *only* by sex, ignoring other statistical factors, presents a partial, and therefore distorted, explanation.

Despite all the data, sex is possibly one of the least useful variables with which to analyze unemployment. People neither lose nor leave their jobs because of genetic inheritance: if anything reflects economic determinants, it is employment. All the analyses of women's employment disclose economic variables: the concentration of women in jobs or locations where unemployment tends to be high, the number of working women in areas subject to rising layoffs, and some association, for married women only, between husband's job location or job termination. None of these, of course, are sexual characteristics; they describe various structural aspects of the economy. However, there is little doubt that rising unemployment has focused a closer look at women in the labor force.

With the onset of depression levels of unemployment in late 1974, other indications appeared of the profound implications of women's participation in the labor force. One is the fact that a working wife represents a kind of secondary unemployment insurance in a family where the working husband has been laid off. Interviews with people at state employment offices or union halls have found repeated comments to the effect that the father can stay home with the kids while his wife switches to full-time work or that the family income will be protected by earnings brought in by a working wife. The multiearner family, which in fact outnumbers those dependent on the "primary male earner," otherwise known as the "breadwinner," is gradually becoming publicly apparent. As more and more workers realize that such families are common, it may not be too much to hope that policy makers will finally become aware of the existence of this social pattern. Some evidence that multiearner families provide special kinds of economic stability appeared in legislation introduced early in 1975 to provide federal health insurance for the unemployed whose former jobs had provided such coverage. Most of the drafts required that unemployed workers could not be eligible if they could be covered by health insurance plans available to another employed family member, thereby recognizing that not only money income but other forms of compensation also depended on more than one earner in a family. And the Supreme Court's decision in March 1975, awarding survivor's benefits under social security to a widower, represented another confirmation.

The other depression phenomenon has been the conflict between affirmative action plans and seniority rights as layoffs increased in industries which had found women entering new jobs during the 1970s. The phrase "last hired, first fired," which had threatened racial tension during the downturn of the early '60s after broad-based attempts to increase minority hirings, became widely applicable to women as well as to minorities in 1974-75. Whether or not seniority rights take precedence over affirmative action plans to remedy past discrimination is a question for court action, and at least four appeals in four different districts were pending in mid-1975. Legally, there seemed every expectation that the question of interpreting Title VII of the Civil Rights Act would reach the Supreme Court. ERA by itself, of course, would not change the course of these cases nor of future action.

The importance of this issue, however, is that it focuses on these women and minorities as *workers* not as special cases or as social problems. Both unions and management, as well as legislators and EEOC staff, have been searching for alternative solutions. The dilemma is typical of social change: the conflict between a well-established, morally defensible right based on length of service and an innovative, untested claim based on new law and a value system not widely accepted. It is interesting to note, however, that this particular threat of economic emergency has called for new modes of *sharing*—of work by accepting shorter hours, or of unemployment by rotating jobs—just as sharing has provided solutions in earlier cases of economic scarcity. There is some evidence that job-sharing succeeds when it can be figured out by the workers themselves and that where they feel a sense of cohesiveness and group belonging, it leads to ready adoption of shorter hours or rotating work. Larger units with more formal interpersonal connections, on the other hand, more frequently refuse to change the impact of unemployment on particular employees. As far as workers themselves are concerned, sharing hardship occurs where the individual is important as a person in need or as someone who belongs to the working group. There is no evidence that the sex of the individual *per se* has any bearing on these decisions.

The acceptance of women in the work force, therefore, has given a new meaning to ERA—women now have equal rights to unemployment and, therefore, to claims for assistance as unemployed workers. Given economic recovery, women will have renewed arguments to demand wider acceptance, because they will have suffered just as men from their labor force participation.

The immediate impact of an economic turnaround, as hirings begin to increase, should be the allowance for ready implementation of ERA. Overall figures on employment and unemployment tend to obscure the fact of labor turnover, the fact that every day and every month some people are getting hired, whether total employment is rising or falling. Not all the jobs that have been reopened get filled by previous workers, and therefore, in a time of rising output, new opportunities for women occur. Furthermore, with firms highly conscious of the need to increase productivity, ERA would allow for a more intensive search for the best qualified worker. To ignore, again, the largely untapped economic resource of women's unused skills and potential capabilities may finally appear clearly unacceptable to a profit-minded management, especially if foreign competition continues to show larger gains in productivity.

WOMEN'S INCOME AND ERA

Widening employment opportunities, plus affirmative action programs, plus suits to raise wages or collect damages for past discrimination, plus new training programs to open up higher-paying positions can all be expected to lead to increased income for women workers. In the short run, however, the gap between men's and women's earnings cannot be expected to disappear, and ERA will have no impact one way or another on this differential. Like the difference in unemployment rates by sex, this difference in earnings represents a complex bundle of disparate factors and needs careful analysis.

The clearest and most precise statement of the differential cites the *median earnings* of *full-time, year-round* workers. In 1963, this figure for women amounted to 63% of that for men; in 1973 the ratio had dropped to 57%. Nothing in these two statements proves that discrimination exists. However, the statements should not be confused with other facts about *income* (which include dividends, rents, transfers, and other payments besides earnings from employment). Nor should average earnings of *all* women workers be compared to those of men because lower earnings among part-time workers obviously lowers an average. The distinction between full-time and year-round is important: the first classification refers to a job providing at least 35 hours of work per week; the second means 50 weeks or more during the previous calendar year. Women outnumber men in both categories, although it is important not to exaggerate the differences. Employment for part of the *year* in 1973 was reported by 17 million men and 20 million women; part-*time* jobs were held by 8 million men and 13 million women. Finally, the 57% ratio of women's earnings to men's does not hold for all occupations: for example, salaried women professional and technical workers earned, in 1973, 65% of what their male counterparts earned, and this ratio has been increasing over the years.

The primary cause of the worsening position of women workers in terms of earned income has been the influx of women into the labor force coupled with stringent occupational barriers. While wages have generally risen, the increase over the past decade for those types of employment known as "women's jobs" has fallen short of the average, simply because, with more women available, competition served to dampen the increases. Exactly the reverse took place in those occupations restricted to men, where wages rose much higher; the overall result was a widening of the earnings gap. To the extent that long-term changes in education and occupational outlook for both sexes reduce segregation by sex, the earnings differential may finally begin to narrow, but its abolition can in no way be accomplished in the short run. The impact of ERA on the gradual process of lessening this differential will lie, in the short run, in the area of educational and training opportunities as well as the broader arena of social and cultural change.

The economist recognizes the persistent and worsening differential between earnings by sex as an indicator of separate markets, in which different prices can be maintained because there is little or no mobility between the two. For men to move into "women's jobs" and women to compete equally with men for all jobs represents a kind of labor mobility that requires similarity among men and women in specific characteristics of acquired skills, previous experience, availability, and so on. This similarity will not be quickly forthcoming.

To work through some familiar examples, beginning with the early years of schooling, girls and boys differ in their mathematical skills and later on in their acquaintance with scientific and technical fields dependent on mathematics. As a result vocational and professional education appears to be sex related, and applicants for jobs or training programs segregate themselves by sex "naturally." Once hired, the "first" woman trainee for the job of police officer or bank loan manager, the few women chemists in an industrial research outfit or on a university faculty face pressures of performance that may, realistically, prevent their acquiring the years of experience, or the kind of on-the-job experience, associated with a typical work history for men. Finally, home responsibilities of a husband and/or children will prevent the working woman's availability from equaling that of the man, if only because of preconceived notions held by those around her. Changing all these circumstances, or even shifting their incidence slightly, is a process that requires time. These influences on mobility consist, in fact, of precisely the types of structural factors identified by economists as long-term determinants of the supply of labor, as described in the beginning of this paper.

Women's earnings have another significance for the impact of ERA, however, in terms of what the legislation will mean for family responsibilities. The single parent family has meant, to all intents and purposes, a mother and children; only 400,000 of the 4.4 million single parent families in 1973 contained a father and minor children. The number of families headed by women has grown rapidly over the past decade, and some structural defects of income distribution and income maintenance programs have probably contributed to this growth. If ERA has any effect on the generally accepted notion that children "ought" to be with their mother or that a divorced woman will automatically receive custody of any offspring, this situation may change. Interpreting the responsibilities of parents as equal in both the nurturing and financial spheres would radically change the opportunities open to women as workers and would also change the demands made on women's earning capacities. Some indications of the possibilities can be found in two instances: work requirements for welfare mothers and child support provisions couched in terms of the financial capacities of parents rather than fathers.

Welfare policies have shifted from the philosophy in the thirties that financial assistance should be provided to enable women to continue their occupations with home and family in the absence of a male earner to the present insistence that able-bodied women should find gainful employment outside the home to finance the family. While this shift may reflect society's acceptance of women as productive workers, it has not, in the design of welfare policies, been accompanied by any parallel acceptance of men as reproductive partners, equally responsible for the care of offspring. However, a man's nurturant or parental capacities have become recognized in nonwelfare cases of divided families or divorces where fathers have obtained custody of the children. Financial contributions by mothers would complete the picture, and to the extent that mothers achieve higher economic status, this type of arrangement will become more common.

Economic Uncertainty and ERA

Probably the most powerful short-term impact of ERA must be its contribution to anxiety via uncertainty. From any point of view, uncertainty is one of the worst possible states of mind. From an economic standpoint, it is a classic source of depression as well as a deterrent to recovery. Uncertainty about future markets, about labor relations, about the availability of material or capital supplies, or about general economic expectations can dampen business investment or retard normal growth. It follows that any additional source of uncertainty must be resented, and to the extent that ERA breeds uncertainty, it will be opposed in the short run. Although some uncertainty surrounding the legislation is inevitable, much of it is probably unnecessary because it represents ignorance or misconceptions about the actual requirements of the Amendment. To the general goal of securing widespread understanding and dispelling the inaccuracies of anti-ERA lobbying efforts should be added the specific aim of reducing economic insecurity by careful explanation before enactment and continual monitoring afterwards.

The Lesson of Affirmative Action for the Equal Rights Amendment

Anne S. Miner

INTRODUCTION

Among those who take an active interest in the subject there is little agreement on how well affirmative action programs in employment are "working." Corporate and other leaders often feel they are working well within reasonable expectations. Some advocate groups feel they are not working at all or, if they have any impact, it is shockingly slow. Many people believe affirmative action programs work but only for the groups of which they are not a member. Most who help administer the programs see significant change as well as disappointing failures. They also see disturbing confusion in the general public about what affirmative action programs *are,* and only a slowly developing understanding of affirmative action principles in their own organizations. Many of the key concepts on which formal affirmative action plans are based are barely understood except by attorneys, and even among the attorneys there is serious dispute on important points.

Nonetheless, there is much to be learned from the principles of and obstacles to affirmative action programs in employment. The first part of this paper reviews some of the fundamental principles of formal affirmative action programs, assesses their broad achievement to date, and describes some of the major obstacles to their implementation. This is followed by a discussion of the potential impact of the ERA on employment and, finally, an analysis of the implications of the obstacles to affirmative action for the implementation of the ERA.

Although, for the sake of simplicity, the main focus of this article is sex equality in employment opportunity, the reader should bear in mind that the phrase "affirmative action" evolved from the long and continuing effort to

85

achieve racial equality in employment. President Roosevelt issued the first Executive Order forbidding racial discrimination by federal contractors during World War II, and the current laws and regulations about employment discrimination are the result of thirty years of struggle to give meaning to the concept of equal employment opportunity.

Expectations about Affirmative Action and Evaluation of Its Progress

The term "affirmative action" is often applied to any set of actions designed to help members of ethnic minorities or women in employment or to active discrimination in *favor* of such groups. Neither is an accurate notion of the formal meaning of affirmative action programs. Although even a summary of the laws, administrative orders, and court decisions that define affirmative action exceeds the scope of this paper, anyone who seeks to understand such programs should be aware of at least the following general ideas.

There is no single, comprehensive, national "law" about affirmative action but rather a combination of state and federal laws about nondiscrimination in employment, a federal executive order that applies only to federal contractors, and many additional riders (about employment) to laws on other subjects. Three major forces shape the national employment picture. First, Title VII of the Civil Rights Act of 1964 forbids discrimination by race, sex, national origin, and religion. This law applies to nearly all employers but does not explicitly require any "affirmative action" unless the employer has been found to discriminate. Many important affirmative action precedents have resulted from court decisions made under this law, however. Some of the court imposed remedies have included explicit hiring quotas to correct the effects of proven past discrimination.

Second, Executive Order 11375 forbids discrimination by major federal contractors and, as interpreted through a document known as Order No. 4, requires each to develop a formal written affirmative action plan. Order No. 4 is not a law; it can and does evolve. It specifies a number of procedural steps each employer must take in order to have an acceptable affirmative action program.

Third, the Equal Pay Act affects nearly all employers and is quite separate from either of the above. Recently expanded in its coverage, this act requires equal pay for "substantially similar" work done by men and women, with provision for merit and seniority systems. Adjustments to correct inequality can be made only by raising the salaries of the lower paid group.

All of these regulations are separately enforced by different agencies, and they are by no means the only ones affecting an individual employer, who may also be subject to regulations specific to the institution (e.g., the Higher Education Act) or its locale (e.g., state employment laws). Whatever other principles guide them, affirmative action programs are also designed to make them consistent (to whatever degree possible) with all of the above.

At the risk of oversimplifying, let us review the basic principles of most formal affirmative action programs. Their specific purpose is to achieve *nondiscrimination* or *effective equal opportunity*. In principle, this means that the employer examines every practice, procedure, and policy and takes steps to insure that, regardless of intent, each has no unnecessary *de facto* discriminatory impact. In terms of hiring, for example, this usually means that the employer is committed to two things: first, to the active recruitment of groups previously absent either from the institution or from a particular kind of job (an activity sometimes known as "taking down the 'white-male-only' sign"); second, to the use of objective and valid selection criteria in hiring. This latter concept relates chiefly to Title VII, under which the Supreme Court ruled that if a criterion excludes minorities *in fact* (regardless of the employer's intent), its use constitutes discrimination and is illegal unless the employer can prove a "business necessity" for using it.

The employer is also committed to correct the effects of past discrimination, normally taken to mean past discrimination *by this particular employer*. The reluctance of most employers to admit past discrimination, the difficulty of sorting out whether the discrimination *is* directly traceable to the employer, and in some cases, the legal concept of a statute of limitations all lead to dispute about the meaning of this concept for an employer who has not been sued.

Another principle of affirmative action programs is a commitment to ongoing complex institutional self-review and planning. The employer actively reviews such things as patterns in the salaries of men and women, comparisons of applicant flow to hiring rates, and the relative promotion rates of individual ethnic groups in order to identify roadblocks to the achievement of nondiscrimination. One of these self-audits is a "work force analysis," in which the employer calculates how many women and/or minority employees now work in each job group and then decides whether or not these proportions reflect the number of women or members of ethnic minorities *reasonably available* for such jobs. If and only if the employer finds that the proportion in his work force does not match the level of "availability" is he required to set numerical goals for hiring and promotion. This approach is least controversial when applied to the number of minority employees in entry level jobs where an obviously reasonable level of expectation is "population parity" (about the same proportion employed as exists in the population at large). Some employers set goals even when such formal "underutilization" does not exist or use high estimates of availability. Others use very conservative estimates. An employer cannot, however, even if he wants to do so, legally set *quotas* without a court finding of past discrimination.

A final component of these programs is some commitment to provide training. However, the extent of an employer's obligation to train women and minorities for a particular job for which he never trained white males is unclear.

Although these formal principles seek to reach the simple-sounding goal of sustained "nondiscrimination" or "equal opportunity," expectations vary widely about what affirmative action will or should lead to beyond this abstract goal and about how we will know when we get there. For some, the key purpose of these programs is accomplished when a woman with precisely the same *current* skills and interests as a man, for example, has precisely the same odds of gaining a management job as does the man. They believe an employer should not have to provide special training for the woman to "catch up" in skills unless clear past discrimination by the employer can be proved and such discrimination was not legal when it occurred.

For others, ending all sex *patterns* in employment is the main issue, and we will not have reached a state of "equal opportunity" until women and minorities reach "population parity" in every occupation, at every level.

For yet others, the workforce *patterns* are not so important as the matter of economic resources. The key matter, then, would not be whether blacks tend to be plumbers or women tend to be laboratory technicians but the economic impact of such employment patterns. Critical measures would be the unemployment rate in the black community or the mean income of women. (At its extreme, this notion leads some people to ask of affirmative action that it accomplish total income redistribution throughout the society, so that not only will a child born female or Chicano have the same odds of becoming a corporate president as a white male, but *also* the gap between the income of any corporate president and a secretary or service worker will be reduced. This is perhaps the least likely outcome of such programs; it would have to be accomplished directly through legislation.)

Finally, an important long-term expectation of affirmative action is that it will indirectly improve the quality of work and institutional life for everyone. At the least, specific institutions will be improved because diversity by race and sex will increase their cultural richness and variety of talent. The expectation further anticipates that the changes needed to reach genuine equal opportunity for women will also lead to more flexible work hours, part-time work, and recognition of the importance of family needs and personal growth for men. Concomitantly, the quality of decision making at work is expected to improve because women will bring additional enriching values and ways of solving problems to institutions. There may be additional options at work for group problem solving (in addition to individual achievement) and for the healthy acknowledgment and enjoyment of emotions (in addition to analytic and power-oriented activity).

Part of the disappointment about the actual implementation of affirmative action is a result of confusion springing from its legal complexity and from these varied notions about its purposes, particularly from the common misunderstanding that its explicit purpose is the unbridled exclusion of white males. But the disappointment springs also from the fact that the results of affirmative action can only be realistically regarded as mixed.

On the positive side, the practice of overt, conscious employment discrimination against women *has* been reduced during the past four years, and machinery has been set up to promote continuing change. This is true in simple quantitative terms. A sizeable portion of the national work force consists of people who work directly for the federal government and of employees of federal contractors. This means that a large number of women work in institutions where overt discrimination is against formal policies and where procedures have been created to implement these policies. In terms of money, both salary adjustments and back pay awards— whether voluntary, negotiated with the federal agencies, or court enforced—add up to significant social change.

On an individual level, there can be no doubt that many women hold traditionally male jobs today because some employers seek actively to end discrimination and to encourage women, because women themselves have challenged discriminatory decisions, and because the laws have been followed or enforced. Notions that would have been considered bizarre if not disastrous in 1970 (such as women police officers and work-crew supervisors) are being realized, however cautiously or reluctantly. Some large employers have long-range numerical goals that, if met, will effect major social change and, in a few cases, will result in the complete eradication of any sex segregation in their work force. That only three or four years of pressure and response have produced such changes is, actually, somewhat astonishing.

In spite of these positive indicators of change, however, a review of the actual *results* of affirmative action programs, in terms either of their simplest goals or of the more idealistic expectations, confirms that the degree of significant change in employment patterns is very slight. It is still true that most people work in sex-stereotyped jobs. It is still true that the vast majority of people earning more than $15,000 per year are white males. It is

still true that minority unemployment rates are often shockingly high. It is
still true that the leaders of most large institutions, whether labor unions,
corporations, or schools are white males. (If all such roles *were* now
distributed in simple proportion to availability in the current work force,
about half of the people in a typical meeting of federal agency directors,
senior union officials, or members of a corporate board of directors would
be nonminority women, male and female blacks, Asians, Chicanos, Native
Americans, or members of other nonwhite groups. While it would be quite
unrealistic to expect this kind of representation to occur within a few years,
even with genuine equal opportunity, it is still interesting to contrast such a
situation with current reality.)

Obstacles to Affirmative Action

It is useful to examine the obstacles that stand in the way of change both to
understand the reasons for the limited success of affirmative action and to
anticipate the impact of these same obstacles on the implementation of the
ERA.

First, there is both personal and organized conscious resistance to the
simplest principles of equal opportunity for women: that a paycheck or sense
of competence is or should be as important to a woman as to a man, that
women "belong" in certain jobs, that an employer or society generally
should actively seek to *change* current aspirations of women at work. Active
resistance by employers to change can take many forms, including lobbying
to change laws and refusing to take certain steps to increase opportunity for
or benefits to women until forced to do so.

There is also organized resistance to affirmative action that has nothing to
do with prejudice or sexism. Most employers routinely resist all outside
intervention in their activities. Some properly resist requirements for waste-
ful collection of data, unnecessary costly analyses or expensive amounts of
documentation. Employers are developing increasingly creative and sophisticated strategies for establishing their immunity to *legal* liability for any
effects of past discrimination. Such defense against charges of discrimination is to be expected. The critical question is whether the creativity applied
to legitimate self-protection is matched by a creative and sophisticated effort
within the institution to implement affirmative action. In its counter-
productive form, self-defense is the employer's only "affirmative action"
activity. Some employers use their resources chiefly for statistical battles
with enforcement agencies, sometimes with both sides attempting to use
data only in their own ideological interests, each feeling they are forced to
do so by the intractability of the other side. In healthy situations, employers

protect their ability to carry out legitimate institutional missions while also investing necessary resources to achieve prompt affirmative action results.

Another kind of obstacle is less dramatic but perhaps even more important than overt resistance to affirmative action. Whole institutions, and certainly many managers or officers within them, bring passivity, complacency, defensiveness, and lack of imagination to the issue of equal sex opportunity. Unless they have recently witnessed a male telling a female, "I will not promote you because you are a woman," many people will argue that sex discrimination does not exist. The concept that the test of nondiscrimination is the *consequences* of one's actions rather than one's *intent* is still far from understood by many employers. Finding that a lower promotion rate for women reflects a low number of female applications for promotion, for example, an employer will often choose to do nothing, feeling that this confirms the belief he began with, namely, that women do not want leadership roles. Only the most sophisticated institutions go on to aggressively assess the institution's own accountability in that situation. The simple fact that the white male has been considered the "normal" employee and leader for decades means that many employers will, either consciously or unconsciously, interpret low proportions of women and members of ethnic minorities in all high status jobs as somehow natural.

There are employers, however, who do seek change and invest resources well beyond what would be required by a defensive analysis. But some obstacles standing in the way of the realization of their own aspirations and the achievement of rapid change are due to the continuing effect of old expectations about how men and women should and can behave and employers' ignorance of the ways these expectations affect opportunity. That is to say that an employer may not even be aware of the *informal* obstacles to effective equal opportunity for women. Some aspects of learning how to be a corporate manager, for example, are tied to informal social activity. The career development of current managers may involve a protégé system in which a senior man "adopts" a younger man and encourages him. In such settings as a golf game, a ride to work, or a poker evening, young male professionals learn the subtle aspects of organizational politics, accepted styles of administrative combat, in-group ways to describe problems, and factual information important to their work. But older males often find it hard to see a woman "taking their place," and further, those informal activities may suddenly become socially awkward and even sexual in implication if a woman joins a senior manager in them.

Moreover, in some cases, males may find it hard to give good negative feedback (critical evaluation) to women on their work, either because the men feel it is unchivalrous or because they have unconsciously low expectations about women's abilities. In the attempt to protect women, they may deny them critical information necessary for self-development. They may avoid giving them hard tasks and expecting top performance. Most people in our culture have been brought up to expect women to be less effective at certain kinds of tasks—particularly leadership roles, analytic tasks, and quantitative problem solving. Successful men and women alike may have difficulty in properly evaluating both the *potential* and the actual performance of women.

The matter of *potential* may be especially significant. An informal review of faculty letters recommending young men and women Ph.D.'s for appointment at other universities, for example, apparently suggested that while the faculty members assessed the intellectual skills of the men and women even-handedly, there was a "missing paragraph" from the letters about women. That paragraph was the one in which the more gifted men were described as potentially outstanding scholars in the field. Such remarks simply didn't appear in letters about women, whether gifted or not.

Women's own expectations about themselves are also obstacles to affirmative action. In particular, many women have been brought up to feel extremely uncomfortable about making direct demands on their own behalf or assuming public leadership (as opposed to more hidden control). Yet these activities may be genuinely necessary for job competence, whether one is the supervisor of a work crew or a manager.

All of these obstacles cluster around attitudes and intent. There are, however, two obstacles to rapid change no matter what attitudes prevail or what aspirations men and women have. First, there are the numerical limits to possible rates of change in the absence of massive compensatory discrimination. To take another academic example, consider a university that hires 50 recent Ph.D.'s each year and has a faculty of 1,000, 100 of whom are women. The school concludes that 20% of all the Ph.D.'s in relevant fields are women and immediately achieves a "nondiscriminatory" hiring rate with 20% of all new appointments going to women. This means the school would hire ten additional women each year. Assuming no woman *ever* left the university, it would still take 10 years for the total number of women to reach 200, or 20% of the faculty. Unless one is willing to adopt compensatory discrimination (hiring proportionally *more* women than exist in the relevant pool), there is no way to achieve dramatic change rapidly.

The example above suggests a second obstacle, that of the real impact of past discriminatory patterns in education and training. Ending discrimination against women Ph.D.'s in faculty appointments, for example, obviously has no *direct* impact on the *underlying* problem of the limited number of female Ph.D.'s. If only 1% of all advanced engineering degrees have gone to women in the past and such a degree is a valid requirement for a corporate research job, for example, the employer is limited in what he can achieve through active recruiting. For work that legitimately requires sophisticated and long training, the effects of cultural patterns and past discrimination will be strong. For such jobs there are sometimes truly few women available. Unless one claims that there is nothing actually learned through professional training, craft, apprenticeships, or management experience (e.g., that it is unnecessary to go to medical school to practice medicine), the rate of hiring women for such jobs will depend on the rate at which they enter such training.

This issue brings us to one final obstacle to affirmative action, which is the confusion about the responsibility for overcoming all these obstacles. Employers tend to see their duty as the immediate prevention of any further overt exclusion of women and good faith attempts to encourage women to seek new kinds of work. Others expect employers to do far more. The fact that all do not share the same agenda sometimes creates unnecessary distrust, wasted effort, and inconsistent action on the part of employers and pressure groups.

THE IMPACT OF THE ERA ON EMPLOYMENT
AND AFFIRMATIVE ACTION

Although it is commonly believed that the ERA will immediately affect employment opportunity for women, patterns of discrimination in work are actually the least likely to be *quickly* affected by the ERA. There are two reasons. First, the ERA is not a law and does not affect private employers directly; it affects state action and how men and women are treated under the law generally. Second, as noted previously, many laws and regulations about employment discrimination already exist, although the ERA might affect court interpretation of some of them.

Nonetheless, the passage of the ERA *will,* particularly in the long run, impact employment in some significant ways. First, it may affect the way in which *current laws* are implemented. This has several aspects. For one thing, it may change the attitude of the courts about the seriousness of sex discrimination. This in turn may lead the courts to accept stronger remedies even in private sex discrimination cases (whether or not state action is involved). There may be increased application of the concept of punitive damages, more complete restoration for the effects of proven past discrimination, and hopefully, more positive and imaginative remedies. (The Bank of America settlement involving training trust funds exemplifies a future-oriented remedy.)

Additionally, ongoing court decisions normally influence large corporations and institutions even when they are not parties to the case. Thus, any changes in court decisions will slowly but predictably change the way employers *interpret* their obligations under existing laws. It should be noted that now, ten years after the passage of Title VII, a dramatic increase in the number of successful sex discrimination lawsuits against employers can be expected in any case. This is primarily because various precedents have been established by the courts, including the assignment of the burden of proof to the employer, making it his responsibility to prove that discrimination does not exist if numerical patterns suggest problems. In addition, more young lawyers, including many women, are now specializing in discrimination law. Thus, the number of professional experts available to plaintiffs will increase significantly in the next few years, and their competence is growing.

For another thing, the ERA may affect employers symbolically, especially small employers who have not taken on the issue of sex discrimination at all; and it may have a symbolic effect on women *employees,* who are likely to be more willing to use existing laws aggressively and to initiate action on their own behalf—whether in individual employment situations or, collectively, in class action lawsuits.

All of these effects on the implementation of present laws would accelerate the rate of change in employment patterns. It should be noted, however, that the ERA may make it *more* difficult for an employer to discriminate *in favor* of women, since it will protect both men and women from unequal treatment under the law. It could support the requirement that any "compensatory" discrimination occur only when past discrimination has been proven.

Second, the ERA will affect employment in ways other than more effective implementation of existing laws. To the extent that it weakens sex roles generally, it may extend concepts of equality to employment-related issues not covered by current laws. If it can change expectations about women's desire and capacity to be dock workers or men's desire and capacity to be secretaries, it will change behavior. While affirmative action is predicated on the notion that behavioral change cannot wait upon attitudinal change (better to be hired by a sexist employer than to be unemployed), experience has taught us that nonconscious expectations are serious obstacles to behavioral change. Because it is impossible to monitor or inspire all human activity through formal sanctions, rules, and threats, the ERA's symbolic influence on expectations should not be slighted.

Specifically, the ERA's most critical long-range effect on employment through attitudinal change will be in the area of family roles. Russia's effort to achieve equality for women *without* redistributing responsibility for housework and child raising has largely failed. Even in Sweden, where family roles have been addressed by public policy, a strong determinant of sex patterns in employment seems to be the degree of change in the family—the liberation of men and their assumption of a more active role at home.

OBSTACLES TO ERA IMPLEMENTATION

Given these possible effects of the ERA on employment, we need to examine the parallels between the implementation of affirmative action and the eventual implementation of the ERA. Since employment laws are perhaps the most well developed (in theory) of all sanctions against sex discrimination at present, whatever obstacles exist for successful affirmative action will exist for the implementation of the ERA.

Our analysis confirms that formal policies and laws accomplish little in and of themselves. As clearly demonstrated through the history of affirmative action and other national mandates that affect deep social norms, formal change—while an important benchmark—is the beginning rather than the end of genuine social change. For most employers, sex discrimination became illegal in 1964. But it was not until women began to use the laws and regulations that their behavior started to change. Thus, active attempts to use the ERA will be necessary to give it meaning.

Such attempts will meet with organized intelligent resistance to the simplest aspects of equality. There will most certainly be sustained opposition to interpretations of the ERA that would require social institutions to spend public money on programs designed to change attitudes about the proper roles of men and women. Even legislators who vote to ratify the ERA may find they do not agree with some of its consequences as implementation proceeds.

Passivity, complacency, and lack of imagination will also impede the process of ERA implementation. Here, the established affirmative action techniques of looking at the objective impact of policies, procedures, and decisions has great bearing. Although numerical analyses are susceptible to manipulation by both pressure groups and defenders of the status quo, they are the best tool available for measuring the *consequences* of action. Constant attention to the actual *impact* of current laws or practices, then, is necessary to identify which of them appear neutral but actually have unnecessarily discriminatory impact.

The idea that the ERA is essentially a *negative* achievement, that its meaning is primarily *restrictive,* will have to be fought with a positive model throughout the society of what "equality" of the sexes will or should mean. The lack of positive models of real equal opportunity powerfully restricts progress. Examination of many actual affirmative action programs shows clearly that the concept of "nondiscrimination" is not enough to guide people to constructive action. An active sense that an institution will improve when women and men work in all occupations and it receives the benefit of the full potential of both sexes is a much better guide to action.

The ERA, in and of itself, is certainly not a sufficient condition to create a society wherein men and women enjoy options traditionally open only to one sex, but it may well be a necessary condition, and that may be more than enough to ask of a single amendment to the Constitution of the United States.

Consequences of the Equal Rights Amendment for the Professions, for the Roles of Professional Women, and for American Society

Cynthia Fuchs Epstein

Passage of the Equal Rights Amendment has been an issue since the first Women's Movement began half a century ago. Proposed as a mechanism to create equality for women, it met the resistance of critics who held that women were *basically* unequal to men and that the laws of legislatures ought to follow the laws of nature in underscoring and enunciating those differences. The thesis that the sexes were unequal was far different than suggesting that there were differences between them. It identified men as more capable and worthy of assuming and administering power in politics, work, and the family and reinforced the subordination of women in all these spheres.

Since the initial campaign for its passage, the arguments for and against the Amendment have focused on a varying array of issues, which, reflecting the cultural biases and issues of the times, are oftentimes inconsistent. In the early days, those who opposed the Amendment insisted that women ought to and needed to be kept in a subordinate position; a current argument is that women ought to be permitted to have special protections and privileges.

Of course, over the past ten years, a considerable reshuffling of ideology, legislation, and public opinion has resulted in significant changes with regard to the position of women in American society. New attitudes and new conditions (such as the ever growing participation of women in the work force) created a climate in which there was increasing support for the Equal Rights Amendment by legislators and by the general public. In fact, the very changes which indicated that passage was possible almost challenged the need for such an Amendment, since considerable strides toward the equality of women were being made without it.

Perhaps one of the most convincing arguments for its passage was the remaining opposition to the Amendment—if there were still people who opposed women's rights to equality in all spheres of American life, then it would appear that the guarantee of a constitutional amendment was still very important.

One might consider for a moment what purposes are served by having a constitution at all. A major power, Great Britain, which has never had one, is yet guided by precedents and traditions which serve as a framework in which its laws have coherence and consistency. The Constitution of the United States, of course, was first devised in an attempt to formulate a *new* framework from that set by the England of the 1700s which seemed inappropriate to the needs and wishes of a new society. The Constitution was, in a sense, a position paper with teeth. It provided a framework immediately, dispensing with the need for a long evolution of traditions. In providing for amendments, a structure was created for the changing definitions a growing society would require.

Constitutional provisions are generally designed for the purpose of setting guidelines for the passage and interpretation of laws. They insure that the guarantees and intentions of government regarding its relationship with the citizenry shall be served without susceptibility to political pressures, differential regional interests, and the strong individual power of those who hold political office or economic resources.

It is in setting the parameters of women's rights under the Constitution that the Equal Rights Amendment should be most effective in all spheres. However, with regard to women in the professions—the subject of this paper—the spelling out of rights to equal treatment is of outstanding importance. This is because the professions are power centers in the society, or gateways to powerful positions. Insuring the rights of women to act as full members of the professions is necessary if they are to have a say in decision making at the highest levels of society.

How would this constitutional amendment serve the purpose? The professions are institutions where entry is jealously guarded by pools of powerful elites. The professions' practices with regard to the recruitment of members and their subsequent socialization into the professions (that is to say, their incorporation as full, working members, privy to inside and privileged information) are largely informal. Specific laws can protect certain formal rights such as access to professional training, but they cannot cover the myriad of activities and mechanisms which prevent women from becoming true members of the professions.

But a constitutional amendment would provide a real umbrella to cover the unforeseen discriminatory events and practices. Of even more importance, it would set the cultural tone, provide the legitimation of women's equality in spheres formerly thought to be out of their realm of competence.

In addition to this overarching cultural support, an amendment would prohibit regression to a former condition of inequality and the overturning of present laws prohibiting such practices as discrimination in employment, housing, and education. Although it is commonly believed that the world generally moves in the direction of progress, a view of history informs us that the freedoms of one period might be denied in another. The professions are especially sensitive to regression. This is because they are linked to the centers of decision making, and small groups wishing to maintain control are apt to limit challenge by competing groups. The Equal Rights Amendment is one way of guaranteeing that access be kept open to women (or even men, if women should take power) and that free entry into the competition for places of power be allowed them.

Let us consider some specific (but by no means comprehensive) consequences which follow inevitably and logically from passage of the Amendment.

ACCESS TO THE PROFESSIONS

Enactment of the Equal Rights Amendment would prohibit restriction of public schools to one sex and would prohibit public institutions from requiring higher admissions standards for women (or men, in case any exist).

For most of American history, formal and informal quotas have been imposed on the number of women permitted to have professional training since they had limited access to higher education, especially quality education. These quotas stood between zero to about ten percent. Although one might have asked why, if women were *inherently* unsuited to the rigors and demands of professional education in law, medicine, sciences, the ministry, and so on, there was any need to impose *rules* against their entrance, elites certainly took no chances. Thus, laws striking down these rules were imperative to open the routes to decision making and activity in the professions. Lifting quotas proved that real opportunity met with no shortage of interested seekers. In the years following the enactment of the Civil Rights Act of 1964, which barred institutions from discriminating against women and minority applicants, the number of women applying and going to professional schools disproved the old myths which supported their exclusion. Women *wanted* to become doctors, lawyers, and engineers and proved they were good in these roles.

The Equal Rights Amendment, in *ensuring* continuation and expansion of equal opportunity in these spheres, will contribute to the newly emerging sex-balanced profile in the professions.

Although there have been fluctuations in the percentage of women in professional schools, at no time in history until the present have women constituted as large a percentage of the student body as they now do. Classes of twenty, thirty, and even fifty percent women have been noted even in Ivy League schools, in contrast to the tiny percentage noted before. This is hardly due to a lowering of admission standards; women's scores on qualifying examinations rank as well or better than those of men. This fact alerts us to the large number of women with aptitude who were barred from entry to professional schools in the past by sheer discrimination.

Consider how the very precepts of the American credo have been violated with respect to women.

Although presumably our best schools operate according to a selection process in which the most functionally qualified are supposed to have priority, we now know the extent to which that has never been the case. The Equal Rights Amendment might press us closer to the practice of the ideal in which meritocratic considerations prevail over the particularistic criteria of social class position and "old boy" networks. Furthermore, as stated earlier, there is the chance that a shift in balance between the sexes in the professions would occur. Since we know that girls often do better in school than boys, an even larger percentage of women may enter training for professional roles than do today. From a change in the sex balance in the professions a more general loosening of the male hold on high prestige positions might follow.

On the other hand, the higher proportion of women entering the professions might decrease the prestige of the professions. This might happen not only because men devalue work done by women but also because women don't seem to demand monetary rewards with the same insistence as do men in the professions. Since prestige and money are interactive phenomena in American society, there is a question as to whether prestige can endure independent of financial enhancement. However, if women "normalize" within the professions and if they step up pressure for equal pay, women may in time go into professions with the same expectations of the financial rewards of success as men. The Equal Rights Amendment might legitimate their rights to the same work and the same rewards of work, reversing the historical pattern.

The opening of training by the guarantees of the Equal Rights Amendment and the subsequent equalization of the balance of recruits should secure greater participation of women in *subdivisions* of the professions and a fairer distribution of them throughout the professional hierarchy. This should occur as a result not only of legal but also inevitable social structural consequences. In the past, the limitation of training to men provided few women in the total pool of eligibles for specialized kinds of training and practice through the disciplines. If only about about six or seven percent of all medical students were women, by the time residencies in specialties were selected, there were often few or no women applicants. Similarly in law, when three percent of all law students were women, the chances of top firms finding a number of women to choose from who were at the top of their class and who met other criteria of personal style and background, were small to nonexistent. When half of medical and legal students are women, there will be more women who will ask for and presumably *be asked* to compete for specialized programs and traineeships. This is, first of all, because there will be fewer men to choose from and, second, because senior professors will see the advantage of choosing qualified women as protégés and associates. As a result, women will have a better chance in the tracking system, be more visible as possible eligibles, and have the credentials through the sequence of training. Since the Amendment would also guarantee equal access to scholarships and fellowships, it would insure that gifted women get the encouragement and means to pursue careers in professions. It would also distribute more equitable resources of financial aid for activities now limited to men students (such as football scholarships). Thus, funds would be freed from a limited sector of the pool of recruits and provided to a wider one.

CONSEQUENCES OF PROFESSIONAL ACCESS FOR OTHER INSTITUTIONAL REALMS

The entrance of women into male dominated professions is apt to have a snowball effect, creating changes in other institutions. The following are possibilities which could flow from the changes in professional access due to the Equal Rights Amendment.

The Family: It is likely that, all other things being equal, women with professional aspirations will want both a career and marriage and that in the changing climate of American society this will be an acceptable choice. Until recently, a half to one third of women professionals tended to be unmarried (divorced or single). This condition has been generally attributed to the consequences of role strain created by the cross pressures of occupational and family demands and to the cultural mandate that women choose between these spheres. Equality would mean that women would have the same options as do men—of both family and career. But the family of the professional woman might look different from what we believe the present "average" family to be.

There is no doubt that families in which both husband and wife have occupational commitments would require more sharing of responsibility in the home. At a minimum, more power balance in family decisions can be predicted. Furthermore, as wives assume more responsibility, there will be greater interchangeability of family roles between spouses. The wife who must now travel to conferences needs to have a husband who can take over management of the home in her absence as she has typically done in his absence. One might also project that occupational choices, like other family decisions, will be made by the family unit rather than the prerogative of the husband.

Organizations: The family situation could also put pressure on organizations and universities to create flexible school and working conditions and accompanying child care centers. The guarantee of equal opportunity in the professions must be accompanied by assurances of structural change in order to achieve that equality. In the same way that racial equality necessitates that black children be bussed to the better schools out of their own neighborhoods to insure their equal access to education, a constitutional right of sexual equality will necessitate provisions 1) to care for dependent children; 2) to provide education at times and under arrangements which mesh with the needs of families; and 3) to offer tax benefits and allowances to compensate for the loss of family services which women now provide.

Of course, this last consideration is quite speculative, but it is not inconceivable that a constitutional amendment would provide a facilitating framework for innovative solutions to the present problems which impede women's participation in professional life.

Work Related Spheres: There will be changes in the disciplines. The impact of women's equal participation in the professions has been anticipated by the present insistence by young entrants into law, medicine, academia, and the ministry that these fields reexamine the ways in which they view women.[1] These are several of the dimensions which can be further changed:

a) Women as clients: Women's second class evaluation in society has been reflected in the professions whcih traditionally view male clients as preferable to female clients. There is good evidence to suggest that women suffered from differential and poorer treatment as medical patients, as legal clients, and as graduate students. There is no doubt that some of this treatment stemmed from the fact that they did not control their own money and that they had no political power to alter institutional attention.

b) Woman as subject matter: Beyond that, women have suffered a general cultural inattention; they have been considered unimportant and uninteresting even in the sciences, where their problems have received less scientific attention. Women's occupations were scarcely analyzed in sociology or in government policy; women's contribution to the national product was ignored by economists. In medicine, gynecological problems were viewed as less interesting to medical specialists, who got less prestige for dealing with them than they did for work on androgynous problems.

c) Professional prestige of women will create a halo effect: As more women become professional specialists, one can predict that they will view women as clients with more concern and respect. Part of this will, no doubt, be an empathetic response of women who have some firsthand knowledge of the social and physical problems women face. But a considerable element will stem from the greater dignity accorded women as a class by male as well as female practitioners when women fully participate in the prestige arenas of the society.

The fact that women will generally be able to earn more money should also be instrumental in changing the way they are treated in professional life. There is no doubt that they will be considered more worthy of attention by the scientific, medical, legal, and business establishment. Not only will there be a greater attempt to deal with their problems, there will also be a greater attempt to make more adjustments to their particular needs and interests.

Credit: One significant impetus to the increased participation of women in professional life should come from the constitutional assurance that women be given equality in financial matters. Of particular relevance to their activity in professional life is the set of guarantees they should receive to obtain credit from banks and other financial institutions. Women typically are employed, rather than self-employed, in the professions as well as in business. They work for government to a much greater extent than do men (the pattern is similar for black professionals). While there is some belief that this is because they do not wish to be engaged in the entrepreneurial end of professional activity, probably a much better explanation is the fact that it is hard for women to get financing to establish their own practices and businesses. In the past, women accepted the fact that banks, and society in general, considered them bad investment risks, and they were loathe to go into debt until such time as they were established. Probably one explanation for the high proportion of women in the medical profession in Eastern Europe and in dentistry in various other countries (Scandinavia and some Latin American countries) is that those governments provide the physical plant and medicine and dentistry are not in the private sector.[2] Dentistry is even more entrepreneurial than medicine in this country, and, proportionately, even fewer women become dentists (one percent of the total) than become physicians (between seven and nine percent at present). When women know that there will be no problem in getting and maintaining credit, we can expect a different distribution of them in the professions and can anticipate that more will go into private practice than before.

One side benefit of this phenomenon is the fact that when women have their own practices, they will have greater autonomy and freedom in managing a work life along with a private life. Women doctors and lawyers can control the flow and amount of client hours and will be able to arrange hours to better coordinate with the demands of other roles. Working as a truly "free" professional gives an individual the maximum amount of flexibility in contrast to the rigid hours set for lower-level occupational workers.

It should be noted that the advancement of credit to women probably will also make it possible for more women to afford professional education. They will be less subject to the priority system in the family which had traditionally favored the education of its male children over its female children and less subject to the enduring prejudices of scholarship committees.

CONSEQUENCES OF PROFESSIONAL ACCESS FOR SOCIETY

Along with the guarantees offered by the Equal Rights Amendment to ease and facilitate women's entry into professional life, we can expect readjustments in other parts of the social structure. This is a set of consequences which has not received attention by social scientists or policy makers. When change occurs in some sectors of the society, it is inevitable that change will occur in other sectors. Examples of such responses are considered in this section.

1) Women will be new kinds of consumers. They will create demands for new kinds of goods and services. Not only will they have needs, they will also be financially equipped to pay for them, and it is not unlikely that this will cause a vigorous thrust to parts of the economy. It is important to consider this positive benefit since typically the cry of workers and labor leaders is that women take jobs from men and cause salary level declines.

As women enter the professional sphere they will also become active and knowledgeable about occupational activity and finance where before they were silent partners if, indeed, they were partners at all. We can expect women to become professional business people and, as professionals, more interested and involved in investment and business opportunities. Here their equality in the professions will be complemented by their equality in business, finance, investment, and insurance.

2) Women will develop an increasing need for transport. They will also require different kinds of transport as more women leave the home for work each day and also for extended work trips away from home. Generally, we might predict a country more on the move and, specifically, with more women on the move. Here, too, a boost to sagging transportation revenues and standards of carriers might occur as women need more and better quality transportation and, in general, feel less inhibited about traveling.[3]

Another offshoot might also be the restructuring of child care with sensitivity to the problems created when women's work takes them away from the home. An example of one innovation of this kind is the European institution of children's hotels where youngsters may spend a weekend to a month while the parents work or travel.

Another set of innovations could center on the creation of transportation facilities intended to make it comfortable to bring children along on work trips. Although this may not be ideal for all persons who wish or need to have their minds and hours totally free for work at conferences and other work endeavors, there ought to be creative solutions for the problems faced by those families who do want or need to bring children with them on business trips.

As women increasingly have professional careers, it will become less common for wives to follow their husbands when transfers occur or to subordinate their own careers to those of their husbands. One response is apt to be more commuting marriages. In this situation wives and husbands may spend work weeks in separate towns or cities and meet for weekends or parts of weeks. This pattern is increasing in the academic world where frequently it is difficult for husbands and wives to get appointments in institutions in the same places, particularly when the institution is in a small community or city. Speedy and convenient kinds of transportation will become more necessary if this pattern is to be facilitated.

A more mundane but relevant issue related to this topic would be the increase in two-car families as women's need to travel increases. Once again, this is a need which would be accompanied by capacity to pay.

To bring this problem into the realm of "rights" rather than privilege is a possible outgrowth of a change in social climate provided by the legitimation of the Equal Rights Amendment.

3) Responsibility for children might be reconsidered. The Equal Rights Amendment might dispel the idea that the nuclear family must provide all care for children and deal with problems individually. This could pressure the community into being responsible for children. People of professional status now tend to cluster in neighborhoods and communities, and as women join the ranks of the professionals, these communities might well gear

themselves to the provision of quality services. Furthermore, child care for children of all ages will be necessary since professional activity is not a 10 a.m. to 3 p.m. proposition. In addition, the demand by professional families for quality care ought to make the society in general reevaluate child care, now primarily custodial in nature. One way to reconceptualize child care is to view education as a requirement from earliest years until independence from the family and as socially important as primary and secondary education. We also might expect a reconceptualization of what is considered the school day.

Other societies, although for different reasons, provide more in the way of care; they have political goals of incorporating the young and use youth groups for this purpose. In a limited way, the United States does this through the scouting movement. One could conceive of politically neutral yet socially significant youth movements which engage the imagination and energy of school-age children. Not only children of professional families would benefit from this activity, but also children in other social strata, where their quest for community presently takes the form of gangs which invariably do mischief and harm. A harnessing of energies into socially useful tasks (conservation, care of the old, building parks and playgrounds) could result from the demolishing of the outdated notion that kids belong with mothers at home—an ideology that serves neither mothers nor children.

4) Probably the pool of professional women, for some time, will come from the same sector as male professionals—the middle class. If this is true, we can expect a dearth of services to the society formerly provided by the wives of professionals as a voluntary service. Those wives will not be side by side with professional husbands. However, in one analytic view, the performance of work for no pay not only caused middle class women a paucity of esteem, it also took jobs away from lower-income, less educated people. Thus, the assembling of energies of the former "leisure class" of women ought to create more jobs. This is not to say that professional jobs ought to be restricted to the middle and upper middle class. As mentioned before, the extension of credit and the rise of a meritocratic system for both admission standards and scholarship distribution ought to create more democracy in training and education and, therefore, within the professions themselves.

A secondary benefit of the change from the present voluntary sector to a committed and rewarded corps of professionalized workers is the greater rationalization for government support. There is some question as to the real benefit of totally voluntary contributions for disease research and voluntary labor for the delivery of certain health services. The generosity and whims of the rich as the only source to satisfy these needs are ineffectual and preposterous; taxation and rationalized allocation would be more in keeping with a modern, complex society.

The arenas of change cited in this article are meant only to be suggestive and heuristic. The impact of the Equal Rights Amendment might be radical or small depending on the times. The lesson of the amendment prohibiting the trade in alcohol, which only resulted in widespread violation, is a lesson in the ineffectiveness of statute when the culture is not consonant with its spirit. But it seems that this is the right time for the passage of a viable and worthy amendment which could have wide range and long-lasting social benefits. The tracing of the steps here indicates that changes can be significant not only in and of themselves, but that they can also create ripples throughout the society beyond their original mandate. The guarantees offered women and men by this Amendment should be among the most significant ever enacted in the United States.

Footnotes

1. See my article, "A Different Angle of Vision: Notes on the Selective Eye of Sociology," *Social Science Quarterly* 55, no. 3 (Winter 1974): 645-56 for further elaboration of this problem.

2. See Cynthia Fuchs Epstein, *Woman's Place: Options and Limits of Professional Careers* (Berkeley: University of California Press, 1970) for further analysis of this point.

3. The social consequences to women's equality which stem from opening the barriers to their traveling have been explored by Rose Coser in her Presidential Address to the Society for the Study of Social Problems, August 26, 1974, Montreal, Canada.

The ERA and Redefinitions of Work:
Toward Utopia

Janet Saltzman Chafetz

INTRODUCTION: THE CENTRALITY OF
THE WORK ETHIC IN AMERICA

The major value system of any group or society generally reflects the orientations and interests of the dominant group of individuals within. For the Unites States, those involved historically in establishing and maintaining our major national values have generally been white, Northwestern European in family origin, and overwhelmingly male. Our national heritage is rooted in both the religious emphasis brought to the new world by dissident Protestants and in English Common Law. The former provided a value emphasis on the importance of work as "calling." The latter embodied a secular emphasis on protecting the propertied and punishing the impoverished, including the unemployed. Moreover, for at least the first two centuries of our history after initial settlement, opportunities abounded for most whites to prosper through hard work on the enormous frontiers of the continent. A nation lacking in an aristocratic tradition learned to elevate those who prospered most through work to an elite status defined not merely as powerful and wealthy but as intellectually and morally superior as well. Occupational success and personal worthiness become one and the same thing.

Contemporary students of social stratification agree that although Americans rank one another on a number of variables, the single most important one is occupational prestige. The higher the prestige of the occupational role filled by a person, the greater the esteem in which others hold that individual. Other perquisites, not the least of which is income, tend likewise to accrue to people on this basis. And finally, self-esteem and related ego gratifications result as well from high prestige occupational roles.

The converse of this phenomenon is that those who are located at the bottom of the occupational hierarchy, not to mention those who are not gainfully employed (i.e., do not receive wages or salaries for their activities), tend to be denigrated as persons. An economy overwhelmingly dependent on high rates of consumption does not seem to create a society in which housewives, one of whose main activities is to consume, are valued. A society which is characterized by media glorification of motherhood, child rearing, and homemaking, nonetheless fails to accord social value to these activities, a fact understood only too well by those millions of women who define themselves as "only" or "just" housewives. A society which, since it's earliest years as a nation, has had a rich tradition of voluntary associations, sneers at the middle class female volunteer. And finally, a society of do-it-yourselfers in fact values the "store bought" over the home produced and sees the woman who sews for her family as either unfortunately poor or engaged in time-filling trivia.

In short, all of the myriad life-enriching, productive, helpful activities in which humans can and do participate, other than gainful employment, fail to provide social prestige and often, in the absence of a work role, entail subtle denigration. It is difficult, indeed, to develop and maintain self-esteem and confidence vis-à-vis the social world in the absence of a social definition that one is engaged in important activities. It is clear that women, much more so than men, spend their lives either at the lowest rungs of the occupational prestige ladder or outside of the work force altogether, and the price they pay is not merely monetary but psychic in the most basic way. Men, too, suffer from this value emphasis. In the first instance, by the very nature of a stratification hierarchy, most males will not achieve roles of very high occupational prestige and will thus suffer blows to their egos as well as pocketbooks. This is, perhaps, even more the case for males than females since occupational achievement is so much more central to the masculine sex role than to the feminine. In addition, the overwhelming commitment to work necessary for those who do succeed often entails the sacrifice of virtually all other activities which, if not socially valued, may at least be personally rewarding. In short, by elevating work to the ultimate measure of the person, our society has created a situation in which almost no one lives a life as rich and ego-gratifying as possible.

The conditions surrounding most jobs today, and especially those at the upper levels of the prestige hierarchy, reflect the value emphasis discussed and exacerbate the problems mentioned. Gainful employment in general, and high prestige occupations in particular, are structured for persons whose main, indeed almost sole, role in life is work, namely, for males and single women without children. Our legal structure places the financial responsibility for the family squarely in the lap of the male (husband-father). Our social conventions place it there as well and, in addition, place virtually all of the child rearing and homemaking responsibility in the lap of the female (wife-mother). As long as such laws and conventions persist, the following aspects of most occupations tend, *de facto,* to handicap married women, and especially mothers, in any job competition with males.

1) The division of workplace from home with child care facilities unavailable at work and totally insufficient in the community.
2) The assumption that a normal work week consists of five days, eight hours per day, generally set between 8:00 a.m. and 5:00 p.m. Lack of flexibility about such things as school hours and family requirements results from these often arbitrary and unnecessary restrictions.
3) The assumption that an occupational slot can only be filled by one person working every week of the year except vacation time and during periods of lay-off.
4) The expectation built into many occupational roles, most notably professional and managerial, that work will entail many more hours than forty per week to demonstrate "serious commitment."
5) The assumption that the serious contender for high-level positions begins a career in her/his mid-twenties and pursues a commitment to that career unbroken by periods of laborforce absence.

It is also noteworthy that most of these conditions of employment, beyond handicapping the female who is assumed, and often assumes herself, to be responsible for home and children, prevent males from participating more fully and meaningfully in other, nonwork roles, especially that of father-hood.

The arbitrariness of many of these employment conditions is evidenced by their manipulation during periods when female labor force participation is needed. Females, more so than racial and ethnic minorities, have truly comprised a labor force reserve to be manipulated by the economic, political, and social powers. During World War II, when manpower was in very short supply, companies found it expedient to establish day care facilities to enable mothers of young children to work. The boom era of the sixties witnessed a growth of part-time arrangements to enable females (especially clerical) to arrange work around children's time in school. Likewise, during those same years, older women whose children no longer needed their supervision could, after prolonged absence, reenter the labor force in areas of shortage, such as clerical-type jobs. Needless to add, with the end of the economic boom and the concomitant labor shortage has generally come the end of such arrangements, as women in large numbers were pushed back out of the labor force.

THE IMPACT OF ERA

The preceding sketch of the centrality of the work ethic and occupational prestige in American society focused primarily on questions of values. New laws cannot be expected to immediately and radically change the values, prejudices, and beliefs of people. However, they can coerce behavioral change. In turn, social scientific theory and research have amply demonstrated that changed behavior patterns often (if not normally) *result* in cognitive and affective mental change. Thus, the potential long-run impact of ERA on the conditions and values surrounding work as well as nonwork activities is enormous.

The first and most direct area of ERA impact on these issues pertains to employer discrimination. Quite simply, ERA would provide constitutional safeguards to all of the myriad nondiscriminatory legislation (state and federal) and executive orders already in existence. Without such constitutional safeguards, legislation and orders are rather easily rescinded and, during a period of high unemployment and economic recession, the temptation and pressure to do so may be very great indeed. Examples abound in the history of this nation, as well as most others, of enormous gains made by disadvantaged groups, later lost during times of hardship. Furthermore, the history of Supreme Court interpretation of the "equal protection" clause is sufficiently variable to demonstrate that only an amendment explicitly extending equality to women will serve to protect females against such arbitrariness in the job market and elsewhere.

There is a far more profound and potentially revolutionary impact of ERA, however. A myriad of state laws explicitly and indirectly render married and formerly married males chiefly, and often even solely, responsible for providing financially for wives (including former) and children. Debt responsibility, alimony, and child support all tend to lay (or at least assume) the overwhelming responsibility on the male, as does the lack of widowers' pensions. Conversely, state laws restricting wives as to legal residence, ability to enter all manner of contracts, etc., and legislation pertaining to age of retirement and pension benefits for women are often designed to further support male financial responsibility by effectively restricting females in their occupational pursuits, encouraging them to leave the labor force and providing them with less retirement income, although substantial widow's benefits. ERA would abolish the constraints on women, thereby enabling them to better earn a living. Simultaneously, it would make both husband and wife (former and present) equally responsible, or responsible according to ability, for financial support. This would strongly encourage females to prepare for occupational achievement, since they could no longer plan (irrespective of the *de facto* misguidedness of such planning in the past) on life-long financial support from a male. The impact on males could be yet more profound. No longer legally responsible for the sole, lifetime support of others, their flexibility in career choice, pattern, and work schedule would be enormously enhanced. In short, law would no longer encourage the constriction of the real options held by men and women concerning whether, in what ways, and for how much time they will participate in the labor force. This, in turn, can be expected to have long-run implications for the values held by Americans pertaining to work and to nonwork activities.

TOWARD UTOPIA

If women were no longer a manipulatable reserve labor force but were constitutionally guaranteed the right to participate fully in the work of our nation, if men were no longer defined (or assumed) legally as having life-long responsibility for the provision of financial resources for their entire families, what changes in our social values and the structure and function of our economic institutions might eventually occur? Before attempting to answer this question to provide a glimpse at utopia, it is important to reiterate a fact of social life that, in this case, makes utopia a bit less unrealistic than it might normally be. Value changes and changes in the structure and function of occupational roles and economic institutions are intimately related in a systemic fashion. This means that any changes introduced into the system tend to effect the other elements within that system. As one area changes, further change accrues to the originally impacted element through feedback, and so on. Thus a relatively modest change in one element may reverberate throughout and produce, in the long run, the most far-reaching consequences. Of course, we cannot antici-pate all of the consequences, nor must we be blind to the high probability that at least some of the unanticipated (as well as some of the anticipated) consequences will be dysfunctional, unpleasant, or costly for many people.

1. Labor Force Participation: Equal employment opportunity will eventu-ally mean that, in general, males and females will have approximately equal earning capacity and approximately equal access to interesting jobs. In a large number of individual families the female's earning potential and/or occupational prestige will, in fact, surpass the male's. Thus, in utopia we might expect that, no longer held legally responsible for the financial state of the family, many males will find it either more feasible and/or more enjoyable to absent themselves from the labor force either temporarily or permanently. Trends toward increased female labor force participation

already exist and can be expected to continue. As some males choose to rely on their partner's income, the social definitions that tie masculinity to breadwinning will decrease; this, in turn, might enable yet more males to choose to leave the labor force. In short, both sexes will be employed in more equal proportions.

2. The Structure of Occupational Roles: It is quite likely that the increased desire on the part of women to enter the labor force will be sufficiently greater than the increased desire for males to leave it, that there will not be nearly enough jobs to accommodate the number of qualified people desiring them. It is also likely that as the emphasis on the male as primary breadwinner decreases, more men will develop greater interests both in their role as fathers and in other leisure-time pursuits. Indeed, this is probably already occurring among younger males.

Either one or both of these factors may produce pressure on employing institutions to develop greater job flexibility in a number of ways. Occupational slots could be carved up into part-time components with two or more incumbents where previously there was one (experiments of this nature involving couples are already underway in some universities). Relatedly, two or more people could share a slot by each working full time for a certain number of months per year and absenting her/himself from the labor market for the remainder. Work hours for many jobs could be rearranged, allowing people to put in their 40 hours in fewer or more than five days in order to have either more hours per day or more days per week free from work obligations. Likewise, there is no reason why many employees need to do their work between the hours of 8:00 a.m. and 5:00 p.m. Some people are "night folks," others early morning, and so on. Allowing workers who do not need to communicate directly and extensively or constantly coordinate work with others to choose all or some of their own hours could yield greater productivity and more efficient use of buildings and equipment. Indeed, the work done on many jobs does not even require that it be done at the office. Part or all of many occupational roles could not only be performed when the worker wished, but where as well. Experimentation in some of these directions of flexibility is already underway, largely in response to urban congestion and commuter traffic problems. As more employees, especially males, demand more flexibility to be able to participate more fully in fatherhood and/or leisure activities, these trends should increase.

In response to the same pressures mentioned above, economic institutions are likely to find that they can no longer move employees geographically with such ease and frequency. Not only considerations of spouse's employment, but other, nonwork roles and commitments have already and will increasingly cause employees to refuse transfers. Likewise, employees may refuse to work extra hours so readily, refuse to follow the dictates of dress and decorum demanded by an employer, refuse to follow a career commitment unbroken by labor force absence. Employees will, in short, become psychically and financially freer to say no to employing institutions if the occupational roles demand too much sacrifice of other aspects of life.

The more occupational roles change in the suggested ways, the more likely workers are to become involved in and come to value nonwork roles and activities which, in turn, increases pressure toward work flexibility. Given the increased number of people desirous of jobs, however, and the greater satisfaction accruing to work under more flexible and worker-controlled circumstances, total output need not suffer and may well improve. It may even be hoped that, as our work force participants are more fully representative of all groups of Americans and as workers develop broader commitments to nonwork pursuits, the nature of the decisions made by economic institutions will become more humane. Persons who utilize the outdoors more for leisure may be less inclined to pollute it, even at the expense of corporate profits. People who are involved intimately in child care may make safer toys and children's goods and may create child care facilities convenient to work sites. Workers sharing the housework may create more durable and efficient household products.

3. Leisure, Volunteerism, and Housework: Much socially desirable as well as personally gratifying activity is conducted outside of the formal economic life of the nation. As such, it is unreflected in our treasured G.N.P. Inestimable billions of dollars worth of necessary work is done by millions in the form of housework, child rearing, volunteer work in hospitals, social service agencies, charities, political organizations, etc., and the creation of goods through sewing, canning, home carpentry, and so on. Many more such efforts, especially in the area of volunteerism, would undoubtedly be of great service to the society in general. By and large, unemployed women have heretofore constituted the vast bulk of those engaged in such activities. They have received no remuneration in the form of income pegged to their labors, usually little social recognition, and often subtle denigration.

Among feminists today we find many who argue that such activities, especially housekeeping and child rearing, should receive recompense. The justification for this rests in large part on the idea that only when income accrues to them will such activities come to be viewed as socially important work. Another perspective, however, is one that questions why only those activities for which money is paid should be socially valued. In a future world where women as well as men are often employed and in which both also spend large amounts of their time in nonwork pursuits, we might expect that the measure of the person will no longer be so closely tied to occupational prestige and resulting income level. Women may, by entering the labor force, spend less of their time engaged in such pursuits, but men will probably spend more of their time in these ways as work schedules become more flexible and demands upon them for ever more earnings decrease. As in employment, the equal representation of both sexes in volunteerism, do-it-yourself production, housekeeping, and child rearing will increase both the definition of these pursuits as worthwhile and the sense of fulfillment and satisfaction among people.

We should not be so naïve as to believe that ERA will result in a problem-free utopia. However, to the extent that work has constituted our most highly valued pursuit at the expense of virtually all other aspects of human existence, the long-run impact of this constitutional amendment may well comprise a liberating and humanizing force for men and women alike. Women will come to make the socioeconomic contributions of which they are capable and from which both our nation and women as individuals have so much to benefit. Men will come to understand the growth-producing, tension-alleviating, and gratifying rewards of a life consisting of more varied roles and activities. Both may come to a deeper appreciation of each other born of their human communalities rather than their sexual differences.

The Impact of the ERA
on Marital Economics

Anne K. Bingaman

On the day a woman marries, her financial situation is altered drastically by the marital property law of the state in which she and her husband reside. If they live in one of the forty-three separate property jurisdictions,[1] her financial rights and responsibilities in the marriage, upon divorce, or upon her death or her husband's death will be governed by laws which are essentially the altered remnants of the English common law much as it existed soon after the Norman Conquest. If she and her husband reside in Washington, California, Arizona, New Mexico, Texas, Louisiana, Nevada, or Idaho, the new wife's financial rights at all stages of her life will be governed by the marital property system known as community property, older yet than the common law system and also substantially altered by legislative reforms to be described below.

In the forty-three separate property jurisdictions, the legal theory under which married persons own property may be simply stated. The earnings of each spouse after marriage retain precisely the status they had before marriage—they are the property of the earning spouse, in which the other has no legal right or interest. Just as each has legal ownership of his or her earnings, each also has the sole right to contract with regard to those earnings, obtain credit based upon them, and manage and control them.[2] Similarly, all property brought to the marriage or inherited is the separate property of the owning spouse and under his or her sole management and control.

In addition to her right to ownership and control of any earnings or property she may have, a wife's financial rights in a separate property jurisdiction include the right to be supported by her husband in the fashion and manner he chooses.[3] In return for this support, she is responsible for

116

rendering the wifely services of keeping the house and tending any children the couple may have.

Under the marital property law of the separate property jurisdictions, the only financial right of the wife who is not employed is the husband's duty of support. She has no legal interest or right to his earnings or what those earnings purchase, unless he deliberately makes a gift to her of some portion of his property by placing it in their names jointly or in her name alone.

The underlying theory of the separate property systems may be simply stated. In application, as we shall see, it becomes more complex.

In the eight community property states, a new wife's financial situation is quite different.[4] If she is employed, her earnings, which before marriage were her separate property, become community property in which she and her husband each have a one-half ownership interest. Similarly, her husband's earnings after marriage become community property in which she has a one-half interest, regardless of whether or not she happens to be employed herself. Each of them will retain as separate property any property brought to the marriage or inherited during it. The other spouse has no legal right or interest in this property, and the owning spouse has sole management rights over such property.

Insofar as ownership of property during marriage is concerned, then, the wife in a community property state is undoubtedly in a better position than her sister in a separate property jurisdiction. As far as management of community property is concerned, however, the situation in community property states is not as simple. Until 1972, no community property state allowed wives to manage community personal property equally with their husbands, although some did allow them to manage their own wages. Since 1972, however, five of the eight community property states have converted to a system of equal management, giving the wife by statute the "equal right" to manage and control the entire community personal property. In Texas, a wife may control her own earnings and may jointly control the community property if her earnings are commingled with her husband's. In Nevada and Louisiana, a wife's right to management and control remain restricted or nonexistent.[5]

What are the practical consequences of these two marital property systems which exist side by side in the United States today? Do their theoretical legal differences make any real difference in married women's lives? To answer the question, the property rights of a married woman under each system at the four principal stages which may occur in her life must be examined.

Property Rights during Marriage

In a credit-oriented society, the most important single aspect of a wife's financial rights during marriage is the ability to obtain credit. Through the use of credit, she may effectively enforce her husband's duty of support —which is otherwise totally unenforceable—by purchasing needed items and deferring payment for them or obtaining unsecured loans to make such purchases.

The Equal Credit Opportunity Act prohibits any creditor in the United States, whether a bank, savings and loan, small loan company, retail merchant, or other creditor, from discriminating in the granting of credit on the basis of sex or marital status. The Act recognizes, however, the pervasive effects of state property laws upon a creditor's decision to extend credit. It specifically provides, among other things, that in making a particular decision as to whether to grant or deny credit, a creditor may consider the application of state property laws which affect an applicant's credit-worthiness. What, then, is the impact of the Act on a wife's ability to obtain credit in separate and community property states?

In any of the forty-three separate property jurisdictions, whether a wife obtains credit under the Act will depend on several factors. If she is employed, a creditor must evaluate her credit-worthiness just as he would any married person's, male or female. However, because most women's incomes are lower than men's, the application of purely objective standards will not give the employed wife in a separate property jurisdiction the same amount of individual credit which the average employed husband would obtain. If an employed wife wishes to obtain a greater amount of credit, she may ask her husband to pool his income with hers in making the application and to expressly agree to be liable on any debts either of them incurs.

If the wife in a separate property jurisdiction is not employed—and over 55% of wives are not—she may obtain credit only in one of two ways. In all credit transactions except those with retail merchants, her husband must sign an agreement stating that he will pay any debts she incurs. The credit so obtained will then be not hers but her husband's.

The second means of extending credit to such wives is used only by retail merchants who, under certain circumstances, will open accounts for the wife alone for the purchase of "necessaries." Under the common law and today, the doctrine of "necessaries" alows merchants to extend credit to a wife for goods purchased without the consent of a husband and to hold the husband liable for the purchase price. However, because the doctrine is hemmed with legal uncertainties, any individual creditor may justifiably refuse to extend credit under the doctrine and thereby leave the unemployed wife in a separate property jurisdiction with only one means of obtaining credit—the express agreement of her husband to pay any debts created. For such wives, who are the majority of married women in the United States, the Equal Credit Opportunity Act is hardly a giant step forward. In fact, for them it represents no advance whatsoever in the crucial matter of obtaining equal credit.

In the five community property states with completely equal management provisions for community personal property, a wife, whether employed or unemployed, may obtain credit on exactly the same terms and in exactly the same amounts as her husband without his signature or consent to any transaction. This is so because she has a one-half ownership of all the community property, which includes both his and her earnings, and has the legal right to manage and incur debts binding the entire community personal property just as he does. Thus, if the community itself is credit-worthy, she may obtain charge cards, retail charge accounts, or unsecured bank or small loans on precisely the same terms as her husband. The credit so obtained will be hers alone.[6]

The situation is not so happy for wives in Nevada and Louisiana. Because those states have not given them the same right to manage the entire community personal property which their husbands enjoy, they are in much the same position as is the unemployed wife in a separate property jurisdiction: they may be granted credit only with the express consent of their husbands or through retail merchants' willingness to apply the doctrine of "necessaries" to their credit applications. In Texas, a wife must be employed in order to obtain credit independently of her husband. The unemployed wife is in precisely the same position as is the wife in Nevada, Louisiana, or any separate property jurisdiction.

During marriage, then, the most important financial rights of a wife are those involving credit. The community property system, as recently amended in five states by the addition of equal management provisions for community personal property, unquestionably offers married women the best chance to obtain credit on the same terms as their husbands.

PROPERTY RIGHTS UPON DIVORCE

As has been noted by a sociologist whose specialty is divorce and its impact on American life, the marital property laws of most of the United States assume that a husband and wife will marry only once and that they will stay married until they die. In fact, American society has long since moved away from that model, as evidenced by a divorce rate of 455 to every 1000 marriages. How does a wife fare upon divorce in separate and community property states?

Two property questions are involved in any divorce, in any jurisdiction—property division and the payment of any alimony or child support ordered in the divorce decree.

Although it is a common belief that alimony awards are a component of most divorces, that belief is simply unfounded. In fact, alimony is awarded in less than 10 percent of all divorces, and, because alimony is deductible from the husband's income and includible in the wife's, payments which are actually for the support of children are often labeled "alimony" to lower the husband's income tax.[7] Thus, alimony is not a large factor to be considered in the property questions which arise upon divorce.

Child support, which is customarily awarded to a wife granted custody of children, is not as customarily paid. The record of child support payments actually made by husbands is a dismal one, as demonstrated by the following statistics:

> 62 percent (of husbands) fail to comply fully with court ordered (child support) payments in the first year after the order, and 42 percent do not even make a single payment. By the tenth year, 79 percent are in total noncompliance.[8]

Thus, with alimony awards infrequent and child support awards difficult or impossible to enforce, the question of the division of property owned by either spouse upon divorce is a crucial one for wives. How does each marital property system deal with the problem?

Theoretically, in a separate property system, the spouse who has earned property is the sole owner of it. In those marriages—over 55% of all marriages—in which the wife does not work outside the home, the spouse who owns property upon divorce will necessarily be the husband. Even in those marriages where the wife is employed, the property she has accumulated is sure to be of less value than her husband's because of women's lower pay scales and the years even most employed women spend outside the labor force rearing children. Theoretically, then, upon divorce, property is divided according to which of the spouses owns it. Obviously, the separate property system gives a husband much-favored odds.

In fact, however, there has been a trend toward dividing property "owned" by husbands alone "equitably" between the spouses where specific legislation in a particular separate property jurisdiction allows it. In 1968, twenty-six of the forty-three separate property jurisdictions had statutes providing for such a division. The theoretical harshness of these systems has thus been mitigated by legislation in the majority of jurisdictions.

The Uniform Marriage and Divorce Act seeks to foster and encourage the same trend toward "equitable" division of property acquired by either spouse during marriage by the explicit provisions of Section 307 of the Act, as amended in 1973. Alternative A of that section, drafted to apply in separate property jurisdictions, states that upon divorce all property, regardless of the name of the spouse in which formal legal title is held, shall be divided between the spouses according to such factors as the duration of the marriage, the skills and employability of each spouse, and the age, health, and station in life of each. The section specifically includes the contribution of the homemaker spouse as a factor to be considered in the division of property belonging to both spouses upon divorce. Thus, the Uniform Act attempts to focus a court's attention upon a variety of factors in making an "equitable" division of property.

Although enacted in only three states as of December 1974,[9] the provisions of the Uniform Marriage and Divorce Act represent movement toward a system of community property upon the dissolution of marriage in separate property states. Were the Act to be adopted widely throughout the United States, it would help to end the inequities of the separate property systems for married women upon divorce. As matters stand now, however, women in separate property jurisdictions are not as well compensated for their years spent as homemakers as are wives in community property states.

In community property states, as Dean Judith Younger has pointed out, although the statutes give each spouse a vested ownership interest in one-half of all community property, only two of the eight states require that such property be equally divided upon divorce.[1] In the six other states, the statutes allow a court in a divorce proceeding to make such division of the community property as it considers "equitable" under the circumstances. In particular cases, such statutes may work a hardship upon the wife, especially in those states where fault is taken into consideration in dividing property upon divorce,[11] but in the majority of situations the wife in a community property state is aided by the unstated presumption that community property belongs equally to the spouses and should be divided equally upon divorce.

Upon divorce, then, while the differences between the two systems may be in fact less great than they are in theory, the basic premises of the separate and community property systems have a substantial effect on the divisions of property ordered. The basic premise of the separate property system, as we have seen, is that property is owned by the person who earned it during the marriage. In a community system, the basic premise is just the opposite: regardless of who earned property during marriage, it is owned equally by both spouses. With such premises as the starting points for the "equitable" property division by courts, it seems inevitable that the wife in a community property state will receive a larger share of the property accumulated by either of the spouses during marriage than will the wife in a separate property jurisdiction. With alimony and child support orders elusive promises at best, property division at divorce is of paramount interest to wives in the United States.

PROPERTY RIGHTS OF A WIFE WHO PREDECEASES HER HUSBAND

Although the majority of American wives outlive their husbands, the right to will property at death for those who do not is severely affected by the property system of the jurisdiction in which the couple lived. In a separate property jurisdiction, the wife will have the right to will only property which she has acquired by her own labor outside the home or which she inherited or was given. As we have seen, she has no legal interest in property earned or accumulated through her husband's labor, and no statutes exist which give her the right to will any portion of her husband's property if she predeceases him. Thus, those women who are not employed during marriage die literally penniless in separate property jurisdictions, with no property whatsoever to leave to children, parents, or others they might wish to care for unless they were fortunate enough to inherit or be given property during their lives.

Women in community property states, by contrast, die owning one-half of the community property and in all eight community property states have the right to will their halves to whomever they choose.[12] Very often, this right can make a real difference to a woman concerned about the care of children, parents, or others. For wives who predecease their husbands, then, the theoretical differences between the two property systems described at the beginning of this article have a very real and important impact upon their ability to assure that persons they care for receive property from them at their deaths.

PROPERTY RIGHTS OF A WIFE WHOSE HUSBAND PREDECEASES HER

The endless permutations of laws concerning the property rights of a wife whose husband has predeceased her make generalization in this area difficult at best. However, it may be said that in all but three separate property jurisdictions,[13] either the common law protection of dower or a statutory "widow's election" offers the surviving wife some share of the separate property of her deceased husband.

In general, the common law dower gives the wife the right to a life estate interest in an amount varying from 1/3 to 1/2 of the real property which her husband either owned at any time during the marriage or died owning. A dower interest is only the right to enjoy the property or its benefits for the lifetime of the surviving wife not an absolute ownership interest. The deceased husband has the right to name those persons who will take the property after the wife's death. A "widow's election," also known as a "forced" or "nonbarrable" share of the deceased husband's estate, gives the wife an absolute ownership interest in 1/3 to 1/2 of all the husband's property which he owned at the time of death, regardless of any provision in his will to the contrary.

Both these forms of protection for the widow constitute implicit recognition of the major defect of the separate property systems—their failure to compensate a wife for the services she performed in the household during the marriage—and in effect affirm the concept of a community of marital interest in property by ignoring the fact that such property was technically "owned" by the husband alone. With regard to these emendations of the concept of separate property, these systems can be faulted only in their assumption that all marriages will last for the lifetime of the spouses and that wives who outlive their husbands will receive their just share of the marital property at that time. When that assumption fails, as it does in all marriages which end in divorce or in which the wife predeceases the husband, the separate property systems offer at best a spotty and haphazard recognition of the wife's labor during the years of the marriage.

In the eight community property states, the wife whose husband has died is left with her one-half ownership interest in the community's real and personal property. Her husband is free to will, just as she is, his one-half interest in the property to anyone he chooses.

THE IMPACT OF THE EQUAL RIGHTS AMENDMENT

In the four possible stages of a married woman's life—during the marriage itself, at divorce, at her death before her husband's, or at his death before hers—the community property system consistently offers wives the opportunity for ownership of greater amounts of property and greater freedom to deal with it. Its assumption of a community of marital interest, and thus of marital property, is more consonant with the manner in which most couples view their marriages, and it gives the woman who works in the home and rears children both fair compensation for her labor and equal dignity with her husband. With two corrections, community property should be the marital property law adopted by all state legislatures in their effort to conform to the Equal Rights Amendment.

The first problem in need of correction is that of equal management. It is imperative that any community property system allow both spouses to share fully and equally in the management of all community personal and real property. Five of the eight community property states have already taken that step. If the system is adopted more widely, such provisions must be included.

The second major defect of most of the community property systems now in existence is their total failure to provide for a wife who marries a wealthy man. If neither of them works, no community property will be accumulated, and under the law of five of the eight community property states, all increments in the value of the husband's separate property will be his alone.[14] At divorce, such a wife is in the same position as the wife of a wealthy man in a separate property jurisdiction: totally dependent upon what a judge feels in "equitable" to award her, either as a division of property or as support. Upon her husband's death, she is in a far worse position than is the wife in most separate property jurisdictions, for she has absolutely no legal right to any of his separate property. This problem could quite easily be cured by enactment of some form of "forced share" provision in community property states, to be effective either upon divorce or death for persons married to spouses with substantial separate estates.

With these two defects cured, community property is unquestionably the fairer of the two systems for married women. But, will the Equal Rights Amendment mandate state legislatures to enact a community property system in the place of the existing separate property systems? Although the answer is by no means clear, there is a legal argument which can be made to that effect.

The argument draws from cases decided under the 14th and 15th Amendments to the United States Constitution and Title VII of the 1964 Civil Rights Act. In those areas, the United States Supreme Court has held that statutes "neutral on their face" which operate in a particular factual setting to discriminate against blacks or religious minorities are unconstitutional. The Court stated explicitly that it could not ignore the facts of the society in which apparently neutral laws operate.

Under these cases, the argument against the separate property systems under an Equal Rights Amendment would be that they also are laws which are "neutral on their face, but discriminatory in impact." These property systems say to all married persons, in effect, "you own what you earn." In the factual setting in which such systems operate, however, it is men in the society who are expected to fulfill the role of wage earners and women who are expected to remain in the home and care for house and children, uncompensated by wages. Even if a wife does work outside the home, the facts of the society in which she must obtain employment mean that she will be employed at a lower level than would a comparable man, will be paid less, will not advance as rapidly, and cannot expect to earn as much in her working lifetime. In what sense, then, are these "neutral" separate property systems truly neutral? The systems are so established as to reward the man who does only what society expects of him—work outside the home—and to penalize the woman who also does only what is expected of her—work inside the home. It is arguable, therefore, that under the Supreme Court precedents in the race and religious minority areas, the separate property systems are "neutral on their face, but discriminatory in impact" and should be declared unconstitutional under an Equal Rights Amendment.

It is possible that the same result could be achieved if the Supreme Court were to hold that sex, like race, is a "suspect" classification under the equal protection clause of the 14th Amendment. Four Justices declared their willingness to so rule, and if such a decision comes down, the constitutional argument concerning the validity of the separate property systems would be the same as that under an Equal Rights Amendment.

Regardless of the Amendment's fate, however, or of the Supreme Court's willingness to hold that sex is a "suspect" classification, women in both separate and community property jurisdictions must become aware of the immense practical consequences which marital property systems have upon their lives—in obtaining credit, in the division of property at divorce, upon their ability to will property, and upon their property rights when their husbands die. It is past time that women debate, discuss, and understand these issues. They are not the exclusive domain of lawyers, law professors, or courts and judges. They are the laws which determine the very amount and extent of property owned by every married woman and man in the United States. As such, they deserve far more attention than they have yet received.

Footnotes

1. All states except Arizona, California, Idaho, Louisiana, Nevada, New Mexico, Texas, and Washington are separate property states. The named states are community property states. The District of Columbia is a separate property jurisdiction.

2. Until passage of the Married Women's Property Acts in the nineteenth century, the husband had sole control of his wife's separate property as well as his own. For a description and history of the passage of the Married Women's Property Acts, see *Am. Law of Property*, Vol. 1, Sec. 5.56 (Casner ed., 1952).

3. The phrase "in the manner and fashion he chooses" is used advisedly. As a practical matter, the husband's legal duty of support is totally unenforceable by the wife because of courts' reluctance to "interfere" in ongoing marriages.

4. There are in reality eight different community property systems, not one, just as there are forty-three varieties of the separate property system described above. For simplicity's sake in a short paper, however, each of the two systems is described here as if all jurisdictions conformed to the common basic patterns.

5. In Arizona, California, Idaho, New Mexico, and Washington, the spouses have the statutory power to equal management of the entire community personal property.

6. The importance of building a credit history in one's own name cannot be overemphasized. If credit which a wife uses during marriage is maintained in the husband's name, the credit history will be his alone on divorce or his death. The wife will be left with no credit history of her own, in spite of the fact that she may have contributed greatly to actual payment of debts incurred. Thus, the name in which credit is granted and held is of the utmost practical importance for married women.

7. Weitzman, *Legal Regulation of Marriage: Tradition and Change,* 62 Cal. L. Rev. 1169, 1186 (1974). The reason for excluding alimony from a husband's income and including it in his former wife's is that the husband is usually in a higher income tax bracket than the wife, which makes the tax savings greater to him.

8. Weitzman, *supra* note 7, p. 1195.

9. Those three are Arizona. Colorado, and Kentucky. Of them, however, only Colorado adopted a provision which closely paralleled that of the Uniform Act.

10. Those two are Louisiana and California.

11. In an attempt to remove considerations of fault from property division questions, the Uniform Marriage and Divorce Act states in both Alternatives A and B to Section 307, as amended in 1973, that property shall be divided "without regard to marital misconduct."

12. Wives in New Mexico acquired this right only after passage of an Equal Rights Amendment to the State Constitution, which required repeal of former statutes denying wives but giving husbands the right to will their respective halves of the community. New Mexico was the only community property state which ever had such a provision.

13. Those three are North Dakota, South Dakota, and Georgia.

14. In Idaho, Louisiana, and Texas, all increases in the value of separate property owned by either of the spouses during marriage is community, not separate, property. Such provisions go far toward solving what is described in the text as the second major defect in the community property system.

The Impact of the ERA on Financial Individual Rights: Sex Averaging in Insurance

Barbara A. Brown and Ann E. Freedman

I. Introduction

This article discusses the application of the Equal Rights Amendment to the sex-based rating systems currently employed by life insurance and annuity providers. These systems rely on sex-based classifications which are purportedly justified by physical differences between men and women. Sex classifications in insurance and annuity rating have a significant discriminatory impact on individuals while appearing reasonable as applied to each sex as a whole. This article describes the nature and extent of sex discriminatory practices in this area and outlines the legal principles which will govern judicial and legislative implementation of the Equal Rights Amendment. It then argues that the ERA prohibits sex classifications of the type now used in insurance rating and that sex-blind systems are both fair and feasible.

The insurance industry has practiced pervasive discrimination against women in coverage, availability, underwriting practices, and rating. The form and extent of discrimination varies from one kind of insurance to another with perhaps the worst record of treatment of women by health and disability insurance providers. The practices of the industry have been documented thoroughly in several governmental reports, which show that, on the whole, the insurance industry has both neglected women as prospective clients and dealt with them less favorably.

The discrimination in insurance reflects and intensifies the discrimination women face in other areas such as employment, credit, domestic relations, and marital property. Several basic assumptions underlie current insurance practices. The first is that women are only marginally connected to the labor force and will therefore absent themselves and overutilize insurance more than men. This assumption leads companies to conclude that women are poor risks for health and disability income plans and to charge them more for similar coverage, give shorter terms of coverage, and refuse automatic renewal options to women.

Second, insurance companies consider pregnancy and childbirth voluntary conditions rather than temporary disabilities. As a consequence, time lost from work for disabilities due to pregnancy and childbirth is excluded from disability insurance plans. Third, pregnancy is considered "acceptable" only for married women, and coverage for pregnancy, childbirth, abortion, and sterilization are often available only to married women at a prohibitive "family" rate based on two adults and two children.

Fourth, domestic work is not regarded as a risk whose loss should be compensated by insurance; only work outside the home in permanent "career-type" jobs is considered valuable enough to insure. Therefore, only women with such jobs can purchase disability or life insurance contracts. The benefits paid by those few disability plans that do compensate loss of work in the home pay only a small percentage of its value.

Fifth, divorced, separated, and even unmarried women are considered unstable. Their financial plight is intensified by the refusal of insurance companies to extend homeowners, automobile, or disability income plans to them. In addition, women suffer in terms of insurance coverage because they are clustered at the lower paid end of the labor market. They lose out on life insurance and annuity and pension plans which have a much higher proportion of employer contributions at the management and predominantly male levels in the economy, and, because of higher turnover rates and interruption of work for childbearing and rearing, they often run afoul of rigid pension vesting rules.

A great deal needs to be done to remedy these forms of discrimination by the insurance industry. Some states have passed, and numerous others are considering, legislation to prohibit sex discrimination in underwriting and availability. Courts, and in their wake, legislatures, are prohibiting the exclusion of pregnancy and maternity-related disabilities from disability income and sick leave plans. Laws or regulations should be promulgated to prohibit the exclusion of the medical costs of pregnancy, childbirth, abortion, and sterilization from standard single person health policies and to require those risks to be spread over the insured populations as a whole. Similarly, the insurance companies must be educated to the value of work within the home and the need to insure against risks to its performance on the same basis as work outside the home.

The last and most difficult sex distinction to attack, from the theoretical point of view, is the insurance industry's virtually universal practice of grouping men and women on the basis of sex to calculate premiums and payment in the forms of insurance that depend on life expectancy. The basic sex distinction works in the same way but with different results in the life insurance and annuity contexts. Women pay lower whole life insurance premiums than men because they live longer as a group and the companies have the use of the money longer before anticipated payout.[1]

Under one common type of annuity, a money-purchase or defined contribution plan, a specified contribution, usually a given percentage of pay, is made. No fixed benefits are guaranteed. Given the use of sex-based mortality tables, the money invested to produce payments after retirement until death will have to last longer for women than for men, so the monthly payments to a woman will be smaller than to a man of equal age. The real life span differential is used for computation in this context, so women suffer the full 5-to 7-year loss in their incremental payments. In the Teachers Insurance Annuity Association plan for college teachers, a woman choosing the single life option receives 13% less in each periodic payment than a man with an equal working record.[2] However, if either person dies prior to retirement, the death benefit to the survivors of each would be identical, since the amount of the total fund is the same. If the annuitant chooses a joint and survivor option with his or her spouse, the amount of the life-time annuity will generally be the same whether the employee was male or female.

Although the present value of the annuity is the same for all annuitants, there is a disincentive for a man to choose the survivor over the single life option. The addition of a female life to his own life increases greatly the anticipated payout period, so the level of monthly benefits during his life will diminish sizeably. Women, already receiving a smaller monthly benefit, lose little by the addition of a male life and therefore have no financial incentive to choose one option over the other. Thus, women are doubly disadvantaged. As annuitants, they receive a smaller periodic payment than men if they choose the single life plan. As spouses, they are less likely to receive protection because their husbands have an inducement to choose the single life option and its larger periodic payment.

A second type of plan is a formula or defined benefit plan, which specifies the rate of benefits, usually a certain amount multiplied by years of service. Contributions to the plan are not fixed but are based on the amount needed to provide the stated benefits. Male and female employees choosing a single life option under such a plan will receive equal benefits, but either employer or annuitant contributions to the plan must be more for women employees. The present value of the annuity at retirement will be calculated on the basis of sex group life expectancies, so that the woman's annuity will have greater present value. If an option other than single life, such as lump sum payment or distribution over a number of years, is chosen, the value of the woman's annuity will be greater.

Employers claim that sex grouping for fringe benefits related to life expectancy is rational (and therefore, legal) because women as a group do live longer than men. They also claim that prohibitions on sex grouping would be unfair to men. In a sex-blind system everyone would be paid a rate based on the longevity of the entire group; it would fall somewhere between the current male and female rates. Since, on the average, men would receive this reduced benefit for shorter periods of time than women, some argue that they would thereby be subsidizing women.

Four federal agencies which monitor sex discrimination in the employment context have grappled with the problem of sex discrimination in life insurance and annuities. Three have thus far taken the position that employers can choose either to pay equal contributions or to provide equal benefits. Unfortunately, this approach allows employers to choose equal benefits in the life insurance context and equal contributions in the annuity context, thus denying women the benefit of their greater average longevity in the former and penalizing them in the latter.

However, the Equal Employment Opportunity Commission, which administers the most far-reaching law governing sex discrimination in employment, Title VII of the Civil Rights Act of 1964, has concluded that the Act's command of sex equality in the terms and conditions of employment means that there must be equal periodic benefits in pension or retirement plans. Greater cost for one sex is no defense. In rejecting an employer argument that the payment of equal monthly payments would discriminate in favor of women because they live longer than men, the Commission stated:

> The logic of this argument is that usually used to support discrimination: an appeal to the average characteristics of a particular sex, race, or other group protected under Title VII. But no person knows when he or she will die. All that [the employer's] sex-segregated actuarial tables purport to predict is risk spread over a large number of people; the tables do not predict the length of any particular individual's life. In our view, any use of sex-segregated tables that results in payment of different periodic pension benefits to males and females is highly suspect. Because actuarial tables do not predict the length of any individual's life, any claim that such tables may be used to assure equal pension payments over a lifetime between males and females must fail. In order to achieve compliance with section 703(a) of Title VII and with the Commission's Guidelines on Discrimination Because of Sex the periodic pension benefits paid to males and females in equivalent circumstances must be equal.[3]

A federal district court faced with a Title VII challenge to an employer-defined benefit plan which required higher contributions from women employees cited the EEOC decision quoted above in holding that the requirement of higher contributions in order to receive equal payments in a plan using sex-based tables was illegal sex discrimination against women employees.[4] Although the court and the EEOC both suggest strongly in their opinions that the use of unisex tables is the proper way to comply with the requirements of Title VII in this area, neither has as yet construed the law to require that method of attaining equality.

Constitutional litigation has not yet yielded any final decisions on the merits of the sex-based rating question. However, an arena in which there has been some activity is state statutory and administrative enforcement of antidiscrimination laws. A number of states have enacted laws which prohibit discrimination in coverage and underwriting policies. Although in many instances sex-based rate discrimination is expressly or by administrative interpretation excluded from the group of prohibited acts, the increased jurisdiction of agencies and strength of antidiscrimination guarantees suggest that state courts and agencies will be pressed to rule on the legality of sex-based acturial tables in the near future.

II. EQUAL RIGHTS AMENDMENT THEORY

Our society has traditionally used a wide variety of sex classifications to assign legal rights and duties. Such classifications may be characterized as legislative statements that, on the average, women are significantly different from men in a particular way. Sex classifications, like most legislative classifications, are imprecise; they range from those which are arbitrary or irrational to those which seem accurate for all but a small minority of women or men.

Significant progress toward eliminating sex discrimination has been made in the last few years due to the increasing willingness of legislators and judges to examine the facts instead of accepting rationalizations or stereotypes about the sexes as justifications for sex classifications. Unfortunately, classifications which bear no factual relationship to the abilities and characteristics of the average woman are not the only objectionable sex distinctions. Equally common are those sex classifications which are true for a large number of women—perhaps a majority or even 90%— but which have a detrimental impact on the remainder. These classifications are "rational" and, on cursory examination, most people may find them acceptable, but they deny qualified individuals rights and opportunities simply because they belong to a sex which usually does not display these qualifications.

Weightlifting limitations are a good example. In 1975, a weightlifting limit which prohibited all women workers from lifting weights of 5 lbs. or more would be considered by most people to be arbitrary and irrational. In contrast, a weightlifting limit which prohibited women from lifting weights in excess of 50 lbs. might be reasonable for the majority of women. However, individual women who would be capable of safely and efficiently lifting weights of that size or larger, perhaps as many as 40-45% of all women, would be harmed by such a limitation. At the same time, individual men who could not lift such weights safely would be denied the protection of the law solely on the basis of sex.

Under the Equal Rights Amendment, according to its legislative history, classification by sex is forbidden in any activity in which the state participates, whether or not the classification is "rational." This absolute prohibition is based on a political and moral commitment to principles of individuality and on the knowledge that sex classifications always mean denial to some people.

Classifications based on average physical differences between the sexes are no exception to this rule. However, the Equal Rights Amendment may be interpreted to permit physical differences between the sexes to be taken into account in two ways. One permissible way might be if the physical difference is a unique physical characteristic of either men or women. If the unique physical characteristic is closely related to the legislative purpose, and it is neither possible to use a sex neutral classification nor to test individuals, the legislature may classify on the basis of the unique physical characteristic. However, it would be quite unusual for a sex classification to be justified under this test.

The other way in which physical differences between the sexes may be taken into account is through classifications based directly on physical differences. For example, it is not permissible to exclude women from a football team, but it is permissible to set height and weight limits and exclude from participation persons outside the limits. However, such superficially neutral rules will be closely scrutinized to be sure that the physical limitations are justified by the legislative goal.[5]

The next section explores the application of this theory to sex classification in insurance rating and the design of sex neutral alternatives to current practices.

III. THE IMPACT OF THE EQUAL RIGHTS AMENDMENT

The use of gender as a rate setting factor is attractive to insurers because sex is easily ascertained and, until recently, has been widely perceived as a fair basis for classification. Sex-based acturial tables are built on the assumption that it is permissible to treat individual members of the class as though generalizations true of the group were true of all individuals. But the fact that the class generalization may be true on the average does not alter the personal injury to an individual who does not possess the class characteristic but who is treated as though she or he does. A woman executive with a real risk of early death is disadvantaged by a grouping which ascribes to her a long life expectancy, for it results in a small periodic annuity; a man who does not engage in similar work and who, consequently, may indeed have a long life expectancy, will be harmed by having to pay the high male rate to obtain life insurance. As in every other area, the vice of sex averaging is that the groups always include some people who do not have the feature assumed to be possessed by the whole sex group and exclude others who do.

The fact that the average difference in life expectancy between men and women as a group does not hold true for many individuals of both sexes is evident. The mortality curves of the sexes overlap significantly; both men and women die over a broad spread of years with more of each clustered within certain ranges but no clear line delineating all women from all men. Averaging inaccurately groups short-lived women with their sex group and long-lived men with theirs. In fact, a sizeable percentage of men and women will live the same length of time. One recent study of 1,000 men and 1,000 women aged 65 shows that the death ages of 68.1% of each group can be paired. Thirty-two percent of the women lived longer than this group and 32% of the men died earlier.[6] This suggests that a large percentage of those grouped together in sex-based tables do not share the characteristic assumed to be possessed by all members of that group.

The reason why actuarial grouping across sex lines appears problematic is that mortality is not like strength or most other physical or mental traits, for it cannot be tested with certainty in any individual and can only be based on guesses derived from earlier experience with persons who have similar features. It is much more difficult for an individual to assert that she will only live to 67, and therefore ought to receive large annuity payments, than to assert that she can lift 50 pounds, since the first assertion can at best only be supported by supposition based on her possession of certain characteristics which are associated with low life expectancy. There can never be a perfect actuarial correlation between risk and rate level; some persons in the group will always receive less for their payment than others, as risk spreading through a group is the essence of insurance. Therefore, it is difficult for any individual to show that he or she is in the wrong group or pays more than he or she ought. As long as the insurance companies group people on a basis (such as sex) that has some consistent predictive value, the group experience will always seem correct, and it will be difficult for those who constitute a subgroup with a different risk to identify themselves as such.

The Equal Rights Amendment precludes penalizing or rewarding women or men because of characteristics which predominate in one sex but are found in both, whether these are derived from social, economic, or cultural sources or from average physical differences between the sexes. Administrative convenience or other state interests do not justify sex-based classifications under this standard. Race, because it is as readily identifiable and as predictive a feature as sex, is also an administratively convenient way to predict life expectancy, yet society has chosen not to allow insurance rates to be calculated on that basis.

As already mentioned, one circumstance in which a physical difference between the sexes might conceivably be taken into account under the Equal Rights Amendment is when the difference derives from a unique physical characteristic. The mere existence of such a characteristic does not justify a sex classification however. Any reliance on it to justify a sex distinction must be strictly scrutinized to assure that the characteristic is closely related to the purpose of the legislation; that the classification is narrowly drawn and is not a camouflage for discrimination; and that no alternative with a lesser discriminatory impact is available.

At the present time, the source of the average differential in life expectancy between men and women is hotly disputed. Most insurance companies and feminists agree that at least a major proportion of it derives from factors which are not inherent in women or men but are more likely, for social and cultural reasons, to be found in one group or the other. Socioeconomic status accounts for large differences in life expectancy for both men and women. Environmental and personality factors deriving from childhood conditioning also play a large part. Boys are generally trained to be more daring, self-reliant, and achievement-oriented than girls. This leads them to more stressful occupations and to more risk-taking which incurs physical danger. Men as a group also smoke and drink more than women, and both of these are related to life expectancy. As more women choose these traditionally male life styles and roles, sex-based rating may become less accurate, thus denying increasing numbers of women the right to be grouped on the basis of the factors which really influence their life expectancy.

Insurance providers contend that these factors do not wholly or even largely determine the difference in mortality, which they claim has a biological or genetic origin. Some studies show an intractable difference between men and women when all other factors are controlled. For example, a group of monks and nuns leading very similar lives were found to have the same differences in mortality as men and women in the population at large.[7] Similarly, a study of men who became annuitants through their own employment and those who were covered through their wives as employees showed similar mortality experience for the two groups.[8] On the other hand, a draft paper by two biologists at the University of Pennsylvania questions the contention that biological or genetic differences between the sexes explain the mortality gap.[9]

While the evidence is not conclusive, it is worth exploring the outcome under the unique physical characteristics test, should such a characteristic be shown to be present in some or all members of one sex but none of the other. As noted above, the inquiry into the validity of the sex distinction depends on several factors, including the closeness of the relationship of the characteristic to the legislative purpose; the proportion of the problem solved by using the sex grouping; the possibility of the physical characteristic being used as a subterfuge for sex discrimination; the availability of less drastic alternatives, with impact on fewer persons or less severe impact on the whole group; and the importance of the legislative purpose being accomplished by the sex grouping.

Were there a physical characteristic in all women which always produced greater longevity by a certain number of years, then the aspect of the test which requires a close relationship between the characteristic and the purpose of the legislation would be satisfied. However, the proportion of the problem solved by reliance on the unique physical characteristic would not be great; many other factors found in some members of each sex have an equally great impact on longevity as do genetic attributes attaching only to members of one sex. There would be some evidence that sex discrimination is the motive for using sex-linked traits as the sole factor for predicting longevity, since other physical and cultural factors which also have a major impact on longevity, such as smoking or overweight, are not taken into account in the rate-setting process.[1] In addition, as discussed below, there are sex neutral alternatives to a system based on unique physical characteristics which would either diminish or eliminate sex discrimination in insurance rates while still allowing insurance companies to function properly. Thus, even if there are unique physical characteristics which explain some portion of the average difference in male and female mortality, it is probable that a court would find insurance and annuity rates unconstitutional under the Equal Rights Amendment.

Under the Equal Rights Amendment, therefore, the insurance providers will have to use a sex neutral system based on factors other than the sex of the insured. This alternative would mean that all insureds in a given group would receive the same monthly annuity benefit or amount of life insurance for the same premium. The rate for the group would be set on the basis of the average life expectancy of that group, which could be calculated either on an occupational or industry basis, on the basis of the composition of the group in terms of various risk factors other than sex, such as smoking, marital status, use of alcohol, and obesity, or on the basis of age alone.

Insurance companies frequently inquire about risk factors such as medical history, overweight, and smoking habits. At the present time, however, this information is used only to decide whether or not to insure a particular individual or to calculate the premiums of particular risky groups to whom only limited policies are available. For members of most groups, rates are determined without regard to information about particular individuals other than age and sex.

It seems likely, however, that the companies will choose to use the occupation-related factors, as a system based on personal health characteristics would be more expensive to administer. Although they could rely on written responses to questions about the presence of those physical conditions, the possibility of fraud or malingering would probably be considered too great to rely wholly on that source of information, and medical examinations of large numbers of people might become necessary. Occupational or industry grouping information, on the other hand, is easy to ascertain, and it is probable that because pension plans on an industry or union basis already exist, longevity statistics that would be useful as a basis for the ratings are currently available. Moreover, personal health factors presently tend in the same direction as sex, so that the rate categories they would produce might still be sex-segregated, still have a disparate impact on women, and might therefore still be constitutionally impermissible.

In addition to occupation-related factors for grouping, another sex neutral grouping is also attractive. Under it, no premium or benefit differences on the basis of sex or longevity-related characteristics, such as smoking, would be made. Distinctions in rates on the basis of age (and salary level for employment connected plans) would be made as under the present system as would different payments based on choice of payout options. There would thus be a single uniform rate for each age group to replace the current sex-based dual rating system.

One form of rating which would not be permissible would be group rating based on the proportion of men and women in the group. This type of rating still attributes to all women and all men the average characteristics of their sex because separate mortality tables based on sex are still used. It simply changes the level at which the sex-based calculation occurs from the determination of individual rates to the determination of group rates. Under this system, individuals would be penalized for annuity purposes if they belong to a group with many women and penalized for life insurance purposes if they belong to a group with many men. This result is no more permissible under the Equal Rights Amendment than individual sex-based rating.

Unisex rating, on the other hand, has several practical benefits in addition to its theoretical advantages. It removes any incentive on the part of employers to discriminate against women in hiring because of sex-based differences in the cost of fringe benefits. It encourages people to think in terms of individual differences rather than in overbroad sex groupings. And it means that union and employee bargaining for decent annuities will produce adequate benefits for employees of both sexes.

IV. CONCLUSION

Courts and legislatures have grown increasingly suspicious over the last several years of the facile use of sex classifications to allocate legal rights and duties. The Equal Rights Amendment represents a moral and political judgment that such classifications should no longer be employed. However, there has been a tendency on the part of many people to accept sex classifications purportedly justified by average physical differences between the sexes while rejecting those based on socioeconomic and cultural stereotypes. This examination of the use of classifications based on average physical differences in the difficult area of insurance demonstrates both the denial of individual rights which such classifications produce and the feasibility of designing sex neutral alternatives to current practices. The implementation of the equal rights principle in this area is the next step. The cost of change from established ways must not be allowed to justify a lessened commitment to equality for women and men in all areas of legal and political life.

Footnotes

1. However, women often do not receive the full benefits of the average age differential. In group policies, there is often no difference in rates on the basis of sex, and when there is, it is at most a three year setback instead of the real five to seven year gap in average life span.
2. Halperin, "Should Pension Benefits Depend upon Sex of the Recipient" (unpublished paper, 1975), p. 1 [hereinafter cited as Halperin].

3. EEOC Decision No. 74-118 2 CCH, Employ. Prac. Guide §6431 (1974), pp. 4152-53.

4. *Manhart v. City of Los Angeles,* Department of Water and Power, 387 F. Supp. 980 (C.D. Cal. 1975).

5. Such rules will also be examined to be sure that they are not subterfuges for sex discrimination and that there are no alternatives with a smaller impact on the protected class. In the football example, for instance, even if the height and weight limitations were not found to be an attempt to discriminate on the basis of sex, a school might be required to have two football teams, one for larger students and one for smaller students, as long as there is no physical reason why smaller students, among whom girls would predominate, could not play football with other small students.

6. This data comes from a study by Dr. Barbara Bergmann, quoted in Bernstein and Williams, *Title VII and the Problem of Sex Classification in Pension Programs,* 74 Col. L. Rev. 1203, 1221-22 (1974).

7. Halperin, *supra,* n. 2, p. 9; see also R. Duncan, *TIAA Female Mortality Experience* 1965-1970 (1972); Bernstein and Williams, *supra,* n. 6, p. 1207 n. 7.

8. Of course the men who qualified as spouses may have held similar jobs themselves and chosen their wives' plans for reasons other than they were not employed. See Kallman and Jarvik, *Individual Differences in Constitution and Genetic Background,* cited in Halperin, *supra,* n. 2, p. 16.

9. Waldron and Johnson, "Why Do Women Live Longer than Men?" (Univ. of Pa.). The biological or genetic difference is said to derive from the presence in men of the diminutive Y chromosome as opposed to two full X's and to the androgen and testosterone levels in men. The University of Pennsylvania paper finds no clear evidence that the hormonal difference contributes to sex differences in occurrence of arteriosclerotic heart disease or cancer. Conditions caused by X-linked recessive mutations constitute less than 2% of the excess of male death before the end of the reproductive years.

10. One physical characteristic which may be relevant to longevity is hormone level in the body. This is a unique physical characteristic in the sense that all men may have a level above a certain point and all women a level below that point, but individuals do vary greatly within the ranges for their sex. It could be argued that because of the individual range within each sex, making some men closer in level to some women than they are to men, insurance companies have a responsibility to base their rates on individual characteristics rather than on sex classifications.

SOCIAL IMPACT

Introduction to Social Impact

This section takes an institutional approach, singling out marriage, education, and the law as the key institutions which will be affected by the Equal Rights Amendment. Each institution is stratified by sex, that is, each is ordered by a hierarchy which assigns greater power, status, and freedom of choice to men. Such a sexual analysis is, however, strikingly absent from sociological investigation. Stratification is one of the major subdivisions of sociological inquiry and much research has been devoted to it; yet, sexual inequality has not been recognized along with wealth, power, and prestige as a determiner of status. The basic reason for this is the implicit assumption that the family and not the individual is the unit of class stratification and that the family's status depends solely on the wealth, power, and prestige of the husband. This is a kind of ironic equality since the wife is assumed to be "equivalent" to her husband. So, as Joan Acker has suggested, what is needed is not just equality in the hierarchy, but *representation* in it for women, the use of sex as a variable in the analysis of status.[1] Presently, only single women are counted in the statistics, and the absurdity of discounting them from those very same statistics upon marriage testifies not only to their symbolic demise as individuals but to the gross inaccuracy of the figures. Each of our writers, therefore, tries to correct for past neglect and to consider each institution from the point of view of sex as a major structural social inequality.

Such basic yet hidden flaws in "objective" science contribute to the fears people have about equality, and consequently, the ERA. What has happened is that implicit *value* judgments of male scientists are expressed as *empirical* judgments. William J. Goode describes the conflict between value and empirical judgments in family sociology by pointing up three pervading themes of the literature: the emancipation of women and children as "destructive evolution" or the "disintegration" of the family; the "strength" or "solidarity" of the family as the authority of the father; and the "unity" of the family as the prerogatives of the husband and father.[2] Because science is a major symbol system in American society, the sanction of scientific or "natural" principles is one drama that creates social order. Such implicit and unidentified subjectivity as pervades the scientific symbol

139

system prevents the changing of the social order through fear of destroying what is "natural" and "pragmatic" and obstructs the search for facts that would belie these traditional biases.

The sanctity of "biological" discrimination or discrimination based on "nature," discussed in our economic impact section as a possible exception under ERA, rears its ugly head again in the social realm. Because of the importance of such symbol systems in creating and sustaining social order, Charles Elkins discusses, in a far different context, the use of biological *terminology* to support prejudices in areas having no relationship to biology or to known facts. Further, the conflict of biological terminology with other terminologies even more valuable to our society causes Dr. Elkins to predict the eventual collapse of biological sanctions for discrimination—with the help of ERA.

In his article, Dr. Elkins also accounts for the realistic problems which legal equality will both encounter and create in an unequal society in which people are afraid of change. He tries to answer three questions: to what extent can constitutional change be expected to provoke significant change in the sex hierarchies of our institutions; *how* will such changes in the social order be effected; and, what problems can be expected to result from the ensuing clash between traditional and newly emerging symbols? It is noteworthy that his "symbolic interactionist" or "dramatistic" approach to the concept of social order is one of the very few sociological perspectives which recognizes and gives value to the sex hierarchy as a basic stratification of society, although studying it only as a drama in and of itself rather than defining its relationship to social hierarchies and institutions other than those in which sex is an obvious factor, like marriage.

Anticipation of change in the relationship between the sexes brings up the question of what "equality" in the social realm really means. Alice Rossi uses the types of relationships of ethnic groups to the dominant culture as possible models for sexual equality. A "pluralist" model of equality retains the diversity of the individual groups forming a heterogeneous society and assumes that the culture's strength will be this very diversity. The "assimilation" model of equality assumes that the minority groups will lose their own identity and take on the characteristics and values of the dominant culture. The "hybrid" model of equality assumes the necessity for change in both the dominant group and the "assimilating" group.[3] The choice of the appropriate model is crucial to our social structure, for it defines the relationship between tradition and equality, between the old social order and the new. Merely giving women greater participation in the old society, assuming they will take on male values, male responsibilities, and male privileges, is not the answer to the problem because inequality is structured into our institutions. On the other hand, the hybrid model would require institutional restructuring in order to make the economic and political worlds accommodate new values, whether "feminine" or "human," which are necessary for the survival of our society. We, of course, anticipate that the legal changes produced by the ERA will increase the strictly quantitative aspect of women's power, but whether the ERA, as a symbolic act, will radically change the social order by a qualitative realignment of values is a matter of speculation explored by Dr. Elkins. The ways in which the ERA may produce qualitative change, its functional limitation in producing such change, and the problems involved in such change are, again, the concerns of his essay.

Marriage, perhaps the key institution around which ERA fears have crystallized, is a good illustration of the choice our institutions face between accommodation (i.e., qualitative change) and decay. What has been defined as "successful" in the past has been so only on its own terms, without counting the human cost. According to Jessie Bernard, happiness in marriage may have been *adjustment,* but now that alternatives to the feminine stereotype are available, that adjustment no longer defines mental health for women. In fact, "sickness" may now be the necessary component for a "happy" marriage.[4] From this point of view, equality itself, let alone the ERA, will not destroy marriage; rather, it will provide an opportunity for freedom of choice and freedom to grow for both partners to be incorporated into the structure of marriage. This doesn't necessitate their making full use of that freedom; but it must be there for those who do want and need it. Morever, because of technology, which reduces housework, and contraception, which reduces child care duties, women will *have* to find something to do with their lives other than being housewives and mothers. Marriage must eventually accommodate this very real need. An ERA future is a world of changed reproductive needs and this change will affect an ever-widening circle of other institutional needs and demands. The benefits to both men and women of a strengthened and more viable union between them are, in and of themselves, incalculable.

The human cost of traditional marriage as well as the demand for change in marriage testify to the need for ERA to help marriage survive. Present sociological reality reveals a trend toward egalitarian family patterns which the law must acknowledge. Lenore Weitzman explores the possibilities of legal change resulting from the ERA that will actually accommodate this cultural change. The ERA, by making marriage more viable for people, will not increase divorce but decrease present unhappiness with marriage. Dr. Weitzman depicts a future which should be welcomed not feared. In discussing the elimination of sex classifications, which the ERA will make almost absolute, Dr. Weitzman describes the very beneficial effects this will have on society, on the family, and on children. It must also be emphasized that the ERA, while expanding individual choice in marriage, will not eliminate the traditional one for those who prefer it and will not limit the state's right to regulate marriage unless sexual classification is involved. It is discrimination within marriage, not marriage as an institution, which will come under review by the ERA.

If the ERA is limited in its ability to change marriage because of the private nature of the institution (i.e., psychological reluctance), there are other kinds of limitations to the ERA's impact, both legal and social. Two complementary pieces by Ruth Cowan and Eloise Snyder explore these perspectives.

Using the institution of education, crucial because of its role in socialization, Dr. Cowan describes the legal barriers to the implementation of the ERA. The progress of equality in education is a case study in implementation paralysis in view of the existence of Title IX of the Education Acts Amendment of 1972, which establishes sexual equality in educational institutions. Nevertheless, discrimination persists and inequality runs rampant. Dr. Cowan proposes that the ERA will face analogous limitations to its impact due to the inability of legal and administrative procedures to facilitate change effectively. Social change is thus blocked by legal and bureaucratic obstacles.

Conversely, legal change is blocked by social obstacles. In dealing with law as an institution, Dr. Snyder discusses the barriers to legal changes in individual rights posed by social values. The interpretation of law is circumscribed by society's values and its willingness to implement legal change in good faith. Law codifies our society's definitions of deviance. Since "deviance" (and this includes crime) is hardly absolute but is totally relative to social definition (including legal definition), changes in the law, like ERA, will conceivably alter our very definitions of female deviance. Women demanding and exercising certain previously unacceptable rights will no longer be "marginal," or "masculine," or "delinquent," or even criminal; rather, the social norms will change to accommodate them. But, as Dr. Snyder emphasizes, any redefinition of deviance and individual rights for women will depend as much on social change as on legal change. The ERA itself is limited in impact precisely because deviance is a social construct which is only *reflected* by the law.

In order not to underestimate the power of the law to effect change in society, Harriet Katz deals with criminal law, an area also covered by Dr. Snyder, from a different perspective. Both writers show how criminal law is rooted in sexism, but while Snyder emphasizes that those sexist values will delimit the range of ERA's effectiveness, Katz sees the ERA's legal reform changing social values and these new social values affecting the incidence and nature of crime itself. Not only can we expect the ERA to result in a more equitable system of justice but in a lowered crime rate. This will not only be due to the above mentioned changes in society's definitions of crime but to healthy psychological changes relative to equality itself.

Both articles, of course, stress the reciprocity of impact between law and society. The possibilities for the future of our institutions designed by the ERA are designed in detail by individuals not by the law as some kind of prime mover, and they will be as real as our efforts make them. So long as we control the change, we needn't fear it.

Footnotes

1. "Women and Social Stratification: A Case of Intellectual Sexism," in *Changing Women in a Changing Society,* ed. Joan Huber (Chicago: University of Chicago Press, 1973), pp. 174-83.

2. "Civil and Social Rights of Women," in *The Other Half: Roads to Women's Equality,* ed. Cynthia Fuchs Epstein and William J. Goode (Englewood Cliffs, N.J.: Prentice-Hall, Spectrum Books, 1971), p. 23.

3. "Sex Equality: The Beginnings of Ideology," in *Voices of the New Feminism,* ed. Mary Lou Thompson (Boston: Beacon Press, 1970), p. 67.

4. "The Paradox of the Happy Marriage," in *Woman in Sexist Society: Studies in Power and Powerlessness,* ed. Vivian Gornick and Barbara K. Moran (New York: New American Library, Signet Books, 1971), pp. 156-57.

Legal Change and Social Value

Eloise C. Snyder

As straightforward as the Equal Rights Amendment seems to be, it must be noted that its ratification may neither realize its proponents' hopes nor its opponents' fears because the ratification of the ERA by no means actually insures legal equality between the sexes. This most important point is exemplified by a statement by Mr. Justice Frankfurter: "The Constitution does not require things which are different in fact or opinion to be treated in law as though they were the same."[1] Justice Frankfurter's statement is based on the legal concept of functionality, and this concept, if applied in the interpretation of the ERA, could result in the upholding of discriminatory treatment of women when such treatment is reasonably based on general physical (functional) differences between the sexes.[2]

The reaction of ERA proponents to the legal concept of functionality is first, that the validity of "general physical differences" between the sexes is being challenged by present research. Such research is attempting to sort out the innate physical causes from the social causes (expectations of males and females by society) of differences in men's and women's abilities. If it is found, as current trends indicate, that male-female differences are not solely based on innate physical components, this could lead to the legal equalization of the treatment accorded the sexes. The proponents believe secondly, that if the legal concept of functionality has any validity at all, it can only reasonably be applied to individual cases of existing differences and not to women as a category (legal class).

Thus, we must take account of the interplay between the concepts of legal functionality and legal equalization in attempting to discern the ERA's effect on individual rights and the legal system. But the interplay of these concepts, although of interest to students of constitutional interpretation, is only of secondary importance in determining the impact which such an amendment might have on society. As an overview of history shows, the interpretation of amendments, and of all law, is ultimately derived from the social definitions of the time, and these social definitions in turn are a direct product of contemporary social values.[3]

This is to say that law reflects social values. It must be noted also that law helps to shape social values; but in this reciprocal relationship between law and social values, analyses tend to support the initial primacy of the social value component. In applying such analyses to the ERA, we find that its impact upon definitions of individual rights as well as the legal system itself will be initially determined, not by the 24 words of the Amendment nor by the application of concepts of functionality or equalization, but rather by the context of social values within which the interpretations of the ERA are made. It follows that when, and if, social values enable the ERA to receive broad and flexible interpretation, without a doubt the ERA will then effect marked changes in the social values themselves. But initially, the very emergence of the ERA shows that some change has been occurring in the social value framework.

Social values define certain behaviors as "right" and certain behaviors as "wrong." It is less important whether the rightness or wrongness of the behavior is based on fact or fiction (myths) and more important that systems of rightness and wrongness do exist. This is so because it is through such systems that society is able to define social deviance (wrongness), and in turn, it is through such definitions of deviance that society is able to define, and indeed defend, its concept of normalcy (rightness).

To expand this idea, we should note that it is through sickness that health is defined; this means that definitions of sickness help society to differentiate health and vice versa. The criminal helps us recognize the noncriminal, and the sinner, the religious. As Durkheim pointed out years ago, the existence of deviance in a society, in addition to its being created by definition of the society itself, serves a number of positive functions,[4] one of which is to set boundaries for what is regarded as acceptable behavior and what is not so regarded (socially deviant behavior). And once the boundaries are established, society, by punishing the unacceptable, defends the acceptable. Although the precise boundaries of acceptable and unacceptable behavior (of Howard Becker's "insiders" and "outsiders") do change in time, such change does not come swiftly or without social stress.

It is not difficult, therefore, to see why the ERA has been subjected to a long and hard battle, unsuccessfully introduced for so many years in Congress and found in the platforms of the major political parties to no avail. The concept of boundary defense is central to understanding such an occurrence.

Maleness and femaleness have long been socially defined and, indeed, are deeply ingrained in our social value system, originating as early as our initial Judeo-Christian literature. In such literature the expectations of men are forcefully differentiated from the expectations of women. For either a man or woman to differ from these expectations is wrong. Indeed, he is to play masculine and she, feminine.[5] Such sex roles are inherent in the socialization process itself, and although they go back to early religious literature, they affect both the religious and the nonreligious. Insofar as the ERA challenges present laws which reinforce traditional sex role differences, it challenges very deeply internalized social values of many men and women.

It is not only important to recognize that such deep-seated values have affected attempts to pass the ERA. It is the concern of this paper to analyze how these social values will further determine the impact which a ratified ERA will have on specific areas of individual rights and the legal system. Such an analysis does not place primacy on such concepts as legal equalization or legal functionality but on the social value framework of contemporary society.

Without a doubt the social boundaries defining appropriate man and woman behavior are changing, but not without great resistance from both men and women. Unfortunately, much of the controversy has centered on such emotional but relatively unimportant legal areas as toilets, dormitories, and cots. The first two, with or without the ERA, can be maintained as segregated units because of the constitutional right of privacy; the ERA might affect the last either by providing men in industry with cots in "their" restrooms or by depriving women of their cots. While the loss of a cot may be very disturbing to some women, others may think of it as more than a fair exchange for obtaining equal rights. We are not going to concentrate on such concerns here, however, except to note that their very existence is indicative of the deep emotional feelings that result from disturbing traditional belief systems, in this case systems pertaining to man-woman behavior.

There are numerous concerns upon which we could concentrate. However, because our primary aim is not necessarily to analyze the specifics of the legal implications of the ERA but rather to analyze the impact of the ERA as it is interpreted through the social value framework of contemporary society, we will select only a few specific areas of individual rights in the legal system, briefly focusing on these as illustrations of the interplay between the ERA and contemporary social values. It is hoped that the reader will be able to apply the dynamics discussed in these areas to other areas of interest.

In attempting this, we will look briefly at four areas, each of which raises important questions of value and provides excellent discussion material concerning the probable impact of the ERA: women's name change and/or retention of the maiden name; military service; criminal law; and juries.

NAME CHANGE AND/OR RETENTION OF THE MAIDEN NAME

It is very uncommon for women to keep their maiden names after marriage. In fact, most people are unaware that it can be done. Actually, only in Hawaii is there a law stating that a woman must take her husband's name upon marriage. Elsewhere it is possible for a woman to retain her name. She does so generally by maintaining with consistency her maiden name as her legal name—which is the name she uses vis-à-vis the state in her dealings with its different agencies. This involves retaining her name on driver's license, car registration, deeds to property, voting records, university registration and teaching, public office, credit, insurance, passports, income tax, social security, work records, and the like.

Although the specific laws may vary from state to state, the ERA can do much to legally clarify and bring about legal procedural uniformity in this matter of maiden name retention upon marriage. It is also probable that the ERA will change the present Hawaiian law. Further, in Hawaii and the remaining states, where it is presently possible to change one's name back to one's maiden name after adopting one's husband's name, the ERA can clarify and unify the specific requirements involved in so doing, such as whether this must be done through court action, with or without a lawyer, etc. Such clarification and unification of legal procedures are important because, although women are now permitted in most states to retain their maiden names and in all states to change back to their maiden names after marriage, and incidentally, in most states to name their children as they please, custom and prejudices are so entrenched in these matters that they may have to take legal action to enforce their rights.

In a recent campaign, in a small university town, an attempt was made to get the local newspaper to accept articles which referred to women as Ms. instead of Miss or Mrs. The newspaper accepted such articles but would then determine whether the woman was a Miss or a Mrs. and change the article accordingly. In fact, newspaper policy was such that one could not even be referred to as Mrs. Betty Smith but only as Mrs. Robert Smith, i.e., only the full name of her husband could be used. The campaign to change the policy of the newspaper resulted in numerous letters written to the editor which broadened the issue from the use of Ms. to the use of surnames. Most letters indicated dismay and shock at the thought that a woman might even think of using any name other than her husband's. These women, and most of the letters were from women, were proud to give up their maiden names for the names of their husbands, and their husbands joined them in this pride. Neither wife nor husband could see any reason for a woman retaining her maiden name, testimony to the readiness with which both sexes accept the absorption of the female by the male upon marriage so poignantly illustrated by the surname structure.

Some letters, however, did attempt to justify maintaining the maiden name. "Exchanging my name for my husband's name is a symbolic denial of all that I was before I married, and allows me little connection with the past. My life did not begin at the time of my marriage. It simply became happier."[7]

And so the battle is waged. Name change or retention, as one can see, is not primarily a legal problem. The Lucy Stoners retained their names back in the 1920s. It is a social value problem because it symbolizes the traditional position of woman as helpmate to the man. Except for legal clarifications and uniformity, name change or retention is not likely to be markedly affected by the ERA initially, not until social values change to the extent that women and men accept a woman's name retention and all that it symbolizes. The ERA, however, can do a good deal to speed up this process by calling attention to the matter and simplifying the procedures.

WOMEN AND MILITARY SERVICE

The impact of the ERA on women and the military service is an even "hotter" issue. Images of women being "drafted" and slogging through rice paddies with M-16's and full 60-pound packs strapped to their backs are offered by opponents of the ERA and effectively create social nightmares resulting in much opposition to ratification.

Proponents of the ERA state that such images, and indeed the actual realities, of men performing these duties should likewise create nightmares and social resistance. Further, they claim that, under the ERA, Congress will still retain its power to exempt certain groups of people from military service, a power it has used at various times in the past, e.g., deferring all fathers and all married men from time to time. This can be done for women as well as for men, in which case *all* married people and/or parents may apply for deferment or exemption. Moreover, ERA proponents state that all citizens, women and men, who have moral objections to bearing arms will be able to seek a classification to serve in noncombat service. This choice is presently available to men. Also, those (women and men) who have ethical objections to any kind of military service could seek classifications to perform community service instead, again a choice presently allowed men.

Moreover, proponents of the ERA claim that the social impact of the Amendment on women in military service would enable them to achieve the first-class citizenship status accorded those groups who serve the society militarily, while at the same time offering much individual choice to both women and men with regard to the form of service. Additionally, such opportunity to serve in the military opens numerous specific benefits to women,[8] such as: valuable in-service training, even for high school drop-outs; correction of physical problems; opportunity to travel; opportunity to learn leadership; educational opportunities and scholarships; veterans' bonuses; veterans' loans; continuation of G.I. insurance; medical treatment at V.A. hospitals; veteran's preference in federal and state employment; civil service listing; extra points on the civil service tests; and less likelihood of losing government jobs during work reductions.[9]

In spite of this beneficial legal impact of the ERA on women in the military, however, the legal component is secondary to the social component. As long as traditional stereotypes of women and men are maintained, the likelihood of Congress "forcing" women into direct military combat is minimal as is the likelihood of mass enlistment of mothers into the military. Therefore, considering the contemporary social values within which the ERA will be interpreted, its primary impact would not be to force women into new and undesired roles but rather to open up opportunities for women to serve militarily in new and more equalized ways than is presently possible. It is further possible that such emerging opportunities might be a factor in ultimately changing the very stereotypes of male and female roles themselves. Such change, however, will not be swift, and the impact of the ERA will be, at best, long term.

WOMEN AND CRIMINAL LAW

We will begin our consideration of women and criminal law by looking first at a most important and invidious interplay between social values based on myths and legal interpretations (and procedures), an interplay which results in a great deal of sexism in the present criminal justice system.

There are two significant myths involved. These myths also play a role in name change/retention and women and the military, but they are best exemplified here because each pervades the criminal justice system. The first myth concerns the Mary image of women, and the second, the Eve image. The Mary image signifies the Biblical unidimensional[10] image of women as incapable of wrongdoing—always performing within the rightness boundaries. Marys are portrayed as pure, devoted, and submissive. They need protection. Eves, on the other hand, are sinful temptresses. They mislead men and, in so doing, are responsible for criminal acts, even those performed against them by men, for which Eves must be punished. Interestingly, most of Eve's misleading activity involves sexual behavior. Women tempt men sexually. This is why, for example, they get raped. They ask for it. And for that matter, deep down within, they even enjoy being raped!!

When it is to the advantage of the interpreting group, however, the Mary image can also be brought into play in the case of rape, as is illustrated by the following story. In one of my classes, during a discussion of rape, it was suggested that when several incidents of rape occur, instead of applying curfew hours to women, as is presently done on campuses, it might be more effective to apply the curfew to men. This suggestion brought forth great hostility on the part of several male students in the class who felt this to be patently unfair since it would punish all men when only a very few were actually involved as rapists! When it was pointed out that it was even more unfair to apply the curfew to all women since none were rapists, the adamant males immediately responded that restricting women to their dorm areas was a protective action—women were being protected by men—and that protecting women in this way was important to both the women themselves and to the society as a whole. There is no better example of using the Mary image to the advantage of the interpreting group.

These Mary and Eve images comprise the most significant value framework for the treatment of women by criminal law. And although specific legal changes in the criminal law system will be effected by the ERA, the social values which produce our images of women and men are without a doubt the most significant factor determining the impact which the ERA will have in this area.

There is no more appropriate category to begin illustrating the effect of these images than that of juvenile delinquency. There are fewer girls than boys involved in juvenile delinquency. The ratio, approximately 1:4, results from at least two factors. First, young girls are socialized in the Mary image pattern. They are taught to be obedient and submissive. Indeed, children's literature is replete with stories portraying boys as very active, running, jumping, climbing, *doing* things, while young girls sit by and watch supportively. This imagery, which becomes part of the socialization experience, decreases the likelihood of young girls performing acts which society defines as delinquent. When they do perform delinquent acts, such as shoplifting small items, they are likely to be treated informally —paternalistically reprimanded by being told that their behavior is not ladylike and sent home with their parents. This is the second factor accounting for less female delinquency, namely, that law enforcement agents themselves have internalized the Mary image of young girls and behave toward them accordingly.

It is interesting to observe, however, that as young girls approach and achieve puberty, their delinquent acts are less likely to be treated informally and more likely to be treated formally through the court system. It is also significant to note that in spite of the numerous behaviors that are involved, the bills of petition sent to the court on these young women (ages 13-18) tend to list acts involving sexual delinquency. Moreover, women show a proportionately higher sexual delinquency than young men, even though the young women's acts are almost exclusively heterosexual; one may wonder where the boys are! This, of course, illustrates the beginning of the influence of the Eve image. Young women tempt men and must be punished. Young men are naturally curious and respond to such temptation. But the naturalness of the young man's sexual curiosity precludes punishment.

Besides, young women get pregnant and young men do not. In several juvenile court systems where I served as a consultant prior to the Gault decision, young women found to be "promiscuous" tended to be institutionalized because, as the judges told me, "They are only going to get pregnant and bring problems to the community." No thought was ever given to the impregnators. The Eve image is here matched with the natural sex interest of men; mythologies all, but when treated as realities, they have an important impact on the juvenile justice system.

At the adult level, very similar patterns occur. Although women commit fewer crimes and fewer women commit crimes, biological and physiological explanations are often invoked. Social causes in terms of role stereotypes and mythologies are all but ignored. This is true in spite of the fact that in at least one study most judges admitted that their view of women influenced their decisions in the cases which they heard.[11]

Social factors are very much involved in the treatment accorded women of all ages by the legal system, and these social factors do not always favor women, as is indicated by the fact that women tend to be more severely sanctioned than men. Women, for example, tend to receive longer sentences than men for committing similar crimes,[12] as illustrated by Arkansas law which sends women to prison for up to three years for habitual intoxication, while the maximum sentence for men is thirty days. Even at the juvenile level such differences in the terms of institutionalization are found. Young men tend to be institutionalized for approximately 9 months and young women, 12 months. Undoubtedly, the legal system views women labeled as criminals more severely than men, perhaps because the system sees these women as having broken the Mary image to become full-fledged Eves.

The ERA should help to abolish the sentencing differences between the sexes. It also may help to improve the vocational and medical services offered in women's institutions. Moreover, since there are fewer women's institutions, they tend to be more remote from the inmates' homes, requiring their families and friends to travel further for visits. The ERA, by creating more institutions for women, may reduce this travel need. However, if the increase in the number of women's prisons is achieved by some type of combination with men's prisons, a less attractive outcome for women may result. Presently women's institutions tend to be small and to have the more personal touches that result from a higher staff/inmate ratio. If these institutions are combined with the larger male institutions, more formal and strict regimes may develop.[13] This may be viewed as a negative impact for women, but it is also likely to result in the improvement of men's institutions and therefore remains beneficial for both.

In the area of criminal law the ERA offers many potential changes, and the reader must decide which are positive and which are negative. We single out for special attention the next two areas to be discussed under criminal law, namely, prostitution and rape, because the ERA can play a very important role in producing change that has been long overdue. Anticipation of this change assumes, of course, that traditional imagery will not preclude its occurrence.

Prostitution and Rape

It has been pointed out that some criminal laws which will be changed or eliminated by the ERA are based on such outdated stereotypes that they simply are not relevant to today's problems. Arrests for crimes such as adultery, abduction, seduction, etc., are so rare that the F.B.I. no longer keeps statistics on them.[14] However, such is not the case with respect to prostitution.

As far back as the writings of St. Augustine, and even earlier, prostitutes, although accorded low status, were regarded as safety valves for men. St. Thomas Aquinas held similar views. It is not difficult, therefore, to understand that such ambivalent views of prostitution would result in the harassment of women prostitutes rather than full legal treatment, including attempts at rehabilitation, and further, in the concentration on the prostitutes alone while totally excluding involved men from any harassment or legal sanction. The Eve myth operates again, so that men with their "natural" sexual curiosity are viewed as simply duped into sexual acts (Adam imagery perhaps?).

The ERA should be able to help equalize the legal treatment accorded women prostitutes and the men who use them, either by punishing both or punishing neither (the legalization of prostitution). The latter is not likely to occur swiftly because legalizing prostitution does not fit well into our contemporary social value framework. Nor would it appear to do a great deal for raising the status of women. It would eliminate the legal harassment of prostitutes which presently occurs, and it would also permit women to make their own choices concerning the use of their bodies. At the same time, however, legalized prostitution would reinforce the "woman as sex object" image which is derived from the age-old Eve image. It therefore seems that the ERA is more likely to effect equal punishment for men and women involved in prostitution. It also should play an important role in the area of rape.

High though the rape figures are today, it is estimated that approximately 3½ times more rapes go unreported. Moreover, about 50% of the rape victims are known to the rapist and at least 80% of the rapes are premeditated *by the rapist*. I must add the phrase "by the rapist" because some contemporary thought on rape implies that women ask to be raped and even enjoy being raped, and this may lead some to think that the premeditation is on the part of the woman victim herself, a totally absurd thought, but nonetheless real. The statistics also prove that the rapist is not simply some demented stranger who jumps out of the bushes and attacks any available woman who happens to pass by.

Such views, however, are supported by and in turn protect the behaviors of those men and women who continue to believe Eve mythology and who also idealize male sexual physical aggression and female sexual passive submission. Indeed, the internalization of such values may result in most rapes taking place in the marriage bed itself. Here again is the repetition of the important interplay between social values based on traditional mythology and the interpretation of law and legal procedure. Attitudes toward rape repeat the Eve-Mary imagery which has pervaded our analysis of criminal law. Indeed, in the area of rape, this Eve imagery is deeply established, going back to the very early period of Moses, who commanded that women be used in rape as part of the spoils of war.[15]

One point that needs to be mentioned, however, even at the risk of being repetitious, is the fact that in rape cases the court procedures frequently treat the woman victim of rape as if she herself were the criminal in the act. In this respect one of the most alarming facts is that in court the allegedly raped woman's previous sexual history is regarded as admissible evidence, while the alleged rapist's record, even if it includes previous sexual offense convictions, is inadmissible. Perhaps no single law better portrays the sexual stereotypes we've been discussing than this law. The ERA should be beneficial in changing this, either by treating both parties' previous histories and records as inadmissible or by allowing both as admissible evidence.[16]

WOMEN AND JURIES

Having concentrated on certain cases of individual rights and criminal law, we will conclude our discussion by briefly focusing upon one of the operational procedures in the legal system, namely, the jury system.

We have already noted that judges acknowledge that their notions about women influence their decisions in court hearings. We have further noted that women tend to receive harsher sentences than men for similar illegal acts. Turning now to jury treatment of women as litigants, we find that women are less likely to win injury cases from juries, and when they do win, juries tend to allot them smaller awards.[17]

Insofar as this may result from stereotyped differences in images of men and women, the ERA may be able to equalize the treatment accorded the sexes and at the same time help to alter those images. It may be, for example, that because men are gainfully employed outside the home, their injuries are regarded as more significantly debilitating; injured women, not being employed outside of the home (little significance is actually accorded women's work inside the home in spite of great lip service paid to it), are regarded as less debilitated and, therefore, are less likely to win injury cases or to receive large awards when they do win. If such reasoning accounts for the differences between the sexes in injury cases, the ERA should be able to equalize this condition and by so doing, be helpful in changing our stereotyped imagery.

The most significant role which the ERA can play in the jury system, however, is to ensure appropriate representation of women on juries. This involves not only numbers but the procedures used in selecting jurors as well. In all states today women can serve on juries. The last state to totally exclude women from jury service, South Carolina, finally gave in to legal pressures and permitted women to serve in 1967. The problem, however, concerns the fact that although the states "permit" women to serve on juries, in 22 states women may be excused from jury service on grounds not available to men; in 11 states, for example, women may be excused solely on the basis of their sex. Moreover, in several states, until most recently, women had to undergo a special registration procedure before they would be considered for jury service; this situation still exists in one state.

The ERA will caution the justice system that women must not only be represented on juries, but that they, like men, can only be excused on the basis of individual circumstances. It is assumed in this paper that jury service is a right of citizenship and that a group so serving, as in the case of the military, gains a type of first-class citizenship not necessarily accorded those who by law are excluded as a class from service.

The exact impact which women on juries will have on the legal system has yet to be determined. I am presently working on one aspect of this, namely, a study concerned with defining precisely what constitutes "a jury of one's peers," and I find this to be a most complex area. Whether the presence or absence of women on juries affects the types of decisions reached is still unclear, though there are studies which indicate a correlation.

In one such study,[18] for example, it was found that the presence of women on juries tended to increase the chances of the "lower status" litigant's winning. This is to say that when litigants appearing before the court were ranked according to the status accorded them by contemporary social values (e.g., industries ran higher than small businesses, small businesses higher than individuals, whites higher than blacks, men higher than women, etc.), the tendency for the lower ranked litigant to win was statistically significantly better when women were on the juries than when the juries were comprised of all men. This may mean that women tend to support the "underdog" in a legal case. However, it was also found that when money was awarded to litigants, the presence of women on juries tended to result in marked decreases in the amounts awarded. Much more work needs to be done in this attempt to analyze the impact of the presence of women jurors on the justice system. But it does seem certain that in this area the ERA can do a great deal to assure women representation on juries and to equalize the procedures required of women and men to achieve participation in jury service.

This matter of juries is most important because our concern for determining the probable impact of the ERA includes not only its effect on specific areas of individual rights but also the ERA's effect on the operation of the legal system itself. For example, it is possible that the increasing presence of women on juries, at least insofar as women and men are presently socialized, will affect the types of decisions rendered by juries. This finding, if upheld by further research, illustrates how the ERA, by insuring the presence of women on juries, can influence the operation of the legal system. Moreover, the very presence of women on juries might, in turn, influence our expectations about roles of women and men, and thereby influence the social value framework.

CONCLUSION

This paper has attempted to determine the impact which the ERA is likely to have in the area of individual rights in the legal system, analyzing this potential impact by drawing attention to the reciprocal relationship between social values and the interpretation of law and noting that when social values result in deeply encrusted stereotypes of women and men, these stereotypes will influence the interpretations given the laws pertaining to women and men. I also noted, however, that the presence of the laws themselves can markedly influence our stereotypes.

Such changes in the social value framework will not occur overnight, however.[19] People cannot be resocialized (e.g., in their attitudes, values, stereotyped images of women and men) by the mere emergence of an amendment. It is a fact, however, that changes in our images of women and men have already begun, as indicated by the very emergence, slow though it has been, of the ERA. This development may be accelerated by ratification, thus demonstrating the manner in which social values and laws work together to effect social change.

Footnotes

1. Justice Frankfurter in *Tigner v. Texas,* 310 U.S. 141, 147 (1940).
2. See Leo Kanowitz, *Women and the Law* (Albuquerque: University of New Mexico Press, 1969), p. 195.
3. Eloise C. Snyder, "Uncertainty and the Supreme Court's Decisions," *The American Journal of Sociology* 65, no. 3 (November 1959): 241-45.
4. For a discussion of this point see Marshall B. Clinard, *Sociology of Deviant Behavior* (New York: Holt, Rinehart and Winston, 1968), pp. 42-44.
5. Betty Roszak and Theodore Roszak, *Masculine/Feminine* (New York: Harper, 1969), pp. vii-viii.
6. For a full discussion of name change, see *Booklet for Women Who Wish to Determine Their Own Names after Marriage,* compiled by The Center for a Woman's Own Name, on file at the International Women's History Archive, 2325 Oak St., Berkeley, Calif. This booklet has a complete listing of up-to-date sources for obtaining the laws pertaining to retention or change of names by married women for each state.
7. Ibid., p. 39.
8. For a discussion of the numerous benefits to the military itself, see Kate A. Arbogast, "Women in the Armed Forces: A Rediscovered Resource," *Military Review* 53 (November 1973): 9-19.
9. Karen DeCrow, *Sexist Justice* (New York: Random House, 1974), pp. 284-89.
10. Some students point out that until most recently men in literature tended to be portrayed as multidimensional characters while portrayals of women tended to be one-dimensional.
11. J. D. Johnston, Jr., and C. L. Knapp, "Sex Discrimination by Law: A Study in Judicial Perspective," *New York University Law Review,* October 1971, pp. 675-747.
12. For an entire journal issue devoted to Women, Crime, and Criminology, see *Issues in Criminology* 8, no. 2 (Fall 1973).
13. Ralph Ardite, et al., "The Sexual Segregation of Women's Prisons," *Yale Law Journal* 82 (May 1973): 1229-73.

14. Lois J. Frankel, "Sex Discrimination in the Criminal Law: The Effect of the Equal Rights Amendment," *American Criminal Law Review* 11, no. 2 (1973): 472-73.

15. Mary Daly, *Beyond God the Father* (Boston: Beacon Press, 1973), p. 116.

16. Camille E. LeGrand, "Rapes and Rape Laws: Sexism in Society and Law," *California Law Review* 61 (May 1973): 919-41.

17. C. A. Davis, "Women as Litigants," University of California, Institute of Governmental Affairs, Reprint series no. 33 (1972), pp. 171-98.

18. Eloise C. Snyder, "Sex Role Differential and Juror Decision," *Sociology and Social Research* 55, no. 4 (July 1971): 442-48.

19. For a discussion of this point in an issue of a journal by the American Bar Association, Section on Criminal Law, entirely devoted to women and men, see *American Criminal Law Review* 11, no. 2 (1973).

Legal Barriers to Social Change: The Case of Higher Education

Ruth B. Cowan

Senator Sam Ervin, arguing against passage of the Equal Rights Amendment, warned that amending the Constitution to deal with sex discrimination "is about as wise as using an atomic bomb to exterminate a few mice."[1] His metaphor, with its implications that sex discrimination is a petty, limited, and localized nuisance readily remedied by household devices on the order of simple mousetraps, is entirely inapt. Sex discrimination, in fact, is a serious problem; it pervades all of our societal processes and structures and it appears not to be diminished by even substantial legislation.

Documentation of the nature and extent of sex discrimination is abundant, especially for higher education, where women faculty have applied their appropriate research skills to reveal the shape and scope of sex discrimination in their own work place and in their own professions.[2] Significantly, the multitude of studies reveal that, despite the large number of separate institutions comprising academe, despite the heterogeneity of its disciplines, and despite the relative autonomy of small organizational units within each institution, the patterns of sex discrimination are consistent. In almost all of the colleges, departments, and disciplines, distinctions by sex are apparent in the representation of students and of staff, in the allocation of institutional resources, and in the distribution of power.

The purpose of this paper is to assess the likely effectiveness of the Equal Rights Amendment in eliminating these distinctions. In making the assessment, it is necessary first to consider the discrimination reality in higher education today and the success of current federal laws in eliminating women's inequality there.

DISCRIMINATION IN HIGHER EDUCATION

Representation of Women as Students, Faculty, and Staff

Throughout higher education, including those disciplines in which women comprise a majority of undergraduates, the representation of women decreases as the status level increases. Women represent approximately 45% of all undergraduate students, but only 37% of the graduate students, 24% of the faculty and less than 9% of full professors. As for college administrators and presidents, women constitute too small a percentage to warrant calculation. This is true for all categories of higher educational institutions and in all disciplines.[3]

Additionally significant is the fact that the representation of women throughout academe today is less than it was in the first quarter of the twentieth century; indeed, less than it was in the nineteenth century.[4] Even in women's colleges, the proportion of women in faculty and administrative positions has steadily decreased.[5]

Women as Students

Although the largest number and proportion of women in higher education are at the undergraduate student status, even here women are underrepresented, not only compared with their proportion in the total population but also compared with their proportion in the population of high school graduates. The Carnegie Commission on Higher Education report documents that "women have been more likely to graduate from high school and less likely to enter college than men in the same age group."[6]

The extent of women's underrepresentation as college students is greater when one considers women's superior high school grades. High school grades are the best predictors of achievement in college. Consistently since 1929, women's high school grades have been appreciably higher than the grades achieved by men. Indeed, grades are higher for females from elementary school through college.[7]

In graduate and professional schools women's underrepresentation increases. In 1970, women accounted for 37% of graduate resident students, and less than 10% of students in first-professional degree programs.[8] A Chancellor's Commission study of the City University of New York noted that the female presence in graduate programs dropped so markedly that the study characterized graduate education at that university as "a male-dominated world."[9]

As in the case of undergraduate women, the underrepresentation of women in graduate and professional schools is minimized by looking at numbers alone, since women admitted to graduate and professional schools have higher academic qualifications than their male classmates. Significant to subsequent discrimination in academe, women maintain their higher academic achievements throughout their postgraduate studies. The Carnegie Commission concluded, "Most of the available evidence suggests that women who receive the doctorate are more able, on the average, than men who receive the doctorate."[10] The Commission study at City University of New York found women "more qualified" than men in all of the graduate fields studied.[11]

While the fact of women's underrepresentation as students is consistent, the extent of the underrepresentation varies significantly according to the type of institution. Generally, women's representation is lowest in the high prestige institutions. For example, among the high prestige private institutions (which the Carnegie Commission designated "Research Universities I"), women comprise about 27% of the undergraduate population.[12] There is evidence that the admissions grade standard for men is lower than it is for women.[13]

Women's representation also varies significantly from field to field. In fields such as business administration and natural science, there are far fewer women than in the arts and humanities. In the City University of New York, a complex of twenty colleges serving approximately 230,000 students, "sex stereotyping of student enrollments [is] immediately evident. Women students are highly concentrated in 'women's fields,' with nearly three-fourths of all senior college undergraduate women students majoring in programs having 90% greater female enrollments."[14] Formerly all-male colleges which now admit women have experienced little strain in accommodating student course demands because women tend to enter academic areas undersubscribed by male students.[15]

In the professional fields which have traditionally offered high prestige for men—such as law and medicine—women's presence is small. In American Bar Association approved law schools, for example, only 12% of the students in 1972 were women.[16]

The Carnegie Commission found "that during the decade of the most explosive growth in the history of higher education—the 1960s—women lost ground as a percentage of members of regular faculty ranks in four-year institutions, especially at the associate professor level and gained ground only at the instructor level."[17]

Women as Faculty and Support Staff

Women are less represented among faculty than they are among students. Like the student pattern of representation, the proportion of women decreases as the status increases. While women as an average comprise 24% of the faculty, they are concentrated in the lowest, noncareer rank of instructor. Their representation declines with each higher rank. At the highest rank of professor they account for 9.8%.[18] Tenure is also likely to be male-related. Women are less likely to hold tenure, another indication of their lower academic status. They are also likely to receive tenure at a later age than their male co-workers.[19]

Like the student pattern, the distribution of women as faculty varies significantly according to the type of institution and field of study. Like the student pattern, the percentage of women faculty decreases as the prestige of the institution increases.[20] At the highest prestige institutions, women in all ranks make up from ten to thirteen percent of the faculty.[21] However, the number of women of associate and full professor rank in these institutions ranges from almost zero to zero. A survey presented by Alice Rossi in 1969 found no women among the forty-four full professors in five major sociology departments.[22] In three high prestige universities, women account for only 6% of the full professors in fine arts and 15% in education—fields in which there is an above-average representation of women students. In the male-dominated fields, women are even scarcer. One percent or less were full professors in the physical sciences and business administration.[23] In the thirty-eight leading law schools during 1968-70, there were only 28 women on the faculty—less than one woman per school—and only seven were full professors.[24] In fourteen out of forty-three economics departments, there were no women at any rank, and in the remaining 29, there were only 14 women with tenure.[25]

In addition to being assigned different status, women faculty are likely to be assigned different work than male professors. Women are more likely to be restricted to undergraduate teaching and to have heavier teaching loads.[26] This has important consequences since it is not teaching which generates rewards in academe.

In sharp contrast to the representation of students and faculty, women are overrepresented among the support staff. That there are large numbers of women in such positions does not, however, reflect nondiscriminatory practices. It reflects, rather, the extensive practice of job segregation. At the City University of New York, for example, there are 82 support staff titles, half of which are entirely segregated by sex. Almost all of the clerical and secretarial employees are women. These jobs pay less than the male-dominated jobs—even those which are unskilled. In addition to discrimination through job segregation, there is discrimination within job titles. Men, comprising about 4% of the clerical employees, are found nearly three times as often as women in the upper ranks of these positions.[27]

Allocation of Resources

Another indication of discrimination is seen in the allocation of institutional resources. Looking at the easiest resource to trace, i.e., money, one sees a lower allocation to women in the form of student services, financial aid, and salaries.

The tremendous gap has been well publicized for college athletics where there is almost an exclusive allocation to the men's activities. The low allocation for women's concerns means that services are often nonexistent. This is true not only for the athletics but for the whole range of services which colleges typically offer their students. In health, for example, it appears that female-related health care is simply not provided.[28]

The disproportionate allocation of financial aid given to students is less extreme. Women and male students, both concerned about money for their education, receive money in about the same percentages.[29] The average amount of money provided by an institution, however, is less for women than it is for men.[30] This is true at the graduate level as well. At the City University of New York graduate women received financial aid in proportion to their representation, but they received an average of $1,000 less per woman.[31] An examination of money given through work-study programs shows that here, too, there is sex differentiation to the disadvantage of women. Women are assigned lower-level and lower-paying jobs.

Women are assigned lower-level and lower-paying jobs throughout academe. Indeed, for women faculty the sex differentials in salaries are even greater than they are in rank. A study by Southern Methodist University reported that the salaries of women range from 5% to 50% of male salaries, when credentials and professional productivity are held constant.[32] A study done for the Carnegie Commission found the average differentials to be between $1400 and $2300, with some men (but almost no women) receiving exceptionally high salaries. Like the maldistribution in faculty ranks, there were variations according to the type of institution and field.[33]

Since staff positions are almost entirely segregated by sex, salary differences here are great. The City University of New York study revealed that only 14 out of 82 staff titles paid less than the office jobs which were held almost exclusively by women, and that several all-male jobs—requiring less skill than the women's jobs—started at higher salaries.[34]

Distribution of Power

The extent of women's presence in higher education and of the resources assigned them illustrates the principle that power is exercised to the advantage of the power-holders. In higher education, power (that is, decision making) is almost exclusively held by men. Summarizing the data of various studies, the Carnegie Commission concluded:

> If women are thinly represented on faculties . . . they are so rarely represented in top academic administrative positions as to be practically non-existent in the upper echelons. In the latter part of 1971, virtually no four-year coed institution was headed by a woman. Even among the non-sectarian women's colleges, there were only eight female presidents—in marked contrast with the situation in the latter part of the 19th century and the early years of the present century. And schools of social work, which used to have women deans quite frequently, were almost exclusively headed by men.[35]

Where women are found in administrative positions, they are likely to be holding posts subordinate to men—as Assistant Deans, for example, or in female-dominated areas. Women are not in positions which control fiscal or personnel matters. The study of the City University of New York reported that women were not entirely absent, though seriously underrepresented, in department decision-making positions.[36]

Is this Really Discrimination?

Defenders of the *status quo* have challenged this statistical picture as evidence of improper discriminatory actions. They offer at least four arguments, three of which are implicitly concerned with assigning "blame." In the course of debate, the implicit concern frequently becomes explicit.

One of the arguments is that the disadvantages in number, rewards, and power occur as a result of women's own preferences. In support of this are such facts as women's higher drop-out rate for marriage and/or childrearing, their failure to apply for admission in male-dominated fields, and their relative noncompetitiveness within academe.

A variation of this argument concedes discrimination, albeit outside of academe. The patterns in higher education, it is maintained, merely reflect the outside discriminatory world. Because of precollege discrimination, women have been conditioned to drop out for marriage, to prefer women's fields, and to be noncompetitive. Because of anticipated postcollege discrimination, they cleave to these patterns. As civil engineers, for example, women expect to find themselves both unmarriageable and unemploy-able.

A third argument more openly concedes discrimination but defends it as rational and justified. Women, according to this argument, are simply not qualified. The facts are, it is pointed out, that fewer women have doctorates and fewer engage in research at the very time when research is of prime importance in their institutions. Further, even qualified women are poor risks as students and faculty because their professional commitments are likely to be both different and weaker than demanded in higher education. The lower career commitment is assumed to be the cause of women's interest in part-time studies and in part-time employment, their presumed lack of geographic mobility, and their willingness to drop out for marriage and motherhood. Relevant to this argument is the fact that more women than male faculty are unmarried.[37]

Finally, there is the argument of insufficient evidence to identify and prove discrimination. Either it is argued that data have not been available to demonstrate discrimination or that data have not yet been assembled at a specific place at a specific time. This is used as a delaying tactic to postpone responsible action.

Advocates of equality have been compelled to respond to these arguments by marshalling the facts for refutation. The refutations show that some of the reasons given for benign discrimination are invalid. Helen Astin's *The Woman Doctorate in America* revealed, for example, that the proportion of women with doctorates who were working full time and the proportion who had not interrupted their careers compared favorably with the percentages for men.[38] A.E. Bayer's examination of career interruptions, for another example, showed men to be less reliable employees in this regard than women.[39] Astin and Bayer together tried to assess the weight of sex discrimination when factors traditionally relevant to rank, tenure, and salary are controlled. They analyzed a large body of data—information from more than 60,000 faculty—and used sophisticated statistical techniques to control more than 30 variables. They found that

> even after control for a large number of significant and relevant variables that account for rank differences among academic personnel, much of the differential could still be attributed solely to sex. Indeed, . . . sex is a better independent predictor of rank than such factors as the number of years since completion of education, the number of years employed at the present institution, or the number of books published. These results clearly demonstrate the biases operating against women in academe with respect to rank.[40]

Regarding salary, they found sex to be a better independent predictor than such other factors as number of years in professional employment or degrees earned.[41] They showed, also, that although persons employed in more prestigious universities and persons employed in larger institutions are paid higher salaries, the women at these institutions earn less than their male colleagues.

> Women generally hold lower ranks and make lower salaries, however comparable their backgrounds, work activities, achievement, and institutional work settings to those of their male colleagues. Considering the many variables in these analyses, one can only conclude that sex discrimination is rampant in academe.[42]

Such evidence, though impressive, is clearly insufficient to "prove" that in each classroom, in each department, and in each of more than 2700 higher education institutions, discrimination against students, faculty, and staff occurs all the time. Such evidence does show, however, that discrimination occurs sufficiently often to characterize higher education.

Discrimination occurs in many forms. There is the most visible, overt, systematic, and direct form, when discrimination is a matter of institutional policy. The restriction of admissions to males is an example. Other examples are found in the use of separate admission standards for men and women or the use of guidance instruments, such as the Strong Vocational Interest test which provide separate tests and separate occupational lists for men and women.

A less visible mode of discrimination—though no less explicit, systematic, and direct—occurs as a matter of department-level action. Discrimination on this level results "from myriads of individual decisions within departments and schools that do the actual recruitment and selection . . . and that initiate the recommendations for merit increases and promotions."[43] Several department chairmen volunteered the information, during a study by Ann Heiss at ten leading graduate schools, that women are purposely screened out as doctoral students and as faculty members.[44] Academic procedures, because they are highly personalized and protected by a screen of confidentiality, maximize the opportunity for biases to operate.

Still another form of direct discrimination occurs in the individual dealings of professors with their students. Professors who make derogatory remarks about women and professors who explicitly discourage women students or colleagues from professional pursuits provide examples. Such discrimination is unsystematic, though perhaps no less pervasive.

There are, in addition, many forms of indirect discrimination. Some may occur as a result of seemingly nondiscriminatory policies, such as rules prohibiting part-time employment.[45] Some may result from the implicit suggestion, contained in the institution's numerous directives, that there are separate tracks for men and women. The same suggestion is made in college catalogues which reinforce sex component of particular fields of study or fellowship announcements which only invite interested men to apply.

Discrimination also exists through cooperation with outside discriminatory organizations, as when the college or university placement office refers only male applicants to the on-campus recruiters.

Whatever the form of discrimination, its results are deleterious. Students, faculty, and staff perceive that women are not taken as seriously as men, that they belong in positions inferior to and supportive of men, and that they are, therefore, by themselves unimportant. The impact of these lessons is durable. It is not irrelevant that women who have gone to women's colleges and to colleges with a higher proportion of women faculty, or women students, appear to achieve more in their lives than their sisters educated in the man's academic world.[46]

The deleterious results of discrimination are cumulative. In academic professional employment, time spent in administrative activities and the quality of one's graduate school are related to rank. Rank is related to job security and to income. Women "often possess," Astin and Bayer note, "few of the characteristics that determine academic success."[47] Thus, obstructed in obtaining one advantage, women accumulate disadvantages as they proceed along their occupational paths.

THE EFFECT OF EXISTING LAWS

There are four comprehensive federal measures which deal with sex discrimination in higher education. The first of these—indeed, the first federal law to prohibit sex discrimination in higher education at all—is Executive Executive Order 11246, as amended by Executive Order 11375 in October 1967.* The Executive Order has subsequently been elaborated by a number of orders, guidelines, and memoranda. Collectively, these measures require that colleges or universities receiving over $10,000 in federal contracts take affirmative action to eliminate discrimination in employment. Each institution is required to have an affirmative action plan which specifies goals and timetables.

The other three laws covering sex discrimination in higher education, all enacted in 1972, are the amendments to the Equal Pay Act, amendments to

---

*Hereafter referred to as the Executive Order

Title VII of the Civil Rights Act of 1964, and Title IX of the Higher Education Act.[48]

The Equal Pay Act requires equal pay for equal work. More specifically, it requires that men and women performing work in the same establishment receive the same pay if their jobs require equal skill, effort and responsibility. The 1972 amendments extended the coverage of the Act to include executive, administrative, and professional employees; that is, to include all but the support staff in higher education. The nonprofessional staff had been covered earlier.

Title VII, as amended, requires fair employment practices for women. It makes it an unlawful employment practice to discriminate on the basis of sex in hiring, firing, "compensation, terms, conditions, or privileges of employment,"[49] or on the basis of sex "to limit, segregate, or classify . . . employees or applications . . . in any way which would . . . adversely affect his [sic] status as an employee."[50]

Title IX, unlike the other laws, deals with discrimination outside of employment. It covers student admissions and student treatment, as well as employment, in education programs and activities. It requires that

> no person . . . shall on the basis of sex, be excluded from participation in, be denied the benefits of or be subjected to discrimination under any educational program or activity receiving Federal financial assistance.[51]

The enactment of each of these laws has been enthusiastically applauded by advocates of equality for women in higher education. As each was enacted, the advocates expressed their firm expectation that the federal government would now successfully proceed to establish equality. Disappointment occurred seriatim. As disappointment arose and hardened for one measure, women's advocates turned their hope to the next. Each succeeding measure was claimed with justification to have avoided the weaknesses of the former. Title IX, which arrived last, was seen, therefore, to hold the most promise. It clearly offered the most comprehensive coverage. It was predicted that now the "gap in the laws protecting women from biased educational policies" would be closed,[52] and the "forms of discrimination which . . . have deep social and legal roots" would be effectively eliminated.[53]

The first of the laws to be judged ineffective was the Executive Order. Its record in eliminating discrimination has indeed proved disappointing. As of September 1974, six years after the law was presumably in effect, fewer than twenty affirmative action programs had been accepted. Much publicity has been given to salary adjustments and promises. But the reality is that by the end of 1971, despite complaints against more than 350 institutions and reviews at about 200, contract funds had been delayed at only approximately 40 institutions. In no case has any contract been terminated; in no case has any school been debarred from funds.[54] The record under Title VII and the Equal Pay Act has been equally disappointing. Interviews with women who have been given pay equalization increases indicate that the much publicized "victory" had only decreased, not eliminated, the sex-based differential. Regarding the effectiveness of Title VII, it was not until January 1974, for example, that the first Commission-level finding of discrimination was made under this law. As for Title IX, three years after its enactment, the implementing regulations have just been promulgated.

The reasons for the failure of these laws to change higher education are neither ephemeral nor particularistic. Many of the reasons will predictably operate to constrict the effectiveness of the Equal Rights Amendment. For this reason, it is well to examine at least some of the persistent obstacles to change through law.

Jurisdictional Limitations and Deferments

All of the laws are limited in their jurisdiction. Indeed, the jurisdiction of the Executive Order excludes more institutions than it covers. Only colleges or universities receiving in excess of $10,000 in federal contracts are covered. While "contracts" have been defined broadly and interpreted to cover certain "grants," there are approximately 1800 institutions not covered, compared to the approximately 900 which are.[55] Of the 900, those receiving less than $50,000 are not required to have affirmative action plans, and all public institutions are presumed to be in compliance until the contrary is manifest.

The Equal Pay Act covers all institutions, and Title VII, which has jurisdiction over institutions of at least fifteen employees, undoubtedly also covers the academic universe. However, both of these measures, as well as the Executive Order, deal only with matters of employment. The Equal Pay Act is even narrower in its jurisdiction since it is concerned exclusively with employment compensation. The Executive Order, at least in official public pronouncements, has narrowed its concern to hiring.

Title IX, though it covers only institutions receiving federal money, appears to have near universal coverage since it is not restricted to schools receiving its money through "contracts" nor to schools receiving large sums of money. However, there are specific exemptions provided in the law. Military schools are given a total exemption. Partial exemptions are given religiously controlled schools, private undergraduate schools, public under-graduate institutions which "traditionally" and "continually" from their establishment have admitted one sex,[56] and undergraduate professional schools, such as engineering or architecture colleges.

In addition to exemptions, the laws provide deferments, thereby reflecting a legislative preference for moving slowly in higher education. Under Title IX, single sex institutions are given seven years to change.[57] Some of the deferments are not explicit but occur as a consequence of following a time-detailed enforcement procedure, as is found in Title VII. Paradoxically, some of the deferments occur because the statute fails to specify time limits. Under the Executive Order, for example, there is no time limit set for issuing a letter of finding consequent to an investigation. HEW has taken years to issue some letters and some letters have never been issued.

Ambiguities and Confusion as to What Discrimination Is and What Compliance Requires

Discrimination must be operationally defined for purposes of law enforcement. The definitions provided by law are ambiguous and inadequate. Under the Executive Order, for example, discrimination is defined as underutilization. Underutilization is to be ascertained statistically by comparing women's representation in the appropriate labor pool with women's representation in the corresponding job categories at an institution. Compliance requires that a "good faith effort" be made to redress the underutilization of "qualified" women. The Equal Pay Act has a seemingly simpler operational definition. Under this Act, discrimination is inferred whenever different compensation is paid for jobs requiring equal (itself defined as "substantially similar") skill, effort, and responsibility.

Definitions under both laws leave much of the institutionalized discrimination untouched. Job segregation, which has substantial salary consequences, is not covered under the Equal Pay Act. The discriminatory foundations on which rest the academic standards for judging merit (i.e., for granting promotion, for permitting the acquisition of seniority, and for determining the qualifications for appointment and advancement) are permitted to stand virtually unchallenged.

The requirements for compliance permit further discrimination. Under the Executive Order, for example, colleges and universities need only show an effort, rather than demonstrate success. At some of the institutions, the effort is more apparent than sincere. Many women charge that the "good faith effort" is made in bad faith.

The ambiguity and inadequacies of the laws undoubtedly reflect the indecision and ambivalence within the body politic and its governmental officers about changing the character of higher education and the character of the professions for which colleges and universities prepare their students.

The ambiguity and inadequacies also reflect a strategic hesitation by proponents of equality to make explicit the full threat which clear, firm, antidiscrimination laws would pose to existing privilege. Discrimination does advantage men and disadvantage women in their competition for the rewards of academe. An effectively implemented nondiscrimination policy would mean a total redistribution of advantages.

The Enormity of the Task

The goal collectively set by the four antidiscrimination laws is to change patterns and practices which pervade entire organizations, which are supported by corresponding patterns and practices in connecting institutions, which are nourished by sanctioned attitudes, and which are highly functional to those with power in the institutions. The nature of the task is enormously difficult.

Adding to the difficulty is the sheer number of the institutions covered (despite the various jurisdictional exemptions) and their complexity. There are approximately 2700 institutions comprising the higher education enterprise. Each of the institutions is itself divided and may encompass several large units. The City University of New York, for example, consists of 20 colleges which, collectively, employ 22,000 persons and serve 230,000 students.[58]

The enormity of the task is further compounded by the structure and style of power within academic institutions. Power, firstly, is highly decentralized. Many decisions are made by departmental committees and even by individual professors acting independently. Consequently, it is difficult to "finger" the discriminatory action.

Secondly, power is typically exercised irresponsibly, that is, without institutionalized accountability. The general absence of accountability engenders a sense of exclusiveness and autonomy. It engenders, that is, the attitude common in academe that the standards of the outside world don't apply, that academe is some kind of sanctuary. This attitude has been manifest in various situations, as when local police have ventured onto college territory to enforce drug laws. Sylvia Roberts, the attorney in what has so far been a precedent-setting antidiscrimination case in higher education, concluded from her experience that "universities don't act like other employers. They don't realize they will ever have to be brought to court.[59] Consequently, there is little sense of obligation to cooperate with law enforcers or to comply with laws.

Lack of accountability, in addition, encourages arrogance in the exercise of power. The explanation by Harlan Fiske Stone when, as Dean of Columbia Law School, he was asked why women were not permitted admission was, "We don't because we don't."[6] This kind of explanation can still be heard today. Despite the sanctions against discrimination, as late as 1973, Phi Delta Kappa, a professional associaton paradoxically in the female-dominated education profession, excluded women from membership and suspended chapters that refused to abide by the restrictions.[61] Significantly, Phi Delta Kappa's action was not that of the last holdout in an otherwise accommodating universe.

Lack of accountability, further, encourages irrationality and sexist biases to operate unchecked in the decisional processes.

Bureaucratic Realities

Laws are implemented by people. The enormity of the task of dealing with sex discrimination in higher education means a substantial workload for the people charged with implementation. The Office for Civil Rights, Higher Education Division of the Department of Health, Education, and Welfare, which enforce the Executive Order and will, in all likehood, enforce Title IX, has a case backlog of years. By mid-1973, about 500 pattern and practice complaints had been filed with the agency.[62] The Equal Employment Opportunity Commission (EEOC), which administers Title VII, had received by late 1974, more than 1600 sex discrimination complaints against colleges and universities.[63] EEOC has not established a record of expeditious case processing. Illustrative is the case of Dr. Sharon Johnson, who filed a complaint of discrimination against the University of Pittsburgh in 1971. The case is still far from legal resolution. After more than two years, she received a finding of discrimination. It was, significantly, EEOC's first commission-level finding. The absence of a case backlog in the Equal Pay Act enforcement agency was a factor regularly cited by women who transferred their faith to that law. Unfortunately for those who hoped to see remedies expeditiously ordered, a case backlog builds up rather quickly in any industry with 2700 employers, almost all of whom are in violation of the law. Title IX, even before its implementing regulations were promulgated, generated more than 100 complaints.[64]

The agencies workloads are even greater than the sex discrimination case record indicates, since these agencies are responsible for handling complaints of discrimination against other classes of persons and for handling complaints in nonacademic employment as well.

The enforcement record illustrates that delay is inherent in the bureaucratic process. Delay must result from the time required to formulate enforcement guidelines. The Executive Order 11375, which added sex discrimination to the previous Executive Order 11246, was promulgated October 1967. It was to become effective one year later. However, it was not until June 1970, more than two-and-a-half years later, that HEW, in fact, began to enforce the law with contract compliance reviews. One and one-half years passed before Revised Order No. 4, requiring affirmative action plans, was issued and almost another year before the Higher Education guidelines were issued to clarify what compliance required of colleges and universities. There was a total of five years between the issuance of the Excutive Order and the guidelines. Title IX was passed March 1972. Three years later, because of "the many complex and difficult issues to be addressed,"[65] implementing regulations have just now been promulgated.

Time is required to process complaints. Either because of bureaucratic sluggishness or bureaucratic thoroughness, delays are substantial. Interviews with complainants at each of the agencies reveal the uniform experience of the passage of years without progress. In the interim, the charge of discrimination can be rendered moot or the complainant can be reduced to hopelessness.

Delays are increased to the extent that the enforcement agencies are understaffed or staffed by persons inadequately qualified. Administrative agencies characteristically complain of understaffing. The complaint certainly appears valid for the Office for Civil Rights of the Department of Health, Education, and Welfare. In 1971, the Office for Civil Rights had 70 contract compliance officers serving all colleges, universities, hospitals, and research institutions in the United States covered under the Executive Order.[66]

In Spring 1974, this same office had filled only 165 out of 618 budgeted positions.[67] Dr. Mary Lepper, Director of HEW's Higher Education Division, explained that the reason these positions remained unfilled was the unavailability of persons familiar with higher education.[68] The lack of familiarity with higher education has been one of the criticisms frequently voiced by both the proponents and opponents of the antidiscrimination laws. The enforcement personnel have been accused not only of ignorance but also of bias. The college and university spokesmen have charged overzealousness, while the advocates of change have charged indifference or worse.

Persons involved in implementing the laws, no matter how sufficient in number or qualification, relate to each other bureaucratically. The realities of bureaucracy complicate and further obstruct the process of advancing rights through law.

One significant bureaucratic reality is bureaucratic discretion. It has many important consequences, one of which is that rules and regulations are changed more readily than they can be through the legislative process. This means that, once established, rules and regulations are unreliable. It also means laws can, in this relatively easy and hidden way, be amended and weakened. The Regulations to Title IX, among other things, amend the law by exempting private undergraduate vocational and professional schools from coverage.[69] Women monitoring the implementation of the federal antidiscrimination laws prepared five finely printed pages analyzing how section after section departed from or weakened the law.

Another consequence of bureaucratic discretion is the shifting of priorities. At one time a regional EEOC office, for example, gave preference to individual complaints. Then it gave preference to class actions. Now it is back to favoring individual complaints.

Priorities may so be shifted as to amount to a policy of inaction. It is rumored that the Secretary of HEW has ordered a "hands-off" policy for high prestige colleges and universities. The National Organization for Women, the Women's Equity Action League, and the Federation of Organizations for Professional Women perceive a more extensive "hands-off" policy in operation and have gone into federal court to force HEW to implement the law.

Another significant bureaucratic reality is internal inconsistency. It is not uncommon to find within a single agency significant variations from regional office to regional office. The opportunities for inconsistency are greatly increased in the case of the antidiscrimination laws in higher education, since at least three different agencies are involved.

The obstructions to law enforcement resulting from the inadequacy of the administrative staff and from the shifting regulations and priorities merely reflect the fact that bureaucracies are part of the political process. They apply pressures in the process, but also, directly and obliquely, have pressures applied against them.

Opposition and Resistance

Pressure against enforcement of the laws prohibiting sex discrimination has been forthcoming from higher education. University professors have written articles and letters. They have circulated petitions and formed committees with high-sounding names. College presidents and chancellors have worked the halls of bureaucracy and written personal off-the-record notes to friends in high places.

Those inclined to a course of opposition have substantial resources at their command. Higher education spokesmen are not strangers to the political

process. College presidents regularly deal with legislators and administrators in order to obtain resources for their institutions. In addition,
academe is organized so that cooperation and pooling of resources can be
readily mobilized. Higher education, further, has prestige. Many of its
members wear a badge of liberalism earned by marching in the South or by
participating in a Vietnam teach-in. These men are also articulate and
imaginative in the use of facts and phrases.

All of these resources constitute advantages in the pressure process.
Higher education's most effective advantage, however, is found in the
strategy of resistance. All that is necessary for the opponents of effective
legal implementation is that they do nothing except carry on as usual. As a
university head indifferently responded when confronted with a possible
court action by faculty women, "Our legal staff is paid to grind them out."[70]

Voluntary compliance, which is critical to effective law enforcement, has
not been forthcoming from higher education. Martha E. Peterson, President
of Barnard, in an address before an audience composed largely of higher
education administrators, noted that "the higher education community
seemed unable to recognize and to take action in correcting injustices until
forced to do so. The disgrace of 'affirmative action' is that HEW had to get
into it at all."[71] That statement was made in October 1972. Title IX, enacted
that year, requires that each covered single-sex institution prepare and
submit a conversion plan.[72] Very few schools have submitted their required
plans.[73] Higher education has generally resisted and continues to resist
compliance.

They are aided in their course of noncompliance by the skills abundant in
higher education, such as the skill of writing reports without substance and
the skills appropriate to myth-making and myth-maintenance. One of the
new myths to emerge is the myth of reverse discrimination. There is also the
carefully preserved arsenal of old myths: that academe is free of the base
motives operative in other societal institutions, that higher education is a
living meritocracy, that government intrusion into higher education
threatens academic freedom, and that all decisions derive from the proper
application of academic judgment as to what is educationally sound.

THE CONSTITUTIONAL STATUS OF WOMEN

The authority for the federal antidiscrimination measures in higher education comes from the Constitution. All of the authorizations have been
indirect. The Executive Order and Title IX, for example, rest on the
constitutional power to spend money. Because of the indirect nature of the
authorization, these laws do not technically prohibit sex discrimination.

They prohibit the use of federal money. If an institution chooses to forfeit federal funding, it can, at least under these two laws, continue to discriminate flagrantly.

The Constitution, without further amendment, could directly authorize equality for women in higher education. However, up until the late 1960s, the courts have seen "divine ordinance" behind the inequality of the sexes.[74]

Since the late 1960s, the federal courts have begun to move slowly and cautiously. As Harry T. Edward has commented, "The evolution of the [judicial] law on sex discrimination has been relatively sparse and equivocal."[75] Until 1971, the U.S. Supreme Court upheld all challenges to legislatively-drawn sex lines.[76] At this moment in history, Title IX goes beyond what the Constitution has been interpreted to require. For example, a Federal District Court in 1971 upheld the constitutionality of separate state supported schools for men and women. They saw the separation not as a denial of rights but rather as a "flexibility and diversity in educational methods" which "often are both desirable and beneficial."[77]

To the extent that the courts have begun to incorporate women's rights into the Constitution at all, it has been through interpretations of the equal protection clause of the 14th Amendment. It has been, as Ruth Bader Ginsburg described it, through "sporadic decisions under a principle pressed into service by extensive interpretation."[78]

The equal protection clause prohibits states, and by judicial extension, the federal government, from denying any person the equal protection of the laws. In determining the applicability of the equal protection right to sex discrimination, the courts have a variety of justifying standards they may invoke. Different standards lead to different results. If the standard invoked is whether the sex differentiation under challenge bears a rational relationship to the legitimate purposes of the statute permitting or mandating it, the answer invariably is positive. If the "strict scrutiny standard" is used—and it is only used when a "suspect classification" or "fundamental right" is identified—the state must demonstrate a "compelling state interest" in maintaining the discrimination. The result is invariably a decision against the discriminatory statute. As Chief Justice Burger observed, strict scrutiny is an insurmountable standard for states to satisfy.[79]

The Supreme Court has not yet found sex equality to be a fundamental right. Nor has it found sex discrimination a "suspect classification," though in 1973, a plurality but not the necessary majority was ready to take this step.[80] Three other Justices amazingly found the pending passage of the Equal Rights Amendment a "compelling reason" to "defer" designating sex classifications suspect. The reasoning offered by these judges was that the Court, "by acting prematurely and unnecessarily," would "preempt by judicial action a major political decision which is currently in process of resolution." Such premature and unnecessary action would not "reflect appropriate respect for duly prescribed legislative processes."[81]

Such reasoning would make the establishment of a constitutional right for women entirely dependent on the adoption of the Equal Rights Amendment (ERA). If it were not adopted, then these same Justices would have to reason that "appropriate respect" mandates that they abide by the negative determination regarding women's rights. Even without the sought-for constitutional protection, the government, in the judgment of constitutional commentators, has unquestioned authority to assure women actual, as well as theoretical, equality to remedy the effects of past discrimination and to deal with the economic and social foundations on which inequality stands.[82] However, the lack of constitutional commitment provides the rationale, eagerly sought by legislators and judges alike, for their predisposition to move cautiously and slowly. The judicial failure to see in the Constitution a direct and firm basis for sex-related equality lends support to the need for ERA, for, as Chief Justice Burger assessed, "In the absence of a firm Constitutional foundation for equal treatment for men and women . . . women seeking to be judged on their individual merits will continue to encounter law-sanctioned obstacles."[83]

THE EQUAL RIGHTS AMENDMENT

Unlike the Constitution's equal protection provision—"pressed into the service of women's rights"—the Equal Rights Amendment was drafted with women's rights specifically and exclusively in mind. It is directed at sex discrimination, though, it should be pointed out, only at sex discrimination under law. The ERA prohibits government discriminatory action. It assures that

> equality of rights under the law shall not be denied or abridged by the United States or by any State on account of sex.[84]

"The basic principle on which the Amendment rests may be stated shortly: sex should not be a factor in determining the legal rights of men or of women."[85] As Ruth Bader Ginsburg summarized, the ERA

> would eliminate the historical impediment to unqualified judicial recognition of equal rights as constitutional principle; it would end legislative inertia that keeps discriminatory laws on the books and it would serve as

a clear statement of the nation's moral and legal commitment to a
system in which women and men stand as full and equal individuals
before the law.[86]

The Amendment, therefore, does not address itself directly to the discriminatory patterns, practices, and consequences in such societal institutions as private colleges and universities. The Amendment does cover state
higher educational institutions and could enter the sphere of private education to the extent that government support in any amount or any form is
given. The Amendment's jurisdiction could prove, in fact, to be as extensive
as is needed. Nevertheless, the claim that there is a private sphere beyond its
reach might well be made. Merely raising the claim would provide the
claimants a deferment until the courts could respond.

There are two exemptions generally conceded to be implied in the
Amendment: discrimination involving either the factor of personal privacy
or physical characteristics unique to one sex.[87] Subsequent exemptions may
develop out of conflict with other constitutional provisions. The
Constitution's religious guarantees, for example, might provide an exemption for colleges whose tenets require sex discrimination in some of its
operations.

Once ratified, the Amendment would not be self-implementing. Legislation for this purpose would be required. Those legislators who are still
cautious, ambivalent, and unwilling to change the character of academe
might succeed in devising the implementing legislation so that it, in fact,
checks the Amendment's jurisdiction even further.

Once the Amendment's restrictions on discrimination in higher education
are formulated legislatively, the laws would still have to be enforced.
Enforcement would predictably encounter the same obstructions which have
impeded the effectiveness of the existing antidiscrimination laws. The
enormity of changing almost 2700 highly diverse and decentralized institutions, of coping with institutional opposition and resistance, and of dealing
with ambiguity and confusion in definitions and procedures as well as with
the inconsistencies of bureaucratic systems will still delay the process of
change.

These delays may be curtailed or further extended by the response of the
courts as cases arise under the new constitutional, statutory, and administrative laws. Certainly, the courts heretofore have not been especially responsive to women's rights. A frequently cited analysis of the judicial record up
to 1971, undertaken by two law professors describing themselves as
"middle-aged, white male[s] [who had never] been radicalized, brutalized,

politicized or otherwise leaned on by the Establishment," concluded

> that by and large the performance of American judges in the area of sex
> discrimination can be succinctly described as ranging from poor to
> abominable. With some notable exceptions, they have failed to bring to
> sex discrimination cases those judicial virtues of detachment, reflection
> and critical analysis which have served them so well with respect to
> other sensitive social issues. . . . [S]exism—the making of unjustified
> (or at least unsupported) assumptions about individual capabilities,
> interests, goals and social roles solely on the basis of sex differences—is
> . . . easily descernible in contemporary judicial opinion.[88]

One of the ways in which the courts can facilitate or impede the process of dealing with sex discrimination is in the time standard it adopts for compliance. A federal district court in 1970 ordered a formerly all-male college to admit women "as soon as is reasonably feasible." In practice, this permitted the college at least two years before being required to admit women on the same basis as men.[89]

HIGHER EDUCATION AND THE EQUAL RIGHTS AMENDMENT

The Equal Rights Amendment symbolizes a national moral and legal commitment to women's equality. Ratification of the Amendment and the subsequent implementing legislation will impose costly obligations on higher education. Given the economic hardships colleges and universities now face and will continue to face, they can be expected to resist stridently the remedial and affirmative actions which impose burdensome expenses.

Colleges and universities could legally reconcile the restriction of economy with the requirement of equality by reducing everything to the level of the resources allocated to women. There would be no legal hindrance to following such a course. The ERA in no way requires that equality rest on the standard to which men in academe have become accustomed. While such a course might be taken in some areas and for some activities, as a general solution it would be politically difficult. There would be too many who would stand to lose too much.

The more likely course would be to move in the direction of enhancing women's status, but in limited areas. Though colleges and universities may perceive themselves as unable to afford total compliance, they will surely see themselves as equally unable to afford total noncompliance. The legal and moral weight of the Constitution cannot be entirely tossed off by institutions which rely for popular support on their reputations for moral rectitude and progressivism.

There are actions colleges and universities could take which would enable them to comply, at least partially, without incurring additional costs. Some of these actions would even provide immediate advantages to the institutions. Nondiscriminatory admission of students would be such an action. There are reports of falling student enrollment and forecasts that this will continue. There is some evidence that women's growing presence as students is already functioning as a compensatory factor for the declining enrollment of men. To the extent that colleges anticipate a shrinking male market for their services, women will be welcomed as customers.

There are other actions which colleges and universities can be expected to take, more out of indifference than out of opportunism. In this category are acknowledgments in the curriculum of the presence and importance of women. Since educators and administrators in higher education, ironically, do not take very seriously the substance of the classroom experience, curriculum modifications will be easy.

Both a nondiscriminatory admissions policy and an education process more respectful of women can have significant impact throughout society. One of higher education's functions, after all, is to train and provide credentials for persons in order that they may participate in other societal institutions. That colleges and universities will be training more women and will be providing both men and women a nonsexist view of reality will be felt in the many institutions served by academe. Because of its socialization function, the impact of change in higher education is multiplied.

While such changes will be important, much more will need to be done both to fulfill the requirements of the law and to meet the rising ambitions of women in higher education. Strangely, the very economic difficulties which should impede the realization of women's rights in higher education could instead work to women's advantage. The turn-around could occur if the federal government were to back its moral and legal commitment with substantial incentives for compliance. There can be no question that the promise of financial benefit, especially when money is badly needed, will go a long way in encouraging institutional change. The question is whether such incentives will be forthcoming.

The answer to that question will rest with the advocates of equality. For, if the experience of the eight years since federal law began dealing with sex inequalities in higher education has validity, the burden of change is on those who want it.

During these eight years, women's advocates have had to challenge their adversaries' claims with argumentation and documentation, to monitor law enforcement, to prod the bureaucracy, to pressure the legislators and, at the same time, to extend their support and enlarge their resources.

Women, in assuming this burden, perceived it to be a transitory one until government could be encouraged to take the one all-inclusive, sweeping action which would eliminate the inequalities in higher education once and for all. Hope was put first in legislation to provide the remedy. When legislation proved disappointing, women turned to the courts. There was a dramatic increase in sex discrimination cases during the 1970s.[90] But the courts also failed to provide more than a tentative, temporary and/or inadequate remedy. Hope has now been placed in the Equal Rights Amendment. But, there is little inherent in a constitutional amendment to indicate that it will provide a final and complete remedy. It is much more likely that, in reality, there is no way of being granted rights. Rights can only be achieved.

There is much to indicate that if women continue to commit themselves to pressing for change, they will be increasingly successful. During the years since the Executive Order covered higher education, women have become more politically sophisticated. They have acquired political skills and have forged effective organizations and coalitions. Most importantly, their demand for equality has intensified. A striking change in higher education has been women's increasing dissatisfaction with what was, just a few years before, either resignedly accepted or even unnoticed. Accompanying the increased dissatisfaction have been expanded aspirations and soaring ambitions. There has been a marked increase in the number of women seeking and getting credentials in previously all-male fields. Women, and men also, have departed from the traditional sex-related academic choices.[91] A study of women political scientists in one region showed the younger women moving into more fields in the discipline and pursuing their careers ambitiously.[92]

If the ambition, sophistication, skills, and resources continue to be joined against discrimination, higher education, with or without universal compliance to the law, will have been irrevocably changed to women's increasing advantage.

Footnotes

1. U.S., Congress, Senate, Committee on the Judiciary, *Hearings on S. J. Resolution 61 and S.J. Resolution 231, Equal Rights Amendment,* 91st Congress, 2nd session, 1970, p. 2.

2. From 1969 to 1973 there were over 125 reports assessing the status of women at individual colleges and universities. In addition, there have been assessments of large samples of academic institutions, such as the following: Lora H. Robinson, *The Status of Academic Women* (Wash., D.C.: ERIC Clearinghouse on Higher Education, George Washington Univ., 1971); Alan E. Bayer and Helen S. Astin, "Sex Differences in Academic Rank and Salary among Science Doctorates in Teaching," *Journal of Human Resources* 3, no. 2 (Spring 1968): 191–200; The Carnegie Commission on Higher Education, *Opportunities for Women in Higher Education: A Report and Recommendations* (New York: McGraw-Hill, 1973).

3. Summaries of a large number of reports appear in Carnegie Commission on Higher Education, p. 2.

4. Association of American Colleges, Project on the Status and Education of Women, *On Campus with Women,* April 1972, p. 8.

5. The Carnegie Commission on Higher Education, p. 70.

6. Ibid., p. 35.

7. Ibid., pp. 50–51.

8. Ibid., p. 81.

9. Chancellor's Advisory Committee on the Status of Women at the City University of New York, *The Status of Women at the City University of New York: A Report to the Chancellor* (New York: The City University of New York, 1972), p. 139.

10. Carnegie Commission on Higher Education, p. 92.

11. Chancellor's Advisory Committee on the Status of Women at the City University of New York, p. 147.

12. Carnegie Commission on Higher Education, p. 51.

13. K. P. Cross, *Beyond the Open Door: New Students to Higher Education* (San Francisco: Jossey-Bass, 1971), pp. 150–51.

14. Chancellor's Advisory Committee on the Status of Women at the City University of New York, pp. 1, 8.

15. Carnegie Commission on Higher Education, p. 52.

16. American Bar Association, *Annual Review of Legal Education,* Fall 1972 (Chicago, 1973).

17. Carnegie Commission on Higher Education, p. 110.

18. Kenneth M. Davidson, Ruth B. Ginsburg, and Herma H. Kay, *Sex-based Discrimination: Text, Cases and Materials* (St. Paul, Minn.: West Publishing Co., 1974), p. 870 fn 42.

19. Carnegie Commission on Higher Education, p. 114.

20. Ibid., pp. 52, 109; and Davidson, Ginsburg, and Kay, p. 870 fn 42.

21. Carnegie Commission on Higher Education, p. 52.

22. "Status of Women Graduate Departments of Sociology," *The American Sociologist* 5 (February 1970): 1–12, cited by Carnegie Commission on Higher Education, p. 115.

23. Carnegie Commission on Higher Education, p. 113.

24. Ibid., p. 101.

25. Ibid., p. 115.

26. Ibid., p. 103.

27. Chancellor's Advisory Committee on the Status of Women at the City University of New York, pp. 27, 38.

28. Association of American Colleges, Project on the Status and Education of Women, "Health Services for Women: What Should the University Provide?," June 1972, p. 2.

29. Carnegie Commission on Higher Education, p. 56.

30. Association of American Colleges, *On Campus with Women*, p. 1; and Chancellor's Advisory Committee on the Status of Women at the City University of New York, p. 153.

31. Chancellor's Advisory Committee on the Status of Women at the City University of New York, p. 8.

32. Reported in Association of American Colleges, *On Campus with Women*, p. 2.

33. Carnegie Commission on Higher Education, p. 116.

34. Chancellor's Advisory Committee on the Status of Women at the City University of New York, p. 38.

35. P. 123.

36. P. 117.

37. Carnegie Commission on Higher Education, p. 111.

38. Association of American Colleges, *On Campus with Women*, p. 1.

39. *Teaching Faculty in Academe: 1972-73*, Ace research reports 8, no. 2 (Washington, D.C.: American Council on Education, 1973), reported in Carnegie Commission on Higher Education, p. 121 fn 7.

40. Helen S. Astin and Alan E. Bayer, "Sex Discrimination in Academe," *Educational Record*, Spring 1972, p. 105.

41. Ibid., p. 108.

42. Ibid., p. 115.

43. Carnegie Commission on Higher Education, p. 119.

44. *Challenges to Graduate School* (San Francisco: Jossey-Bass, 1970), pp. 93-95, reported in Carnegie Commission on Higher Education, p. 93.

45. Carnegie Commission on Higher Education, p. 98.

46. M. E. Tidball, "Perspectives on Academic Women and Affirmative Action," *Educational Record* 54, no. 2 (Spring 1973): 130-35, summarized in Carnegie Commission on Higher Education, p. 73.

47. P. 117.

48. The Education Amendments of 1972, more popularly referred to as the Higher Education Act, amended the Equal Pay Act. The Education Amendments of 1972 also contained Title IX. The Equal Employment Opportunity Act amended Title VII of the Civil Rights Act of 1964.

49. Sec. 703 (a) (1).

50. Sec. 703 (a) (2).

51. Sec. 901 (a).

52. Remarks of Senator Birch Bayh, Floor Debate, 117 *Congressional Record* 30 (1971), p. 403.

53. Alexandra P. Buek and Jeffrey H. Orleans, "Sex Discrimination—A Bar to a Democratic Education: Overview of Title IX of the Education Amendments of 1972," *Connecticut Law Review* 6, no. 1 (Fall 1973): 25 fn 84.

54. Davidson, Ginsburg, and Kay, p. 872.

55. 1 *Women Law Reporter* 1.22 (September 15, 1974).

56. Subsec. 901 (a) (1) and (5).

57. Subsec. 901 (a) (2).

58. Chancellor's Advisory Committee on the Status of Women, p. 1.

59. Statement made at Northeastern Women's Caucus in Political Science Meeting (New York, March 23, 1974).

60. Davidson, Ginsburg, and Kay, p. 882 fn 80.

61. *New York Times*, 19 March 1973, p. 25.

62. Marion E. Doro, "The Carnegie Commission, the Lester Report and the Status of Women" (Paper delivered at the 1974 Annual Meeting of the American Political Science Association, Chicago, Illinois, August 29-September 2, 1974), p. 12.

63. Association of American Colleges, *On Campus with Women*, November 1974, p. 2.

64. 1 *Women Law Reporter* 1.22.

65. Letter from Elizabeth Athanasakos, Chairperson, Secretary's Advisory Committee on the Rights and Responsibilities of Women, Dept. of Health, Education and Welfare, August 2, 1974.

66. Davidson, Ginsburg, and Kay, p. 873.

67. Cathe Wolhowe, "HEW Guidelines," 1 *Women Law Reporter* 1.18 (September 15, 1974).

68. Ibid.

69. Regulations for Title IX, Sec. 86.2 (m) & (n).

70. Source confidential.

71. "Keynote Address" (delivered at American Council on Education Annual Meeting, October 1972), reported in the *Chronicle of Higher Education*, 16 October 1972, p. 3.

72. Sec. ℵ91 (a) (2).

73. Buek and Orleans, p. 7 fn 20.

74. Davidson, Ginsburg, and Kay, p. 8.

75. "Sex Discrimination under Title VII: Some Unresolved Issues," 24 *Labor Law Journal* 411 (July 1973).

76. Davidson, Ginsburg, and Kay, p. 3. The 1971 decision is *Reed v. Reed*, 404 U.S. 71.

77. *Williams v. McNair*, U.S. District Court, D. South Carolina 1970, 316 F. Supp. 134, aff'd 401 U.S. 951, reported in Davidson, Ginsburg, and Kay, pp. 828-29.

78. Davidson, Ginsburg, and Kay, p. 115.

79. Ibid., p. 104 fn 2.

80. *Frontiero v. Richardson*, 411 U.S. 677.

81. Ibid., reported in Davidson, Ginsburg, and Kay, p. 83.

82. Davidson, Ginsburg, and Kay, ch. 1, secs. A & D.

83. Cited in ibid., p. 64.

84. *Proposed Amendment to the U.S. Constitution*, S.J. Res. 8, S.J. Res. 9 and HRJ Res. 208, 92nd Congress, 1st session (1971), sec. 1.

85. Senate Comm. on the Judiciary, *S. Rep. No. 92-689*, 92nd Cong., 2nd session (1972), p. 2.

86. Davidson, Ginsburg, and Kay, p. 116.

87. Ibid., p. 108.

88. Johnston and Knapp, "Sex Discrimination by Law: A Study in Judicial Perspective," 46 *N.Y.U. Law Review* 675-677 (1971), cited in Davidson, Ginsburg, and Kay, pp. 3-4.

89. *Kirstein v. Rector and Visitors of University of Virginia*, 309 F. Supp. 184, reported in Davidson, Ginsburg, and Kay, p. 823.

90. Davidson, Ginsburg, and Kay, p. 115.

91. Carnegie Commission on Higher Education, p. 64.

92. Committee on the Status of Women, Northeastern Political Science Association (Report Delivered at the Annual Meeting, Nov. 7-9, 1974).

Legal Equality in Marriage and Divorce: The ERA's Mandate*

Lenore J. Weitzman

The Equal Rights Amendment provides a unique opportunity to bring the structure of legal marriage into line with social reality. The present structure of legal marriage is archaic: it continues to enforce outmoded and inflexible roles on husbands and wives. These roles are based on sex stereotypes and strongly contradict the living reality of most marriages. The passage of the Equal Rights Amendment will necessitate fundamental changes in family law to make legal marriage more closely reflect an egalitarian partnership between husband and wife. In this way the Equal Rights Amendment will revitalize and strengthen marriage by making it a more viable and equal relationship, a structure more in accord with the needs and family patterns of most people in our society.

In the first section of this article, we will review the traditional legal structure of marriage and show how it tries to impose an outmoded paternalistic structure on family relationships. The second section will examine the recent changes in family patterns which point to the "popular mandate" for a new legal structure of marriage. The final section discusses the anticipated effects of the Equal Rights Amendment on the legal structure of marriage and outlines its potential for insuring more viable egalitarian relationships.

I. TRADITIONAL LEGAL MARRIAGE: STATE IMPOSED INEQUALITY

The legal marriage contract is unlike most contracts: its provisions are unwritten, unspecified, and typically unknown to the contracting parties.

*Adapted from "Legal Regulation of Marriage: Tradition and Change," *California Law Review* 62 (1974). Copyright © by Lenore J. Weitzman. Revised by and printed with permission of the author.

One wonders how many men and women entering marriage today would freely agree to the provisions of their marriage contract if they were given the opportunity to read it and to consider the rights and obligations to which they were committing themselves. However, no state gives them the opportunity to read the terms of their "unwritten" marriage contract, nor does any state ask them if they are willing to assume the duties, rights, and obligations it specifies.

What is in this unwritten contract? The four essential provisions of the traditional marriage contract are those which: (a) recognize the husband as head of the household, (b) hold the husband responsible for support, (c) hold the wife responsible for domestic services, and (d) hold the wife responsible for child care. Each of these provisions is rooted in common law, and each remains alive in 1975. However, their endurance is anachronistic and the need for change pressing. Let us briefly examine each of these.

A. The Husband as Head of the Family

In the common law of England, the husband and wife merged into a single legal identity, that of the husband. As the authority William Blackstone explained:

> By marriage, the husband and wife are one person in law. . . . [T]he very being or legal existence of the woman is suspended during the marriage, or at least is incorporated and consolidated into that of the husband, under whose wing, protection, and cover she performs everything.[1]

Under this doctrine of coverture, a married woman lost the control of her real property and the ownership of her chattels. She could not make a contract in her own name, either with her husband or with third parties, and she could neither sue nor be sued in her own name.[2] If she worked, her husband was entitled to her wages, and if she and her husband separated, he invariably gained custody of the children. In fact, the concept of the unity of the husband and wife as a single person even prevented her from full criminal responsibility for her own conduct. Criminal acts done in her husband's presence were assumed to be committed under her husband's command, and he was therefore held responsible for them.[3]

Most of these legal barriers to *property* ownership were removed by the passage of Married Women's Property Acts in the nineteenth century.[4] However, today, one hundred years later, the basic legal obligations between husbands and wives are still defined by English common law—and thus remain fundamentally the same. The present marriage contract, i.e., the legal contract in both statutory and case law, continues to enforce these common law obligations. The first of these is the basic common law assumption that a woman must assume her husband's identity upon marriage. Today when a woman marries, she still loses her independent identity: she assumes her husband's name, his residence, and his status—socially and economically.

The married woman's loss of an independent identity is clearly symbolized by the loss of her name. Women who try to retain their maiden names may have difficulty voting, obtaining a driver's license, running for office, and securing credit.[5] In some states a woman with children is forced to retain her husband's name even after they divorce. As recently as 1972, the United States Supreme Court upheld an Alabama law requiring a married woman to use her husband's surname on her driver's license.[6] Although many women may want to assume their husbands' names when they marry, a coerced change of name, as Professor Herma H. Kay has noted, is "resented by the woman who wishes to retain her birth name in order to establish a continuity of identity throughout her life."[7] A career woman in public or professional life may suffer a real loss of recognition when she marries and adopts her husband's name, more so if she marries more than once.

Recently some states have adopted a more progressive attitude and have held that common laws do not require a woman to assume her husband's name even though such a custom might be followed by the majority of married women.[8] However, in other states a married woman who does not want to assume her husband's surname may still have to contend with laws and administrative regulations which restrict her freedom to do so.

The second area in which a woman assumes her husband's identity is in her domicile—the legal term for a person's residence. A married woman is required to accept her husband's choice of residence. If she refuses to accept his choice, she is "considered to have deserted him." If "deserted," the husband has valid grounds for divorce, and in some states a wife found guilty of desertion is "at fault" in the divorce action and can be deprived of her right to seek alimony.

The location of a person's legal domicile also affects a broad range of legal rights and duties, including the place where he or she may vote, run for public office, serve on juries, receive free or lowered tuition at a state school, be liable for taxes, sue for divorce, register a car, and have his or her estate administered. For example, a woman who is, and always has been, a state resident, and therefore receives free tuition at the state university, may suddenly be charged out-of-state tuition if she marries a male student whose legal domicile is in another state.

In some states married women who must assume their husbands' domicile are subjected to unfavorable tax consequences or lose the privilege of running for public office in their home state.[9] In other states a woman cannot retain her own domicile for voting, and in still others she cannot for paying taxes. As of 1971, only three states in the United States—Alaska, Arkansas, and Wisconsin—permitted a woman to have a separate domicile from her husband for all legal purposes.[10] As Professor Leo Kanowitz has observed, the practical function of the domicile rule is to "deprive wives of certain governmental benefits they would otherwise have."[11]

In addition to the law of domicile and surname, there are other areas in the law which recognize the husband as head of the household with his wife's identity subordinate to his. Some of these are found in administrative regulations regarding unemployment insurance, social security benefits, federal survivors and disability insurance, and public assistance.[12] Other regulations, such as those governing consumer credit, are derived from legal principles but have acquired an authority of their own. For example, the restrictions that a married woman faces in the credit arena are a direct outgrowth of the traditional marriage contract. At common law, the husband gained control of his wife's property upon marriage and therefore assumed responsibility for her debts as well as her support.[13] Today, however, despite the fact that married women earn money, hold property, and acquire debts in their own names, in most cases they are still required to apply for and obtain credit in their husbands' names—and need their husbands' explicit permission to do so.[14] A married woman's independent right to seek bank loans, home mortgages, federal housing loans, department store charge accounts, and credit cards in her own name is thus severely circumscribed by the prevailing assumption that her husband is the head of the household.[15] The result in this area, as in many others, is a series of social customs and regulations which surround and enlarge the husband's strictly "legal" rights as head of the household and consequently further diminish those of his wife.

The legal system's insistence that the husband be head of the household appears anachronistic in a society where marriage is becoming more of an equal partnership between husbands and wives and marital decisions are made by both parties, not the husband alone.

B. The Husband's Responsibility for Financial Support

The courts in our country have a strict, conservative view of the necessity for a clear division of roles within the family, holding that the "husband has a duty to support his wife, that she has a duty to render services in the home, and that these duties are reciprocal.''[16] When major judicial decisions are examined, one finds that this system has not changed in over 200 years.

> The husband is to provide the family with food, clothing, shelter and as many of the amenities of life as he can manage, either (in earlier days) by the management of his estates or (more recently) by working for wages or a salary. The wife is to be mistress of the household, maintaining the home with the resources furnished by the husband, and caring for the children. A reading of contemporary judicial opinions leaves the impression that these roles have not changed over the last two hundred years.[17]

All states, even those with community property systems, place the prime burden of family support on the husband: he is to provide necessities for both his wife and his children.[18] In contrast, a wife is *never* held responsible for the support of her husband in two-thirds of the states, and in the remaining minority of states, a wife is held responsible for her husband's support only if he becomes incapacitated or a public charge.[19]

Because the courts have held the traditional view of the husband bearing the total responsibility for the family's financial support, husbands and wives are not allowed to make private contracts that would alter or limit the husband's responsibility. Even in cases where the wife is independently wealthy and has no wish for financial support from the husband, the courts have deemed the husband responsible. The law's position on this subject is absolute: "A husband may not be absolved from his duty to support his wife, nor can this duty be qualified or limited. The husband's duty as a matter of policy is an obligation imposed by law and cannot be contracted away.''[20]

One effect of placing the primary support obligation on men is to further reinforce the husband's position as head of the household and, more specifically, his authority over family finances. While the husband's obligation for support does not alone bestow upon him the mixed blessings of financial authority and financial responsibility, most of his financial power stems directly from this obligation. For example, in most states, because the husband has the primary responsibility for family support, he has the power to manage and control family income and property. In some states, again because of his responsibility for support, his permission is necessary before his wife can open a business or trade in commodities.[21] As we have already noted, the husband's financial powers are also used to justify granting married women credit in their husbands' names. This is especially harmful to the wife in the event of a divorce. She (not *he*) automatically loses "her" credit rating and is then forced to begin again and reestablish her credit by proving that she is financially responsible.

Of course, we can take this one step further and ask, "What if a wife divorces, loses her credit rating, rebuilds it on her own, and then decides to marry again?" The law hasn't changed, and thus she would have to begin again and assume her new husband's identity, name, credit, etc. One might say, "It's the same old merry-go-round."

An assumption underlying the husband's legal responsibility for support is the continued economic incapacity of the wife. As Professor Kay has recently noted:

> The support laws embody the legal view that a married woman is an economically nonproductive person dependent upon others for the necessities of life. . . . [T]he married woman continues to be treated as a legal dependent, like the children and insane persons with whom the law formerly classified her.[22]

This automatic assumption of a wife's dependency is clearly anachronistic in 1975. Today, 43% of all married women are in the labor force and are actively contributing to the financial support of their families.[23]

Such absolute laws have the effect of perpetuating unnecessary sex stereotypes in the lives of individual people. The modern man becomes bitter and resentful when the courts force him to support a woman who is well employed or wealthy. On the other side, the employed wife feels insulted because the law assumes she is incapable of supporting herself and doesn't recognize her important contribution to the family's income. The legal adherence to these sex-stereotyped roles appears unrealistic and unnecessarily rigid in modern day marriages where many women voluntarily share the burden of financial support with their husbands.

The law diverges from social reality in a second respect. In practice, the spousal support obligations of the husband are rarely enforced because the courts have been reluctant to interfere with an ongoing marriage. In the leading case in this area, *McGuire v. McGuire,* the wife complained that her husband had not given her any money nor provided her with clothes for the past three years. Although he was a man of substantial means, her husband had also refused to purchase furniture and other household necessities (beyond the groceries which he paid for by check). The court, however, refused to consider the wife's complaint because the parties were still living together and the court did not want to "intrude" on the marital relationship. In the language of the court:

> The living standards of a family are a matter of concern to the household, and not for the courts to determine, even though the

husband's attitude toward his wife, according to his wealth and circumstances, leaves little to be said in his behalf. As long as the home is
maintained and the parties are living as husband and wife, it may be said
that the husband is legally supporting his wife and the purpose of the
marriage relation is being carried out. Public policy requires such a
holding.[24]

If a wife does not receive the court's assistance in obtaining support
during her marriage, then it becomes meaningless to speak of the husband's
legal obligation to support his wife. The Citizens' Advisory Council on the
Status of Women[25] aptly describes the present situation: "[A] married
woman living with her husband can, in practice, get only what he chooses to
give her." Thus, for the married woman, the law's promise of support is a
hollow guarantee — one that affords a married woman no more protection
than her husband will willingly grant.

Women do not fare much better after divorce, although the husband's
theoretical responsibility for support continues with his obligation to provide
alimony for his former wife.[26] The guarantee of alimony is based on the
continuing assumption that women, like children, are incapable of supporting themselves. Alimony was originally awarded by the English ecclesiasti-
cal courts which gave only divorce *a mensa et thoro* (from bed and board),
authorizing the husband and wife to live apart but not freeing them from the
marital bond.[27] An alimony award under these circumstances was an
enforcement of the husband's continuing duty to support his wife. Since the
husband retained control over his wife's property and employment opportunities for women were lacking, alimony alone provided a woman's
essential means of support.

The survival of alimony today, despite recent changes in women's status
and labor force participation, reflects the law's continued assumption of the
wife's dependency on her husband (and perhaps its cognizance of the
realistically poor employment opportunities for a middle-aged woman who
has devoted her productive years to full-time housework and child care).
Because the law encourages a woman to give up her independent earning
potential in favor of her marriage, the provision for alimony is based on the
assumption that women have done just this—and are, as a result, incapable
of independent financial survival.

Yet, if a woman relies on the law's promise that her husband will continue
to support her, she will find her expectations thwarted. Even though most
states continue to hold the husband theoretically liable for alimony, in fact,
alimony is actually awarded in less than 15% of all divorce cases. Since
alimony is a tax deduction for the man and child support is not, the husband
is likely to want to label some of his child support as alimony. Thus, *true*

alimony may be given in less than 10% of all divorce cases. Although the myths of "alimony drones" and of wives "taking their husbands to the cleaners" persist, it should be emphasized that for over 90 percent of the divorced women in the United States, alimony is just that—a myth.

C. The Wife's Responsibility for Domestic Services

As already noted, legal marriage assigns specific roles to both the husband and wife. The man exchanges financial support for his wife's services as a companion, housewife, and mother. The services a man can legally expect from his wife are enumerated in *Rucci v. Rucci:*

> [S]he has a duty to be his helpmate, to love and care for him in such a role, to afford him her society and her person, to protect and care for him in sickness, and to labor faithfully to advance his interests. (Citations omitted) Likewise, she must perform her household and domestic duties, . . . without compensation therefor. A husband is entitled to the benefit of his wife's industry and economy.[28]

Traditional law has fostered and nurtured the role of woman as housewife and mother for generations. "The paramount destiny and mission of women are to fulfill the noble and benign offices of wife and mother. This is the law of the creator."[29] Today, the law continues to assume that a wife will fulfill the role of housewife and mother, reasoning that she owes these services to her husband in return for his protection and financial support.

In the past century, the courts have been remarkably consistent in upholding the wife's domestic obligations *above all else*. Because "a husband is entitled to the benefit of his wife's industry and economy," the courts have reasoned that a wife owes domestic services to her husband, and they have therefore refused to honor contracts whereby a husband agreed to pay his wife for her domestic services. Even when husband and wife have agreed that her work was extra, such as working in her husband's business or doing farm labor, the courts have voided contracts which obligated her husband to pay her.

Even if an engaged couple wishes to clarify their relationship for their future married life and wants the wife to receive an income for her housework, the law states: "An agreement for personal services made while the parties are unmarried is terminated by the marriage of the parties since one of the implied terms of the contract of marriage is that the services will be performed without compensation."

On the other hand, if a woman decides the homemaking role is not her style and chooses a full-time job or career, as many are doing today, the law does not accept her decision to change roles. By law, she is still expected to cook, clean, and maintain comforts for her husband even though this results in a clear inequality: she must handle two jobs, one at work and one at home, while her husband has only one.

The law's assumption that a wife "owes" her domestic services to her husband undermines the value and importance of the wife's labor in building the family wealth and property, both during the marriage and at the time of dissolution. When a woman's labor is "seen as a service she owes her husband rather than as a job deserving the dignity of economic return,"[30] the contribution and value of the housewife is greatly underestimated. Although there is "much rhetoric about the value of homemaking and child rearing," the law does little to ensure that these tasks are accorded "status, dignity, and security."[31]

The National Organization for Women has urged that housework be treated as a bona fide occupation with compensation and fringe benefits.[32] Using estimates of the value of housework (such as the computation used by Galbraith that the average housewife's yearly services are worth $13,364[33]), feminists have suggested paying the housewife for her work to lessen her dependency status.

The current dependency of housewives and the undervaluation of housework could also be reduced if women covered as independent workers under social security. Clearly, housewives work even though they do not receive monetary compensation for their work. Yet today's housewife does not have an independent right to benefits from her husband's social security (although her work at home clearly contributes to family support) until she has been married to him for twenty years. Without independent coverage a wife cannot provide for her retirement or old age as an independent person. If, instead, the wife's contribution to the family were recognized as work, she would be independently entitled to insurance based on her homemaking and child care services.

Recognition of the housewife's contribution to the marriage may be even more important at the time of divorce. In many states, the woman discovers that her contribution to the family wealth and property is ignored upon dissolution. Although marriage is considered a partnership in theory, when the partnership profits are divided, the woman's contribution is devalued in all but the eight community property states. "The shocking unfairness" of the "obsolete and archaic marital property laws" of many states which do not subject the husband's separate property to equitable distribution upon divorce is illustrated by the New York case of *Wirth v. Wirth:*

> Both husband and wife were employed and for 22 years of their marriage their earnings were pooled. She also raised two children. In

1956 it was agreed between them that the husband would start a "crash" savings program and that family expenses would be met out of her income and his would be used for investments. According to the wife, the husband said that the program was "for our latter days" and "for the two of us." All of the investments were taken in the husband's name and none were held by joint ownership. Upon divorce it was held that she had no interest whatsoever in the assets they had accumulated as a nest egg for both of them, and that although she might be entitled to alimony (after some forty years of marriage), he got to keep all of the investments. No social or economic justification for the result was offered by the court which insisted that for the imposition of a constructive trust fraud or concealment had to be shown. The decision makes a fetish of how title is held and ignores the tradition of equity courts in effecting justice.[34]

Foster and Freed criticize the unfairness of the separate property concept because it ignores the wife's contribution to the family property:

The system disregards the division of labor in the family and leaves the wife without family assets. . . . At current prices the replacement value of a wife's services may not be an insignificant sum. There also are such intangibles as a wife's help and encouragement in furthering her husband's career.[35]

Thus, the separate property system, the system in all but eight states in the United States, disregards the wife's contribution to family property. The woman who has contributed to the growth of her husband's business, career, property, or income during the marriage generally finds that her contribution to the partnership is unrecognized in law. Upon dissolution the partnership is treated as a one-man business, and she is cheated out of a fair share for her half of the effort.[36]

It is a strange irony that the law seems to punish a woman who has devoted herself to being a mother and wife at the same time that the law encourages all women to remain housewives. The law thus puts women in a double bind: the legal structure of marriage seems to provide incentives and rewards for women to remain in the domestic role but also penalizes them for this role if their marriages dissolve. Since a woman cannot insure the survival of her marriage, the marriage may be dissolved, and she may be punished through no fault or intention of her own. The double bind is such that whatever a woman chooses she stands to lose. If she follows the legal and cultural mandate and chooses marriage above all else, she will sacrifice her earning potential for her family, and she and her children may suffer upon divorce. On the other hand, if a woman chooses a career, the law forces her to do two jobs, and she (and her family) may suffer because of the legal priorities in taxation, social security, etc., given to families with a single earning partner and a housewife.

D. The Wife's Responsibility for Child Care

The fourth provision of the state imposed marriage contract places almost total responsibility for child care, both during marriage and after dissolution, upon the wife. The woman's role as mother remains at the very core of our legal conception of her place in society, and it is likely to meet the most resistance to change. It provides a fertile ground for stereotype and the "most stubborn and intractable bastion of discrimination."[37] As the Supreme Court said:

> [H]ealthy mothers are essential to vigorous offspring, the physical well-being of woman becomes an object of public interest and care in order to preserve the strength and vigor of the race.[38]

Although women have been given great deference because they are mothers, they have also faced many exclusions because of their mothering roles. Our courts have allowed the exclusion of women from specific occupations, such as bartending, from job classifications, such as those requiring weight lifting and over-time work, and from certain periods of employment, such as the time just before and just after childbirth.

The continued legal assumption that the woman is the natural and proper caretaker of the young is most clearly reflected in child custody dispositions. Women continue to be awarded custody of their children in over 90% of the cases.[39] Although most divorcing women want custody of their children, the extreme deference to the mother as custodian may have the social effect of further reinforcing woman's social roles as housewife and mother and—in many cases—her dependency on her husband for support.

The practice of automatically giving the mother custody of the children may have two other detrimental effects. First, it may not take sufficient, if any, account of the needs of the children and the qualifications of the parents involved. Second, in practice, it has the ultimate effect of causing the mother to bear the greater, if not the total, financial burden of child support.

The current preference for the mother in custody cases is so pronounced that fathers may be denied an equal right to custody because the presumption of a mother's fitness is so hard to overcome. Fathers who would be better custodians face an uphill battle in most courts, and many are discouraged from trying. Children may also suffer when their interests are ignored or undermined by this a priori custody assumption.

Further, it is not clear that the mother benefits from the presumption in her favor. Because it is assumed that all mothers will want custody of their children, there is a strong social pressure for women to assume this role without considering its consequences. Since custody awards to the mother are so routine, the woman who admits that she would prefer not to have her children is viewed suspiciously and made to feel deviant and guilty. She may therefore be coerced into a role which is harmful to both her and her children.

The legal deference to mothers comes from a time when our country was young, needed population, and wanted to encourage women to have many children. This may have been appropriate for that period in our history. But what about our present need for a zero population growth? Forced mothering has been a difficult burden for many women, but until recently, women would seldom express a dislike for children or say that they did not want to have children. Today, however, a real choice is open to women, and the law should allow women who don't want to be full-time mothers to exercise this choice.

Once again, the law seems to be based on stereotyped assumptions about the proper roles of men and women. Women who may not want to be full-time mothers are coerced into it, and fathers who want custody are prevented from it by the legal priorities given to women. Certainly public policy would be better served by eliminating these rigid role prescriptions and increasing the options available to both sexes.

When the mother is awarded custody, she is expected to perform child care services without pay. The father's obligation is limited to direct support for the child. Even the Uniform Marriage and Divorce Act, which represents the enlightened vanguard in family law, makes no provision for the custodial parent to be compensated for his or her labor in caring for the children.

The father, as the noncustodial parent, is typically ordered to pay child support. However, most fathers do not support their children as ordered.[40] Indeed 62% fail to comply fully with the court ordered payments in the first year after the order, and 42% do not make even a single payment. By the tenth year, 79% of the fathers are in total noncompliance. Yet, despite the alarmingly high rate of noncompliance, legal action against nonpaying fathers is rarely taken.[41]

In summary, our review of the provisions of the traditional marriage contract has shown that the law imposes duties on husbands and wives which are based on sex role stereotypes, and it is highly questionable whether the law should enforce outmoded sex roles in an increasingly egalitarian society. Morever, for the woman, the effect of the marriage contract is to allow, encourage, and sometimes compel the primacy of her domestic roles. The law gives the young woman an apparent guarantee of financial security—support and alimony—if she gets married and performs her marital role well. The law tells her that she need not develop her individual capacity, for her economic security will be dependent on her husband's (not her own) earning ability. Of course, as already shown, these guarantees are illusory. In reality, a woman's "right" to support depends on the goodwill of her husband, in both marriage and divorce. But by the time the woman discovers that the law's guarantees are hollow, it is too late; she has typically passed the point where she could easily choose a different course.

II. FAMILY PATTERNS WHICH CHALLENGE TRADITIONAL LEGAL MARRIAGE

In the past 200 years there have been profound transformations in our society which have impelled corresponding changes in the nature and the functions of the family. With the increasing industrialization and urbanization of our society, the central role of the family as the basic productive and economic unit of our society has declined. The typical family has shifted from an extended intergenerational form to the smaller nuclear or conjugal unit.[42] Yet, at the same time that the productive and economic functions of the family have declined, there has been an increase in the family's role as the major source of psychological and social support for its individual members. Sharing, companionship, and emotional solace in the marital bond have become primary for most couples in our society.

However, despite these profound changes in the internal structure of marriage in our society and the relations between husbands and wives, the legal structure of marriage has remained stagnant and is consequently a rigid and outmoded vestige of the old social system. The increase in egalitarian family patterns challenges the traditional marriage contract and points to the need for a more flexible legal model, a model which is more suited to the nuclear family unit and to the diverse roles modern husbands and wives must assume. Let us consider specifically how this movement toward more egalitarian relationships within the family provides a fundamental challenge to the provisions of the traditional legal marriage contract.

The first provision of the traditional contract, the recognition of the husband as head of the family, is inconsistent with an egalitarian family form in which both authority and responsibility are increasingly shared. Today it is typical for husbands and wives to talk over family problems. Decisions on financial matters such as budgeting, purchasing, saving, and the "general struggle for survival" are now being made jointly or apportioned on a less sex-stereotyped basis.[43] Similarly, decisions on the family residence—of when and where to move—are no longer made by the husband alone, nor are they solely based on his career.

The assumption that the husband is head of the family, with his wife's identity subordinate to his, is also being challenged by the increasing number of women who are retaining their maiden names and by their independent social and financial identity. Many married women are discovering that they may be better off in the long run if they keep their own names and maintain their driver's license, diplomas, tax records, and credit cards in their maiden names.

The second provision of the traditional contract, that of holding the husband primarily responsible for family support, is similarly challenged by changing social reality. Married women now constitute 60% of the female labor force, and these 20 million married women certainly contribute to the financial support of their families.[44] Contrary to the myth that married women are working for pin money or extras, the facts show that the wages of these married women are of vital importance to their families.[45] Today, when 43% of all married women are in the labor force, social reality strongly contradicts the legal assumption that the husband should and does support his family alone.

The third provision of the contract, that which holds the wife solely responsible for domestic services, is similarly challenged by the egalitarian family norm and the extended range of domestic responsibilities which are now being shared or alternated between husbands and wives. An increasing number of married couples are interchanging the traditional household roles, with men playing a greater role in cooking, shopping, cleaning, and women assuming more responsibility for family budgets, working in the garden, and fixing things around the house. There is a growing acceptance of the idea that when a woman returns to the labor force, and thus shares the responsibility of supporting the family, the husband in turn must share equal responsibility for the household.

This general trend toward more egalitarian relations within the family may be noted in other areas not directly affected by family law. For example, the current sexual revolution has focused increasing attention and emphasis on the wife's participation and satisfaction in sexual relations and, consequently, on a more mutual and egalitarian sexual relationship. Similarly, the growing acceptance of sharing responsibility for birth control, entertainment, recreation, and vacations may be noted.

The final provision of the legal marriage contract, that of holding the wife responsible for child care, may also be challenged by changing family patterns. Parenthood is coming to be defined more and more as the joint enterprise of both husband and wife, not only because women are insisting that men share some of the load but because many young professional men themselves no longer accept as their fate the compulsive male careerism that dominated the 1950s.[46] The removed, austere father of yesteryear is fading away as today's father plays a greater role in nurturing and caring for his children. Fathers are enjoying the pleasure and affection that women have had for generations, and some men are delighting in it. By sharing child care responsibilities with their wives, men are also coming to appreciate the difficulty of assuming the full-time job of child care alone.

In the past, it was widely believed that children of a working mother suffered from "maternal deprivation." Today, however, social scientists have shown that working mothers provide more positive role models and are better parents for growing children of both sexes. In contrast, the woman who is too devoted to motherhood may have a negative effect on her children by binding them too closely to her, dampening their initiative and resenting their growth.[47] In addition, women who are preoccupied with motherhood may suffer in later life. Pauline Bart has reported extreme depression among middle-aged women after their children leave home, when the mothers have been overly involved with, and have too closely identified with, their children.

Although some of these egalitarian patterns, such as the father's assumption of responsibility for child care, are not readily accepted in all segments of our society, the long-term trend appears to be in this direction. This trend is supported by three important societal forces. The first is the increasing male dissatisfaction with the occupational burdens of the male role. For the first time, men are rebelling against an exclusive preoccupation with a career and are seeking to humanize their lives by assuming a greater role in and getting more satisfaction from their relationships with their wives and children.

The second force is the changing expectations of a marital relationship, with multiplied emphasis on the emotional and psychological needs of the spouses[48]—love, sex, intimacy, companionship, emotional support, security, and ego enchancement. At the same time that the economic functions of the family have declined, the emotional interdependence of family members has increased, and these emotional and psychological needs appear to be better met in an egalitarian relationship. They thus serve as a further force in pushing intrafamilial patterns in that direction.

A final and most significant thrust toward more egalitarian family patterns is coming from women's increasing dissatisfaction with the traditional role of the housewife and mother and their resulting demands for more independence, greater participation and compensation in the labor force, and more sharing of domestic chores by husbands and children.[49] Dr. Jessie Bernard has shown that marriage puts a greater emotional strain on women and that "traditional marriage makes women sick—both physically and mentally."[50] As Dr. Bernard explains, in every marriage there are really two marriages: the husband's marriage and the wife's marriage. The husband's marriage is a beneficial one in that it enhances the husband's mental health, happiness, career success, income, and life expectancy. The wife's marriage is a destructive one. Married women are more depressed, have more nervous breakdowns, have more feelings of inadequacy, and are generally less healthy, both mentally and physically, than single women. Dr. Bernard writes that women are "driven mad, not by men but by the anachronistic way in which marriage is structured today—or rather, the life style which accompanies marriage today and which demands that all wives be housewives."[51]

The disaffection of women with marital and family roles should provide a powerful force in the restructuring of relations between the sexes in marriage. As Betty Friedan recently noted: "If there is anything that makes a feminist, it is growing up and believing that love and marriage will take care of everything, and then one day waking up at 30, or 40, or 50, and facing the world alone and facing the responsibility of caring for children alone. . . . [It is] the obsolete sex roles on which our marriages were based [which are to blame]."[52]

These changes only highlight the profound modifications in the internal structure of marriage taking place in our society today. Although we have covered them very briefly, the implications of these trends are nothing less than revolutionary. There can be no doubt of the fundamental alteration in the relations between husbands and wives today and of the very inadequate nature of the present legal assumptions.

III. THE EQUAL RIGHTS AMENDMENT
AND THE MANDATE FOR CHANGE

The Equal Rights Amendment seems to offer the most promising route for challenging and altering traditional legal marriage. The question of the ERA's effect on laws regulating marriage arose several times in the debates surrounding its passage. Senator Ervin, who opposed its passage, argued that the Amendment would so change present marriage laws that it should not be passed.[53] Ervin praised the way current law establishes "the institutions of marriage, the home, and the family," and makes "some rational distinctions between the respective rights and responsibilities of men and women" within these institutions. He expressed regret that the Equal Rights Amendment would eliminate such distinctions.[54] According to Ervin, if the ERA should be interpreted by the Supreme Court to forbid any legal distinctions between men and women, it would nullify all state laws requiring women to be homemakers and mothers and precluding them from pursuing gainful occupations. It would also nullify laws that impose upon husbands the primary responsibility to provide homes and livelihoods.[55] These laws, of course, are the very laws which are cited as objectionable in the first section of this article and which, in the author's opinion, are in the most need of change.

Although Ervin's minority report finds the impact of the ERA objectionable, his delineation of its practical consequences are similar to those of the Amendment's proponents. The Majority Report of the Senate agrees with Ervin that the Equal Rights Amendment would nullify many present state laws regulating marriage and would require changes by all states to bring their domestic relations law into conformity with the Amendment: "State domestic relations laws will have to be based on individual circumstances . . . and not on sexual stereotypes."[56]

Let us briefly examine the probable effects of the Equal Rights Amendment on each of the provisions of the traditional marriage contract.

The first provision of the traditional contract, that which establishes the husband as head of the family, would clearly be illegal. The married woman's loss of identity and the traditional network of legal disabilities imposed upon her with marriage would have to disappear.[57] For example, since name and domicile regulations continue to subordinate a woman's identity to her husband's, these laws and any other laws which require a married woman to assume her husband's identity would become a legal nullity. No married woman could be required by law to take her husband's name upon marriage. In addition, married women would have to be granted the same independent right to choice of domicile as married men now have.[58]

Since the Equal Rights Amendment would prohibit enforcement of sex-based definitions of conjugal functions, it would invalidate the provisions of the traditional contract which assign specific roles to husbands and wives. The Equal Rights Amendment clearly prohibits legislation which dictates different roles for men and women within the family.[59]

Thus, the second provision of the traditional marriage contract, that requiring the husband to be solely responsible for family support, would be illegal. The responsibility for family support would no longer fall on men alone. Each spouse would be equally liable "based on current resources, earning power, and non-monetary contributions to the family welfare."[60] Similarly, the Equal Rights Amendment would require that alimony be available to both husbands and wives, although laws could be passed to grant special protection to any spouse who had, in fact, been out of the labor force for a long time in order to make a noncompensated contribution to the family's well-being. Such laws would tend to benefit the traditional wife and would provide legal recognition of her contribution to the family. Thus, the ERA would not remove the housewife's right to support either during marriage or after divorce. It would only extend this right to men if they have assumed the "housewife" role while their wives supported the family.

The third provision of the marriage contract, that of requiring a wife to do. housework, to provide affection and companionship, and to be available for sexual relations, would likewise be prohibited as yet another example of sex-based assignment of family roles. These obligations could be required of wives only if they were also required of husbands. Although it is likely that such obligations would be removed from the laws of most states, some states might require domestic services of both spouses.

Finally, the fourth provision of the traditional contract would have to fall, as wives could not be held responsible for child care unless equal obligations were imposed upon all husbands. It is probable that most states would extend these obligations to husbands so that both parents would be responsible for their children's care. In addition, it is likely that most states will hold men and women equally responsible—according to their financial ability —for child support after divorce.

Thus, the Equal Rights Amendment would nullify the existing marriage contract and would require that marital rights and duties be based on individual functions and needs. In both marriage and divorce this would mean that spouses would be treated equally or on the basis of their individual capacities. Today's network of legal disability for married women would have to disappear.

The possibilities for truly equal marriages under the ERA appear to be very positive and exciting. Although some women have feared that the passage of the ERA would eliminate all the protections they currently enjoy in law, it is clear that this would not be so. If a woman has spent her productive years in homemaking and child care, then it would be reasonable to award her alimony on the basis of her past functions and her need. The Senate Report on the Equal Rights Amendment quotes with approval a New York Bar suggestion that "alimony laws could . . . take into consideration the spouse who had been out of the labor market for a period of years."[62]

However, although the ERA will not remove the possibility of support for the homemaking spouse, it is useful to recall that the law's promise of support for divorced women has often been a hollow guarantee. Today 90% of the married women in this country have not received the law's guaranteed support upon divorce. Similarly, most divorced women have not received court ordered child support. Thus, it is difficult to think of the ERA threatening rights which have rarely existed in practice.

On the very positive side, the Equal Rights Amendment allows for and encourages a complete redefinition of marriage as a true marital partnership. This modern conception of marriage might well include provisions for compensating a spouse who contributes, as the housewife does, to building the family's wealth and property.[63] Thus, it could be argued that many wives have a right to half of the family property and to alimony—or to some monetary reimbursement after divorce—irrespective of their financial need. If a wife has contributed to her husband's employability and helped to advance his career, as most married women have, she should be considered his economic partner with a financial investment in his earnings and property. Traditionally, the law has assumed that family property is limited to items of real and personal property. However, in a mobile urban society, the spouses' earning powers have become the major assets of most families. Thus, a modern conception of marital property might well be broadened to include the "earning power" of the marital partners. The recognition of earning power as marital property would legitimately compensate a non-income earning spouse for contributing to the other's education, employability, and job success. In cases of a single-income family, the single career should be conceptualized as a "two-person career" or the product of a cooperative effort by the partnership,[64] and both partners should have a future share in it.

Another possibility open under the ERA would be the treatment of housework as a bona fide occupation with compensation and fringe benefits. With the fall of the wife's traditional obligation to provide domestic services, the law could then recognize the wife's services as an independent contribution to the marriage. Further, married women could be covered as independent workers under social security. Even more important, when it comes to divorce, the value of their contribution to the building of family wealth and property would be recognized by law.

Although my interpretation goes beyond the current legislative history, it would seem that the Equal Rights Amendment would require all states to assume a "community property system at the time of dissolution," as the Uniform Marriage and Divorce Law now does. It would thus force all states to recognize the wife's contribution to family property. In the event of divorce, the homemaker's role in building the family property would entitle her to an equitable share of the property in return for her share of the effort.

The Equal Rights Amendment thus provides a unique opportunity for revitalizing legal marriage and for bringing it into accord with modern reality. As we have seen, the ERA has a popular mandate for reform that would eliminate an archaic legal system and bring it into line with social changes in family patterns which have already taken place. Once the Amendment is passed, all states will have to remove each of the sex-based provisions of the traditional marriage contract, allowing men and women to maintain a true partnership in marriage for the first time. It is important to stress that the Equal Rights Amendment will not destroy marriage and the family but will help accommodate them to social reality by providing a realistic legal structure for egalitarian families. In fact, the rate of divorce may decline as a new legal equality in marriage makes it a more viable institution.

Footnotes

1. *Commentaries,* 4 vols. (Boston: Beacon Press, 1962; orig. 1765), 1:442.

2. Max Radin, "The Common Law of the Family," in *National Law Library,* 6 vols. (New York: P.F. Collier, 1939), 6: 79-175.

3. Homer Clark, *The Law of Domestic Relations* (St. Paul, Minn.: West Publishing Co., 1968), p. 223.

4. Leo Kanowitz, *Women and the Law: The Unfinished Revolution* (Albuquerque, N.M.: University of New Mexico Press, 1969), p. 40.

5. Barbara Brown, Thomas Emerson, Gail Falk, and Ann Freedman, "The Equal Rights Amendment," *Yale Law Journal* 80 (1971): 871.

6. *Forbush v. Wallace,* 405 U.S. 970 (1972).

7. *Sex-based Discrimination in Family Law* (St. Paul, Minn.: West Publishing Co., 1974), p. 125.

8. *Stuart v. Board of Supervisors of Elections,* 226 Md. 440, 295 A.2d 223 (1972).

9. Kay, p. 127.

10. Brown et al., p. 941.

11. P. 52.

12. Colguitt Walker, "Sex Discrimination in Government Benefit Programs," *Hastings Law Journal* 23 (1971): 277.

13. Clark, pp. 219-20.

14. The National Organization for Women, *Women and Credit* (Chicago: N.O.W., 1973), p. 1.

15. Brown et al., p. 61.

16. Clark, p. 181.

17. Ibid.

18. Kay, p. 133.

19. Ibid., p. 139; Clark, p. 186.

20. Isabella Grant, "Marital Contracts before and during Marriage," in *The California Family Lawyer* (San Francisco: Continuing Education of the Bar, 1962), p. 160.

21. Kanowitz, p. 57.

22. Pp. 140-41.

23. United States Department of Labor, *Women Workers Today* (Wash., D.C.: Government Printing Office, 1971).

24. *McGuire v. McGuire,* 175 Neb. 226, 59 N.W.2d 342 (1953).

25. *The Equal Rights Amendment and Alimony and Child Support Laws* (Wash., D.C.: Government Printing Office, 1972), p. 38.

26. Clark, pp. 420-21.

27. Vernier and Hurlbut, "The Historical Background of Alimony Law and Its Present Statutory Structure," *Law and Contemporary Problems* 6 (1939): 197.

28. *Rucci v. Rucci,* 23 Conn.Supp. 221, 181 A.2d 125, (Super. Ct. 1962).

29. *Bradwell v. Illinois,* 83 U.S. 130 (1873).

30. Kay, p. 142.

31. Citizens' Advisory Council on the Status of Women, *Recognition of Economic Contribution of Homemakers and Protection of Children in Divorce and Practice* (Wash., D.C.: Government Printing Office, 1974), p. 6.

32. *Task Force on Marriage and the Family: Suggested Guidelines in Studying and Comments on the Uniform Marriage and Divorce Act* (Chicago: N.O.W., 1971).

33. John Kenneth Galbraith, "The Economics of the American Housewife," *The Atlantic,* August 1973, p. 78; A. Walker and William Gauger, *The Dollar Value of Household Work* (Ithaca, N.Y.: State College of Human Ecology, 1973).

34. *Wirth v. Wirth,* 38 App.Div. 2d 611, 326 N.Y.S.2d 308 (1971); discussed in Henry H. Foster and Doris Jonas Freed, "Economic Effects of Divorce," *Family Law Quarterly* 8 (1974): 174-75.

35. Ibid.

36. A recent report by the Citizens' Advisory Council on the Status of Women (1974) urges a careful evaluation of the economic effects of divorce laws to insure that the homemaker's contribution to the marital property is not ignored. They have specifically urged states adopting no-fault divorce laws to change their laws on the division of property, alimony, child support, and enforcement so that the law explicitly recognizes the contribution of the homemaker.

37. Brief for Appellees, *Geduldig v. Aiello,* 94 S.Ct. 2485 (1974).

38. *Muller v. Oregon,* 208 U.S. 412, 421-22 (1908).

39. William J. Goode, *Women in Divorce* (N.Y.: Free Press, 1965; orig. title *After Divorce,* 1956), pp. 29, 209.

40. Stuart Nagel and Lenore J. Weitzman, "Women as Litigants," *Hastings Law Journal* 23 (1971): 190.

41. Kenneth Eckhardt, "Deviance, Visibility, and Legal Action: The Duty to Support," *Social Problems* 15 (1968): 470.

42. William J. Goode, *The Family* (Englewood Cliffs, N.J.: Prentice-Hall, 1964), p.108.

43. C. Foote, "Changes in American Marriage Patterns," *Eugenics Quarterly* 1 (1954): 254.

44. Bureau of the Census, U.S. Dept. of Commerce, *The American Almanac: The Statistical Abstract of the U.S.* (Wash., D.C.: Government Printing Office, 1974), pp. 222-23.

45. Mary Jean Suelzle, "Women in Labor," *Transaction* 8 (November 1970): 50.

46. Arlene Skolnick, *The Intimate Environment: Exploring Marriage and the Family* (Boston: Little, Brown and Co., 1974).

47. Alice Rossi, "Equality between the Sexes: An Immodest Proposal," in *The Woman in America,* ed. Robert Lifton (Boston: Beacon Press, 1964), p. 113.

48. Norman Ryder, "The Family in Developed Counties," *Scientific American,* September 1974, pp. 123, 128.

49. Foote, p. 246.

50. *The Future of Marriage* (N.Y.: World Press, 1972), pp. 3-53.

51. Ibid., p. 48.

52. *New York Times,* 21 January 1974, p. 32.

53. *118 Congressional Record* S4372 (daily ed. March 21, 1972).

54. S. Rep. No. 97-689, 92d Cong., 2d sess. 49 (1972).

55. Ibid., pp. 40-42, 47-48.

56. Ibid., pp. 17-18.

57. Brown et al., p. 937.

58. Ibid., p. 941.

59. Ibid., p. 953.

60. Ibid., p. 946.

61. Ibid., p. 952.

62. S. Rep. No. 92-689, 92d Cong., 2d sess. 17-18 (1972).

63. Lenore J. Weitzman, "Legal Regulation of Marriage: Tradition and Change," *California Law Review* 62 (1974): 1185 fn 82.

64. Hannah Papanek, "Men, Women and Work: Reflections on the Two-Person Career," *American Journal of Sociology* 78 (January 1973): 852.

The Impact of the ERA on Criminal Justice and Crime

Harriet N. Katz

I. INTRODUCTION: SEXISM AND THE CRIMINAL LAW

At first glance, the task of predicting the impact of the elimination of sexism from the criminal law on society seems one that calls for wild speculation. Fortunately, however, feminists working on law reform have developed a sensitive understanding of sexism in the criminal law system and have already devoted considerable thought to the goals of reform.

Sexism permeates the criminal justice system. It appears most strikingly in the definition of substantive crimes involving sexual behavior; in law enforcement practices concerning sex crimes against women and assaults by husbands on their wives; in the double standard of delinquency that is common for male and female juveniles; and in the very different treatment of male and female offenders in penal institutions. Most of the differences have been harmful to women. Both adults and juvenile women are imprisoned for activity that is tolerated if carried on by men or boys; rape law enforcement is so inadequate that it has been blamed for widespread underreporting of the crime; and opportunities available to male prisoners are routinely denied to women, while, at the same time, men's prisons stand out as the more oppressive institutions.

The movement for legal equality of men and women has caused a reexamination of these distinctions. Feminists have exposed not only the day-to-day difficulties these discriminations cause but also, and more importantly, the crude cultural prejudices that created them. The thrust of the feminist critique is that classification by sex is always arbitrary and unjust. If some conduct is so deleterious as to require legal control in a free society, then we should apply criminal sanctions fairly to all rather than tolerating behavior in one sex while criminalizing it in the other.

The ERA will be a powerful tool for the elimination of sexism in the

206

criminal law. The first step will probably be the revision, through legislative change and court challenges, of explicitly discriminatory provisions in the statutes and regulations comprising the criminal law and governing law enforcement and correctional practices and facilities. As implementation of the equal rights principle proceeds, enforcers and administrators of the law, as well as the lawmakers and judges, will gain greater understanding of sexism in this area of the law, and hopefully will reexamine the sexism in their own behavior. The process of change will go further than the substance and administration of criminal law, however, because the movement for legal reform reflects a widespread movement to change the consciousness of men and women and to eliminate sexist relationships throughout society. Therefore, to the extent that some forms of criminal conduct are encouraged and generated by sexism, the movement for equal rights for individuals of both sexes offers hope of change in the nature and extent of criminal conduct itself. Such change will not appear overnight, nor is it guaranteed. This paper is an analysis of the long-range results of a conscientious reform effort, and is, therefore, a hope as well as a prediction. Moreover, by articulating the goals and possibilities inherent in Equal Rights Amendment-related reform, we can begin the educational process which must inform our efforts.

II. CRIMES AND LAW ENFORCEMENT

A. Male Crime against Women

1. Sexual Assault

Rape, from the act itself through the investigation and trial, is probably the most obviously sexist crime. The causes of rape are too complex and various to be thoroughly explored in this brief essay. Nevertheless, the frequency with which rape occurs suggests the dangerous effects of sexist ideology which portrays women as victims and men as tough aggressive conquerors. Males learn to express anger against other people violently. At the same time, females are taught to fear men and to believe themselves weak and men strong. Men are encouraged to develop physical strength and personal assertiveness; women are taught that athletic prowess and speaking up for oneself are unfeminine. As a result of this socialization, women's physical weakness is accentuated by their emotional readiness to be intimidated by men.

These features alone do not explain why men's attacks on women are so often sexual, however. To understand that, one needs to consider some of our society's views on sexual intercourse. One is that sex, even under normal circumstances, is a form of attack upon the female; another, that sexual experience, at least outside certain approved situations, is degrading to a woman. It isn't surprising, then, that an attack or effort to degrade a woman should take a sexual form.

The growth of the Women's Movement will change the sexist attitudes and behavior patterns of both women and men that seem to be related to sexual assault. Women are increasingly asserting their right of personal freedom of movement, refusing to confine themselves out of an inordinate fear of attack. Casual predictions have sometimes been that such conduct causes an increase in the number of rapes, but those comments are an outgrowth of the continuing pattern of blaming women victims for the assaults upon them. We will see in the discussion of law enforcement that this attitude must end if we are to have adequate rape law enforcement. In addition, women's assertiveness and self-confidence will ultimately aid in decreasing violence against them as they become less easily intimidated by men and even learn to defend themselves effectively. Greatly increased acceptance of women's sexuality and consequent changes in the relationships of women and men may also decrease the use of sexual assault to degrade women. Such a development will certainly increase women's willingness to report and prosecute rapes and improve the attitudes toward them of law enforcement personnel and juries. These changes themselves would aid in combating this crime.

In the investigation and trial of the attacker, more prejudicial attitudes about women and sexual attack are revealed. Women who were attacked under circumstances of not restricting their activities severely—by being in a public place alone, by permitting seemingly innocent contact with a stranger, by appearing or acting sexually attractive—find their credibility severely undermined. The average juror from the community apparently assumes that women lose the right that any male citizen enjoys to be free from physical attack if they step outside their cultural roles.

The message is: male sexual attacks on women are to be expected and, in that sense, are accepted by the community. It is women and not men who are responsible for preventing such attacks by being unavailable or unprovocative. Only if women behave according to the accepted rules are they entitled to a chivalrous containment of normal male aggression.

The anger of men against rapists on behalf of women victims has even been considered to grow from a threat to a property interest in the female's sexuality which society seems to give them. This point of view is reflected in differential law enforcers' attitudes toward rape victims, which vary, for example, from solicitous concern for a married white woman of good repute to callous disregard of a young black woman's complaint.

Furthermore, previous sexual history of the complainant is often permitted to color the jury's view of her credibility, despite its remoteness and irrelevance to the incident in question. "Force" under state law may be measured by the victim's resistance, even to the point of injury rather than by the defendant's own behavior. In investigation, police detectives are reported to be unbelieving and sometimes mocking. At trial, women have said they feel it is they who are being tried. The victim is treated so differently from ordinary prosecution witnesses that she is even called the "prosecutrix," as if she is in court only to present a peculiarly personal prosecution of the defendant, while any other victim of crime is a witness for the District Attorney who represents the "People's" or the "State's" interest in law and order.

Reform in the standard for admissibility of evidence and improvement in the treatment of rape victims by the law would increase the proportion of rapes reported because women's confidence that the criminal system will take such complaints seriously will increase. This change alone will remove one of the principal impediments to reporting rapes and following through in prosecution. In addition, social attitudes will gradually change, so that the woman victim is no longer implicitly blamed for the attack upon her; this, too, will aid in the willingness of women to report the crime.

2. Domestic Violence

Wife beating and its inadequate handling by the law is one of the most serious consequences of sexism. Although statistics are not precise because it has not yet been thoroughly studied, domestic violence has been cited as the cause of more than half of the citizen calls for police aid and one-fourth of all homicides. The problem is definitely not limited by social class despite common stereotypes.

In law enforcement, violence inflicted by a husband upon his wife is often not considered a serious crime, even when she is injured as a result. There is, in fact, a very troubling tendency to dismiss brutal treatment of a wife as deserved or provoked by disobedience, a cavalier attitude much like the legal exclusion of husbands from the prohibition against rape. Criminal handling of the complaint is further reduced as the man is usually charged with a "harassment" type of offense rather than the more serious assault and battery that it would be if committed outside of a marriage. Finally, an attempt is made to negotiate a peace between the parties oriented toward persuading the woman to drop charges. State attorneys are so uninterested in encouraging abused wives to press charges that, as in the case of rape, the burden of pressing forward with a prosecution in such cases is left to the woman herself. Yet, if she does not do so, her subsequent complaints of mistreatment are very likely to be discounted by both police and prosecutor.

Thus, both as a behavioral phenomenon and as a distinct problem in law enforcement, domestic violence raises critical issues arising directly from sexism, some of them similar to those of rape. Some men express anger at women by striking them rather than by more effective communication, possibly because they don't believe women and men can ever understand each other. The very different spheres and interests of wives and husbands in sexist society support such beliefs. Meanwhile, the extreme economic dependence of women on men, creating heavy burdens for both, create ample opportunity for built-up resentment. Some women learn to expect male aggression and will tolerate abuse.

Interest in solving the problem of domestic violence is beginning to increase as respect for women—and women's self-respect—increases. The minimal demand which will be made on the legal system to aid in this solution is immediate intervention on behalf of the woman's safety. At present, there are complaints that when police are called to intervene, violence sometimes resumes, even escalates, after they leave the home. As husbands' treatment of their wives is accepted as a legitimate matter for law enforcement, intervention will be increasingly effective in stopping a pattern of violent aggression. Also, the increasing demand by women for equal employment opportunity on police forces may aid this trend. Preliminary findings indicate that use of women officers reduced violence in domestic disturbance calls.

The most far-reaching hope offered by women's changing status and attitudes is the end of domestic violence as a common occurrence. All of the attitudes and behaviors which cause such behavior are rooted in sexism and are challenged by the movement for equality. It is most likely that fewer and fewer women will be willing to endure mistreatment. Their new self-confidence may itself reduce the likelihood of abuse to the extent that their abuse has been psychologically encouraged by their passivity. In the shorter run, women will be more willing and able to defend themselves vigorously. Finally, the equality of women and men offers a much greater possibility of mutual communication replacing violence as a means of resolving disputes.

3. Seduction, Adultery, and Similar Crimes

At present, the laws in an appreciable number of states include statutes which discriminate against women in such areas as seduction and adultery. Statutes such as those providing criminal punishment for males seducing females, usually under a certain age, obviously discriminate against men, but they are equally discriminatory against women in a variety of ways which are less evident. The presumption of seduction statutes is that women lack the emotional maturity to share in the decision to engage in sexual relations, that the male is the aggressor responsible for the act which shames the female. Even if it is agreed that a female may seduce a male, once again the woman and not the man is the degraded party.

Statutes which assume that adultery is a crime only when a married woman is involved make similar assumptions that women are not responsible for their own decisions in this area of private sexual behavior. Additionally, such laws reflect the classic societal bias that a woman is the property of the male, the husband being the proprietary party sinned against. While the male participant in the illicit relationship may be criminally liable, the woman generally receives a greater share of societal approbrium. Another aspect of such laws is that traditionally it has been not only legal but often acceptable to the point of being societally approved for married men to engage in sexual relations outside their own marriages.

As women are recognized as responsible for their own decisions about sex, societal control of women's sexual behavior will decreasingly take place through laws. Statutes which explicitly or implicitly allow proprietary treatment of women in sexual matters by husbands or fathers must disappear from the criminal codes. Only thus can equality exist in this area of life. Private decision making and institutionalized pressures such as those exerted by religion may then be of greater importance in determining trends in personal behavior.

B. Female Crime
1. Prostitution
Prostitution is considered a woman's crime. In the few states which provide criminal penalties for customers of prostitutes, enforcement is nonetheless biased, in part because of arrest strategy which ordinarily involves officers acting as decoy customers. Thus, only females are arrested and prosecuted, although men are obviously involved in the activity in equal or greater numbers. The uniformly discriminatory arrest patterns and the history of discriminatory statutes have provided wide open and unfortunate opportunities for police abuse and corruption. This discrimination is firmly based on a double moral standard that declares the female prostitute's conduct shocking (and, erroneously, the sole source of danger to public health), while it quietly accepts the conduct of her male customer.

Sex discrimination is only one and not the principal ground for criticism of prostitution laws, which has primarily emphasized the waste and discrediting of law enforcement resources that result from attempts to enforce them. From the viewpoint of constitutional rights, prostitution laws and related statutes are often case studies in the denial of due process resulting from vagueness, overbreadth, and infringement of the right of free speech and association. Sex discrimination itself has prompted some courts to uphold challenges to prostitution statutes as denial of equal protection; therefore, the Equal Rights Amendment would also seem to require careful review anywhere that discriminatory enforcement is prevalent. But the most irremediable defect of criminal prostitution laws is their conflict with the right of privacy, a personal constitutional right that is of growing importance. Privacy is a well-established right with respect to birth control and marriage and is certain to be firmly established as applying to all sexual matters between consenting adults. This principle will eventually result in decriminalizing much prostitution-related conduct.

Arguments concerning privacy and the abuse of law enforcement resources will probably have the most impact on the future of law in this area. Nevertheless, the equality movement can have considerable effect. First of all, sex discriminatory drafting or enforcement of statutes will not be permitted under the Equal Rights Amendment. In addition, public expectation is increasing that women and men will be treated equally before the law. Because the feminist movement has a strong respect for individual capabilities and interests, complementing its criticism of enforced sex roles, equality between the sexes in this area is likely to take the form of the decriminalization required by the privacy right.

2. Juvenile Offenders

The separate system of criminal courts and institutions for juveniles was instituted to improve their treatment by segregating them from adult prisoners and giving courts broader power over juveniles than they have over adults. "For their own protection" juveniles are detainable for unruly behavior that might be a forewarning of future criminal activity. As a result, minors may be declared "delinquent" for acts which would not be considered criminal if committed by adults. For instance, laws refer to "immoral, lewd or incorrigible behavior," a vague standard which can be interpreted as the court sees fit. Detention is also seen as a way to protect juveniles, to prevent them from engaging in criminal or antisocial activities or from associating with persons who do so. This protection has often meant that adults who are disturbed by a youngster's behavior can have the youngster placed in detention for acts such as running away from home, being truant, staying out late, or engaging in sexual relations.

Since the definition of what is prohibited behavior for minors is so vague, sexism is reflected both in the different definitions of delinquent behavior for and the treatment of girls and boys. The overwhelming majority of incidents for which boys are placed in detention are acts which would be criminal if committed by adults, many of them acts of violence. Girls, in contrast, are incarcerated primarily for sexual misbehavior, behavior which may be encouraged among boys. Furthermore, because the behavior considered appropriate for girls is so limited, girls who break out of the roles established for them are believed to be in need of more severe punishment than boys for doing similar things. As a result of these different standards, girls are usually placed in detention for longer periods of time than are boys even when less serious offenses are involved. In some states, boys and girls are even tried in different courts under explicitly different standards.

The disparity in both the types of behavior considered delinquent and the length of sentencing is clearly discriminatory and will be replaced by equal treatment for members of both sexes. Boys and girls will be allowed the same range of behavior; if the courts want to punish or ignore sexual behavior, they will do so equally for boys and girls. Once that standard is established, it will be impermissible for arbitrary distinctions to be made as to what is delinquent for girls only. Moreover, activities for which girls are now punished but which fall outside of what is considered criminal in adults will probably be removed from the laws. Sentencing will also become the same for both sexes.

The use of a juvenile detention system to "protect" girls by punishing their displays of strong or independent behavior is indicative of the extent of the patriarchal need to control women and will disappear as the system becomes more equitable. The tendency of girls to "act out" by engaging in sexual behavior frowned on by society and perhaps by becoming pregnant is further indication of the restrictions on women's life options which lead girls to see sexual relationships with men or motherhood as the only way to escape from parental and societal pressures. As women's roles in society change, girls will become able to explore the entire range of activities that contribute to the development of human character, which includes taking risks now only permitted boys. Adults will learn to reevaluate their stereotyped expectations of girls' behavior and needs, so that girls can find out what they are capable of handling instead of being controlled by rigid conceptions of how they must act.

The other side of social change in this area is the potential for reducing violent acts by boys as they are also permitted to depart from stereotyped roles. Boys' traditional conditioning in toughness and fighting often leads them to think that if being tough is good, being tougher is better, and that respect can best be won through violence against each other, property, and females rather than from responsive interaction with other people. As young boys begin to see girls as equals, they will change their behavior towards them. If they are allowed positive feelings towards girls and are allowed to express their feelings without fear of being labeled sissies, perhaps they will not develop the hostility that accounts for their violent behavior, including crimes like rape.

III. CORRECTIONS

Most correctional systems at both the federal and the state level maintain separate and very dissimilar institutions for incarcerated women and men with severe disadvantages to both. Segregation itself, because of the small number of incarcerated women, produces some of the differences. These include the relatively small inmate population of women's institutions, which is generally seen as an advantage, but also their extreme geographic isolation from family, lawyers, and familiar environments, their lack of a meaningful classification system, and their inaccessibility to many programs available to larger or more urban populations.

Program differences between men's and women's facilities were, at their inception, justified by extraordinary assumptions about the distinct nature of women offenders and the very different correctional philosophy which should be applied to them. Historically, male offenders have been viewed as inherently dangerous, therefore requiring not only extreme physical restrictions in the guise of security but also safe outlets for their energy. If rehabilitation is a goal, job skills are emphasized for men. Women, on the other hand, have been viewed as weak persons who were somehow led astray by others and were inadequate in their roles as wives and mothers. They need to learn homemaking skills and to live in a relatively comfortable cottagelike environment but have no particular need for education, employment, or exercise. It has even been noted that women's sentences for similar crimes are longer than men's because of the belief that their impressionability makes them particularly good candidates for rehabilitation by institutions. The result of these stereotypes has been that men's institutions tend to be large, lacking in privacy, oppressively structured, but reasonably close to the inmates' home community and providing some variety of rehabilitative opportunity; women's prisons are remote, provide virtually none of the opportunities afforded men, but are more comfortable physically.

Equal opportunity for programs and facilities in the prisons will be required under the ERA. Efforts to equalize prison opportunities will automatically raise the question of ending the sex segregation of prisons. As assumptions about women change and especially as the law no longer tolerates such vague assumptions, prison officials will no longer attempt to justify differential treatment as an intentional policy. Even now, the main excuses for unequal opportunity have shifted from ideology to more practical reasons of cost, security, and differential interests. The cost or even possibility of providing separate equal facilities to the much smaller women's institutions is a very real problem and will be resolved by integrating existing programs. Integration may be required wholly apart from the question of programming because of the severe impact of the remoteness of women's institutions as well as the clear impossibility of having separate facilities which are, in fact, equal.

Increased equality of opportunity for prisoners will provide a chance for improved rehabilitation and prerelease preparation. There will, first of all, be equality at the margin for those women and men whose interests do not fall into the average pattern for their sex and for those who might change their interests because of the opportunities. Secondly, sexually integrated populations will aid in the process of preparing prisoners for the community into which they will eventually be released. In the context of prerelease transition facilities, in fact, the irrationality of the security argument against sexual integration is most evident. Prisons will still need to be organized so as to protect women—or any prisoner—from assault by others. And an adequate classification and internal discipline plan should accomplish that goal without sacrificing all other aspects of equality.

The Social Order and the Equal Rights Amendment

Charles L. Elkins

Nature has given women so much power that the law has very wisely given them little.

—Dr. Johnson

Despite its being one of our few growth industries, future forecasting is a risky business. With all of their devotion to a rigorous methodology and to "hard data," contemporary futurologists have gained little advantage over their great nineteenth century predecessors—Comte, De Tocqueville, Spencer, and Marx—and their record is characterized by almost as many abysmal failures as limited successes. My students, for example, have been more than a little amused when I assign them Edwin Dale's "The Economics of Pollution," written in 1970.[1] Dale's gloomy predictions concerning our ecological crisis are based on what he calls the three "iron laws" of economic growth, one of which is the "inevitable" growth in production and the simultaneous increase in the Gross National Product. At the moment I am writing this, the GNP has been down for five consecutive quarters and is now "off" by more than ten percent. So much for the "iron laws" of economics. The issue, of course, is that if by knowledge we mean empirical knowledge, then we cannot "know" the future at all. We cannot know something which by definition does not exist.

On the other hand, whatever the logical validity of these observations, they are beside the point. We act as if we can determine the future. Indeed, it is only by creating images of the past and future that we can act at all. Our images of the future provide us with goals which direct our action in the present, and it is only by reference to a future that we can determine the efficacy of present action. Thus, those who oppose and those who urge the passage of the ERA do so by reference to their differing images of its effect on an imagined future state of affairs which each believes it will actualize. In a very real sense, all action is a leap of faith.

216

Nevertheless, taking these observations into account and trying to avoid any claims to certainty or even a privileged vantage point, I will make the leap and speculate on the impact that the ERA will have on the social order. Beginning with the premise that the sex hierarchy is a fundamental structural and functional component of the social order, I will try to address three major questions. Can the sex hierarchy (i.e., the relative status of women and men) be influenced by changes in one (i.e., the constitutional) sector of the legal hierarchy? How will these changes be brought about? Finally, will the passage of the ERA and these concomitant changes create problems, i.e., social disorder (a term relative to the status quo rather than a value judgment)? Basing my argument on our use of language to communicate and legitimize roles (in hierarchical communication) as well as the tendency of the "ultimate" hierarchical symbols upon which our Constitution is based to "spill over" into all areas of social hierarchy, I conclude that the answers to the first question must be "yes," and to the third question "temporarily," as the new and better order is being created. As for the second question, I assert that role changes are effected through "symbolic action," which may be described as a process in which traditional roles are symbolically demystified and new roles are sanctified by appealing to the very powerful symbols which are believed to sustain social order.

I

In an outlandish attempt to justify his burying the Equal Rights Amendment within the House Judiciary Committee for 47 years, Representative Emanuel Celler argued: "Men and women are as different as a horse chestnut and a chestnut horse. . . . Vive la difference."[2] Without commenting on the mentality which offered this argument, one should note the Congressman's resort to that familiar natural or biological analogy to justify existing social relations. Historically, the importation of words defining a biological state of affairs into the area of social relationships has served not merely to describe but to *legitimate* traditional social arrangements. Celler is presenting his *terms for order,* drawn from the "natural" order and superimposed on the social order. He justifies his actions by grounding them in nature rather than society.

There are many different "orders" with accompanying terminologies, the four major ones being: (1) the physical or natural order, (2) the supernatural or celestial order, (3) the social order with its role, class, and status distinctions, and (4) the order of language itself. There are also terms which "bridge" these four realms as well as terms which are explicitly of one realm but implicitly of another order (e.g., the designation of God as "Our

Father"). Moreover, these orders can be thought of as hierarchical in structure. The natural order can be seen as a development from the "lower" to the "higher" organic forms, or from "simple" to more "complex" molecular structures. One can think of the celestial order as proceeding from Humanity, through the various orders of angels, to God. The social order is expressed in terms such as "low," "middle," "high" class and exists in relations among "inferiors,""superiors," and "equals." The linguistic order can be seen as moving from "simple" structures, such as phonemes, to more "complex" structures, such as sentences, and in the semantic hierarchy as climbing the ladder of abstraction from terms of relatively "low"-level abstraction to terms of very "high" levels of abstraction.

The *social* and *linguistic* orders are inevitably commingled because language is a social product and society is a linguistic product. Their interaction makes possible the transformation, borrowing, and smuggling of symbols from one order to another that is characteristic of humankind's symbolic activity—call it "metaphoring"—which allows us to experience our world from an almost infinite variety of perspectives. We borrow terms from the physical world to describe ourselves and our society. We describe a person as a "thinking machine"; we say that someone is as "solid as a rock"; we talk about the "social bond," "organic communities," and social "forces" on the "body politic." Conversely, computers become giant "brains," ants are "social" animals, and mountains are "noble." We borrow terms from the social world to characterize the metaphysical and vice versa: Mary is the Mother of God, and kings once ruled by "divine right." And the metaphysical can invade the physical, as when we recognize the "spirit" of a place and designate it a church, temple, or synagogue. The nature of language and the symbolic process allows us to borrow terminology appropriate to one hierarchy and apply it to other hierarchies. It is a characteristically *human* process which, when abused, can create distinctively *in*human situations. Let us, then, consider the particular linguistic connections between the social and natural orders, transformations which create the sex hierarchy and provide the rationale for sexism.

Notwithstanding the possibility that we are giving Celler's pronouncement a more serious treatment than it manifestly deserves, we must point out that his analogy is even more preposterous than it might appear to be. The analogy has nothing to do with legal rights. In nature, neither the horse chestnut nor the horse have any rights. There are no "rights" in nature. Rights are human creations and have nothing to do with nature.

All living things need space. All animals respond to the "territorial imperative." However, space is not a "right"; it is a necessity. The horse chestnut and the chestnut horse must have space. However, we have created symbolic analogues for this "need." The biological necessity for space in the natural world has been transformed into "property rights" and "private property" in the social world. With our facility for universalizing symbols, we have extended this concept of "rights" where no biological necessity exists. "Rights" and "obligations" are, then, particularly "human" (as opposed to "natural") creations whose forms are determined by the possibilities of language. Unlike the "laws" of nature, they are neither eternal nor immutable. While they may be grounded initially in the natural order of biological necessity (i.e., unconscious drives, instincts), they are expressed and take on meaning *only* within human symbol systems.

Nevertheless, historically, terms such as "natural law" and the "laws of nature" are prescriptive. They are tied to norms. It is often believed that there is a close relationship between "natural" human laws and physical laws. Moreover, the same basic laws of the universe are believed to govern human conduct as govern physical nature. Although modern science insists that the latter are purely "descriptive," they are often considered to regulate the phenomena to which they refer. From the very beginning of political and legal philosophy, the concept of natural law has exercised enormous influence. The order of nature has served as a ground for social order, and the social order has influenced the "order" we see in the natural world.

Thus, sexual differentiation, which is a consequence of biological evolution, is given meaning within the sociolinguistic realm that it does not possess in nature. What does the male-female difference signify in nature? Nothing; it simply exists. But *we* have made much of the difference. For example, the English word for *woman* comes from the Old English *wif-man,* i.e., "wife man." The suggestion is that the female is merely an effeminate male and, in a patriarchal social structure, the male represents "true" humanity. As a consequence, in many languages including English, *man,* as in *mankind,* refers to the total population as well as to males specifically. In fact, all Germanic languages associate hu*man*ity with the male. The German *Mensch,_* signifying "man" as a human being comes from the word *mannisko,* the adjectival form of *man;* it indicates that the "human" is not simply "man" but "mannish." The conclusion is obvious: if the male represents total humanity, the woman has little to say. (A sidenote: because the "woman" does not represent humanity in her own right but is derived from the man, her name is often taken as a derivative of a male name.)[3] Hence, the *male-female* "biological" distinction perceived in the natural order takes on enormous social implications when it is transformed into the *man-woman* polarity in social terminologies.

II

At the same time, this ordering of terms constitutes the social order, which is created and sustained by the communication of hierarchy. One learns one's role in the social order in communication with others. In addition, these terminologies usually originate in public documents which function to legitimate institutions whose power rests on their ability to maintain social order. In any complex social order there are several institutions which compete for an individual's allegiance. Religious, political, economic, social, artistic, scientific, familial, educational institutions—sometimes in concert, oftentimes in conflict—vie for our loyalties. This paper focuses on a limited change in the terminology of our legal hierarchy—the Constitution; however, changes in the legal hierarchy are particularly significant because the Law is so closely linked with the very foundations of social order. American democracy is founded upon and legitimated through the rule of law.

The ERA will, in a very literal sense, alter a basic document which has given form to our particular social order. Again, social order is always expressed in specific forms, and these forms must be communicated and interpreted to everyone. Symbolic creations, such as the Constitution, the Federalist Papers, the Monroe Doctrine, the Gettysburg Address, the Pledge of Allegiance, and the 1954 Supreme Court Decision on segregation, are documents serving as "charters" for our social order. They articulate the structure of the social hierarchy, and, in particular, they express those "god terms"—the ultimate symbols—upon which all of the various hierarchies are structured and integrated. They are similar in function to the various myths of origin which serve as the foundation for social order in more "primitive" societies. A more familiar example of a social charter would be the Bible, which served as a myth of origin and the foundation for Western social order in the Middle Ages; practically all medieval institutions and personal relationships were legitimated and hierarchically ordered through an interpretation of Scripture.

Our Constitution operates as a myth of origin and as a social charter. The very definition of *constitution* reveals its basic *formative* function; in Webster's *Third* (unabridged), one finds the following:

1. a. an authoritative ordinance or enactment;
   b. an established law or settled custom;
2. the act of establishing, making or setting up; . . .
4. the mode or manner in which something is constituted, constructed, or organized: the structure, composition or physical make up, or nature of anything; . . .

5. the mode in which a state or society is organized; . . .
6. a system or body of fundamental rules and principles of a nation, state, or body politic that determines the powers and duties of government and guarantees certain rights to the people.

A legal constitution is a symbolic act created to serve as a motivational ground of "subsequent actions, it being thus an instrument for the shaping of human relations."[4] The Constitution and similar documents, functioning as myths of origin, express the "god terms"—"justice," "domestic tranquility," "one nation under God," "the general welfare," "government of the people, by the people, for the people"—by which hierarchical conflicts are resolved. They are the symbols of ultimate appeal.

The ERA will revise one of our basic myths of origin, one of our basic social charters. At the very least, it will codify and make explicit the belief that "equity" and "justice" transcend the various conflicts engendered by the meanings we attach to the man-woman polarity in our culture. As a constitutional amendment, the ERA will provide legal sanction for resolving those social contradictions which result from the clashing of roles sanctified by tradition with the obvious need for hierarchical change.

I have used the expression *social order* without elaboration. However, it may be helpful for an understanding of the effects of the ERA on our society to examine the social order and the ways in which it changes.

Society originates in and is sustained by the communication of significant symbols which makes cooperation possible. (Significant symbols are those symbols that have essentially the same meaning for the person communicating as they do for the person receiving the communication.) This communication allows people to relate to themselves and to others.[5] Social *order* within a specific society is crated in hierarchical communication in which people are distinguished as inferiors, equals, or superiors in terms of their sex, rank, class, status group, and other styles of life. While many of these distinctions may function in harmony with one another (i.e., they are "socially integrated"), it is also often the case that these differences may be in contradiction or competition with one another. Hence, it is also the function of communication to resolve these contradictions through reference to the "ultimate" principles upon which the hierarchy is grounded.

Conflicts are resolved, and loyalty and obedience are given when order is legitimated. These "legitimations," as Max Weber calls them, may refer to tradition, usage, charisma, and law. We may resolve conflicts by reference to a revered past (tradition); we can rule others by virtue of demanding what has always been done in a specific way (usage); we may be advised to follow the dictates of a leader because he has access to some sacred Truth or power (charisma); we may appeal to the Law because law creates equality among people. Legitimations, rights, or whatever term we use to designate the integrative factors in social life, may refer to nature (human or physical), to a particular role, to methods, ways, instruments (i.e., when we believe that how we do something determines the validity of what we do), or to awesome mystifications, such as those symbols which refer to the nation itself, an ideology, a way of life, God, or some cosmology.

Moreover, at any particular historical moment some of these legitimations will be more legitimate than others; to paraphrase George Orwell, all god terms are equal but some god terms are more equal than others. In the eighteenth century, for example, the "law of Nature" became equated with God's "law"; the laws of nature were an expression of the will of God, and God the Father became God the First Cause. Where before social terminology had invaded the metaphysical, now the natural—the mechanistic —invaded the supernatural. We have discussed the possible consequences of this kind of linguistic transformation. For example, racial differences (i.e., natural differences) could be thought of as expressing God's will. Furthermore, if a political constitution were an expression of God's will and natural law, it would be obliged to take these "differences" into account. And if the God of the framers of the Constitution happened to be white, so much the worse for those "colored" folk who happen to come under the law. These ultimate symbols resolve contradictions which arise in any hierarchical system by "transcending" those terms upon which the contradictions are based. Traditionally, the rationale for denying equality to blacks was grounded in Nature, i.e., their supposed "natural inferiority." The same argument has been used against women. The laws of God and Nature transcended any human-made laws based on equality, i.e., were considered more universal, more ultimate in priority. Though neither God nor Nature has the majesty and power it once did, both are still effective in providing the motivational ground for human action.

However, as nature is increasingly subject to human control, as it becomes more secularized and its laws understood, hence demystified, it becomes more and more difficult to use nature as a sacred principle for social order. Its powers of "legitimation" have become less than ultimate. As Herman Kahn and Anthony Wiener point out, Western society has moved and continues to move inexorably toward "institutionalized secular, manipulative rationality."[6] More and more, the Law itself (i.e., the laws of government) asserts its primacy. Samuel E. Stumpf, the distinguished legal scholar, makes the observation, "Modern man's life is controlled more effectively, forcefully, and in greater detail by law than by any other agency of social control."[7] Stumpf goes on to say that few laws can command unanimous approval, but there is now a kind of morality which compels one to *obey the law because it is the law*.

> The fact that a law is morally deficient does not immediately lead to disobedience of the law, for there is still the second basis [other than conforming to existing morality] of obligatoriness, namely, that the system of law, the rule of law that encompasses the remaining rules and procedures, must be upheld.[8]

The Law, the rule of law and the rules of law, as well as those transcendental principles upon which the law itself is based—"order," "equity," "right," "justice"—are now legitimations which transcend both sacred and natural symbols of legitimation. Today, it is generally accepted that social order is grounded not in Nature or God but in Law. As the Watergate affair has demonstrated, even the charisma of the Presidency, or the appeal to the "national interest," or the tradition of "executive privilege" —legitimations in their own right—are not more ultimate than the law. We say that no person is above the law; the law applies equally (in theory at least) to all.

III

The ERA will alter our present social order, but it will not change the way in which this order is attained. In fact, the symbolic appeals made by those urging the enactment of the ERA provide a clear illustration of the way in which social order is achieved. The immediate result of the ERA will be the alteration of the Constitution and the legal precedents, anchored in constitutional law, which have historically been advantageous to men. (The intimate relationship between the legal and the moral order makes the ERA's consequences a great deal more far-reaching; however, for the moment my concern is limited to the legal order.) The ERA will make explicit what has until now been merely implicit (if that), namely, that women cannot be denied equal rights because of their sex. Notice, however, that the proponents of the ERA are not attacking the law as such. Quite the contrary, they are trying to "purify" the legal order by appealing to its ultimate principles, the god terms upon which the legal hierarchy is based, i.e., "equity," "justice," "the general welfare," "inalienable rights," etc. These ultimate terms are believed to transcend any contradictions and conflicts within the legal order. They are the terms which are invoked to enact or repeal laws legitimated by some assumed social, natural, historical, or metaphysical differences. (Although it should be noted that laws based on "discrimination'' are not automatically considered unjust, e.g., the age and citizenship requirements for voting and holding public office, the ''rights'' of a convicted felon, the ''rights'' of minors.)

From one perspective, it can be argued that the ERA will simply alter constitutional law, merely one of the hierarchies in our social order, and will not significantly change the other hierarchies in our society. Indeed, this is one of the arguments voiced by some ERA advocates. A flyer put out by the League of Women Voters says that the ERA ''will remove sex as a factor in determining the *legal* rights of men and women. It will primarily affect government action. It *will not* interfere in private relationships.''[9] The choice of the word ''interfere'' is obviously a conscious rhetorical strategy. It helps to placate those who are anxious about the unknown and perhaps unintended consequences of the ERA on the entire social structure. Certainly the passage of the ERA will affect our private lives. Indeed, it is inconceivable that it would have no influence on other hierarchical relationships. The various hierarchies which constitute our social order are not separate, autonomous entities which have their own dynamics and are unaffected by other hierarchical shifts.

In the first place, pressure brought to bear on our legal system for the passage of the ERA originated not solely or even largely within the legal hierarchy itself—a notoriously resistant, conservative institution—but from without, from contradictions generated in the economic, social, political, and cultural arenas, all of which found and are finding powerful voices within the contemporary feminist movements. The ERA is the recognition, the formal acknowledgment, of principles that are now beginning to assert themselves as rules and precepts governing the conduct of everyday social relationships.

In the second place, society is a seamless web of relationships in which the deformation of one strand produces harmonic distortions throughout the entire network. This reverberation effect is particularly characteristic of legislative action. Any accurate prior determination of the ultimate scope and ramifications of the ERA is quite impossible. As Professor Stumpf observes: ''The breadth of the law's concern is in no wise suggested by what the nature of the law is. Whether the law will be used narrowly or widely is a matter not of the meaning or nature of the law but a consequence of a society's decision about its use. . . . And in the United States the law has gradually absorbed many areas of behavior that might well be considered the proper province of morals.''[10] Discussing the expanding role of law, Stumpf makes some comments which seem particularly relevant for speculating on the future impact of the ERA:

> The scope of the law seems to increase as a society becomes more sensitive to how men "ought" to be living or how the social life of man can be improved. At each step in the march of law there is resistance to its invasion into previously "free" domains of human behavior; at the same time there is constant pressure for the law to move into these previously uncontrolled areas. What at one time were considered the minimal concerns of the law have been over the years so elaborately reconceived as to proliferate the law's influence with astonishing thoroughness.[11]

Undoubtedly, Sebastien Chamfort was correct when he said that "it is easier to make certain things legal than to make them legitimate." The obverse is also undoubtedly true: it is easier to make certain things illegal than to make them illegitimate. The failure of Prohibition taught us this.

Nevertheless, all institutions, including our legal institutions, seeking to legitimate and sustain their influence on society, must compete with other institutions for power. This struggle is manifest in each institution's attempt to "universalize" and "perfect" the ultimate symbols upon which its hierarchy rests. That is to say, terms such as "justice," "equality," and "fairness," the ultimate terms upon which our legal hierarchy is founded, are symbols of such power and majesty that they are capable of taking on a life of their own outside the legal hierarchy and of gravitating toward and linking up with other hierarchies. For example, we apply our legal terminology and its ultimate symbols to religious doctrine. Some religions would maintain that God himself is "legally bound" by concepts of "justice" and "fairness." God must be "fair" and "equitable" in his dealings with humankind. Similarly, we apply our legal terminology to the inanimate world; we talk about the "laws" of nature and label as "lawless" those irregularities which we discover but cannot explain. Law pervades the natural and supernatural worlds as well as the social order.

Our veneration for the law, its institutions, its documents, and the symbols which legitimate this hierarchy, and our belief that the law is an accurate reflection of our moral order as well as the foundation for social order, make such ultimate symbols as "justice" and "equity" very powerful indeed. By the same token, once these symbols are linked with other powerful symbols—God, Reason, Order—they become effective in resolving contradictions outside the realm of the strictly legal. If such appeals to "justice" and "equity" can be used to resolve legal conflicts between men and women, it is in the very nature of symbolic activity that these same potent symbols will be applied to other areas of human relationships.

IV

How will this work in practice? The ERA will significantly modify one of the basic documents which defines power relations in our society. It will change one of the criteria by which social classifications are made, especially the criteria by which one is classed as an "inferior," "superior," or "equal." Perhaps it may be easier to understand what this change entails if we conceive of society as a "drama of human relations," in which each person is assigned a variety of roles. The ERA will be a revision of an existing "script" (the Constitution) which has historically left undefined the legal rights and obligations attached to being a woman. More accurately, while the ERA does not define specific roles, it will expand the parameters within which society must accommodate women, both in their traditional roles and in new roles. Traditionally, the law "has frequently been considered as playing the role of an umpire, watching the race only to insure that nobody is pushed off the track or tripped. It is not the function of law to make sure that everybody wins the race but only that the lanes are kept clear."[12] At the same time, given the historical handicaps forced upon women, think of the implications of Stumpf's comments! For the first time, the "lanes will be clear" for women. With no one around to push them off the track, women will run a different race. Indeed, it will not be the same race, or to use the dramatic metaphor, the passage of the ERA will change the meaning of the roles themselves. We know this: a change in the script changes the play. For better or worse, it will no longer be the same drama.

In this play of social relationships we call society, roles are created and sustained by communication. No one is born knowing a role. The script is written by society as a style of behavior which must then be internalized by the individual. Michael Banton offers a definition of "role" which uses the dramatic metaphor:

> Every member of a social unit, be it a ship, a football team or a nation has one or more parts to play. He has tasks to perform and is entitled to receive services from other people in recognition of his contributions. These clusters of rights and obligations constitute roles.[13]

Roles are not private; on the contrary, they are public and are not created by specific individuals but are ongoing forms of social behavior which exist prior to and after any one individual who fills them.

The theatrical metaphor is particularly appropriate because it allows one to examine how the changes in women's roles will affect the rest of the social order. For example, it is clear that every dramatic role entails the cooperation between the actor who plays the role and the other actors in the drama. Desdemona can play her assigned role—e.g., she can be Othello's "property"—only if Othello, Iago, her parents, and the other actors permit her to do so. In his classic study of social roles, Florian Znaniecki argues: "We shall find in every social role a social circle within which the individual performs it, that is, a set of agents who accept him and cooperate with him. If no such circle exists, the individual cannot actually perform a social role, though he may imagine that he does, like a daydreaming child who identifies himself with some person he wishes to be, or a pathological adult who believes that he is some great hero."[14]

Legislative fiat cannot force cooperation in all areas of social life. Roles are "played out" as we relate to each other as inferiors, superiors, and equals. The ERA will insure equality under the law, but friendship—a relationship possible only among equals—can never be forced; it must be freely given. However, as one of the many "Thou shalt nots" which constitute our social order, the ERA (having the prestige of constitutional law) will legitimate equality in other areas of human relationships and provide the symbolic ground for cooperation. Once the script has been altered, there will be a drive to make the other roles and the drama itself "consistent" with the new legal status of one of the principal actors and to overcome whatever contradictions result from this newly acquired status.

Extending the theatrical metaphor further, one can argue, as Znaniecki does, that "every theatrical role is *culturally patterned*—every actor who later creates it has to learn the pattern from the author's work, and is supposed to follow it." Similarly, "social roles are also culturally patterned; individuals who perform them are supposed to learn the patterns and follow them." Each role is "defined and evaluated according to certain standards, and it is [the actor's] duty to act in accordance with definite norms. [But] he cannot perform his role adequately, unless the participants in his circle have also learned to follow certain cultural patterns."[15]

With the passage of the ERA, a new cultural pattern will come into being which will alter the traditional relationships among men and women. If the ERA is an idea whose time has come, then it will simply codify what has already become custom. However, if the custom itself is creating serious problems, the process can be reversed, and custom may be changed by legislative action. There is an obvious difference between the external complusion of the law and the pressure of cusom. Law *commands* us to act; whereas custom influences us to *choose* to act in a specific way. However, we do not obey the law solely because it is commanded. We are willing to be bound by law because, in addition to the instrumentalities available for enforcing the command, the command is legitimated in powerful symbols. It "makes sense" (reason); it is "fair" (justice); it is "for our own good" (the general welfare); it is the "law" (order). Naturally, society runs smoothest when legal imperatives become merely the codification of moral imperatives which accurately size up the particular historical situation out of which they arise. However, one must keep in mind that it is a reciprocal relationship: on the one hand, social change undermines custom, and the new custom becomes codified as law; on the other hand, law itself is a force for social change.

As it is incorporated into one of our basic myths of origin, the ERA will establish the framework within which new roles can be legitimated. It is, in a sense, as if the "author" of a drama had changed one of the fundamental hierarchical relationships in his play, as if Shakespeare initially assumed that Desdemona was a "free woman," that she could not be the possession of any man. What could have served as the motivational grounds for the action in *Othello?* What if there had been a dramatic convention which said in effect: Thou shalt not treat women as inferiors! What kind of drama would have been possible?

Finally, just as actors seldom interpret a specific social role in exactly the same way (there have been almost as many "Othellos" and "Desdemonas" as actors who have played Othello and Desdemona), so too when individuals perform a social role which conforms to some cultural pattern, their performances also vary. These variations, Znaniecki argues, should also be examined,

> for they may be socially significant to other participants in social life, e.g., the authoritative judges who maintain established cultural patterns of specific social roles, the social circles within which these roles are performed, the other performers who are supposed to follow the same cultural patterns, and the community members who are concerned with the influence such variations may have on their own lives. Just as in theatrical roles, while many variations are treated as minor manifestations of personal differences within the cultural pattern, some variations are judged to be undesirable transgressions which must be repressed; whereas certain other innovations, on the contrary, are considered desirable by thinkers who are critics of traditional patterns, and these can eventually lead to the emergence of new kinds of roles.[16]

The ERA will function as a symbolic court of appeal for those seeking to repress the traditional and justify the emerging roles for women.

The concept of human social life as a "drama" is as old as the beginning of social philosophy and dates from Plato's use of it in his *Philebus,* through the sixteenth and seventeenth century with their *Theatrum Mundi* and Shakespeare's declaration that "all the world's a stage,/And all the men and women merely players," to such modern theorists as Kenneth Burke, Hugh

Duncan, and Erving Goffman. While the metaphor has no special claim to absolute Truth, it is useful in thinking about the nature of social roles (the term *role* itself is derived from drama) and the effect of the ERA on our social hierarchy.

V

The ERA will not create specific roles for women, but it will establish the legal rights of women to play certain roles. "Rights," as Stumpf observes, "have their initial form in morals, and the legal rule is the official recognition and technical means of enforcement of rights."[17] The ERA will create new parameters around which roles will be constructed and construed. Ultimately, the various roles assumed by women and the status of these roles in the social hierarchy will be determined, in a large measure, by those institutions which control the creation and distribution of symbols: government, business, religion, the mass media, and art most pointedly. Power is influence; influence is power. Power rests on the ability of an institution to persuade its audience to share its view of reality, to use its symbols to create social order. Let there be no mistake about it: the struggle for women's rights will be fierce. Some institutions have a vital stake (so they believe) in maintaining traditional roles. Those who benefit from the status quo will not surrender without a fight, and the institutions which are male-dominated will share power only when they are convinced it is in their interests to do so. The threat of legal sanctions may be necessary for them to become convinced. As long as business can reap enormous profits by depicting powerless, mindless women who please their families only through appropriate forms of consumption, it will try to keep women in that role.

On the other hand, institutions maintain power only to the extent that they are able to convince us that they can create social order by solving the everyday problems confronting us. Further, they must not only communicate traditional roles, but when traditional roles are no longer functional, they must offer us new roles as well as passage from the old role to the new one. This is done through symbolic acts. Traditional roles are "demystified" through satire, comedy, and ridicule. New metaphors are created to gain new perspectives on and to explore the meaning of the traditional role as well as the new role. Finally, our sacred symbols, our "god terms," are associated with the new role and function to legitimize it in the social order.

One would suspect that initially there will be a period characterized by a conglomeration of symbols (words, images, metaphors, etc.) which redefine (demystify) the role of women in the social hierarchy. Indeed, this is already the case, and this redefinition is affecting all institutions. Women have been identified with oppressed minorities and have taken on many of their attributes. Our best symbol makers, the artists, are making a sustained symbolic attack on traditional female stereotypes. For example, in "The woman in the," Marge Piercy writes:

> The woman in the
> ordinary pudgy graduate student girl
> is crouching with eyes and muscles clenched.
> Round and smooth as a pebble
> you efface yourself
> under ripples of conversation and debate.
> The woman in the block of ivory soap
> has massive thighs that neigh
> and great breasts and strong arms that blare and trumpet.
> The woman of the golden fleece
> laughs from the belly uproariously
> inside the girl who imitates
> a Christmas card virgin with glued hands.
> It is time to bust out of girlscout camp.
> It is time to stop running
> for the most popular sweetheart of Campbell Soup.
> You are still searching for yourself in others' eyes
> and creeping so you won't be punished.
> In you bottled up is a woman peppery as curry,
> a yam of a woman of butter and brass,
> compounded of acid and sweet like a pineapple,
> like a handgrenade set to explode,
> like a goldenrod ready to bloom.[18]

The language itself is undergoing revision. Children's textbooks are examined for instances of sexism. The social address, *Ms.*, is no longer a joke and has been officially adopted by many institutions. It is standard procedure nowadays to speak of *chairperson*. These symbols are functioning as bridging devices as old roles are changed and new roles emerge. Women have had their consciousness "raised" (note the hierarchical symbol!) by words such as "liberation," "unisex," "androgyous," etc., which encourage the blurring of traditional roles. Other symbols, very powerful symbols, are being attached to new female roles, e.g., "freedom," "equality," "partner," "friend"; these symbols sanctify and legitimate new, nontraditional styles of life. Many of these same terms will be employed in the future because they are the ultimate "terms for order" upon which our society rests.

At the same time, we are witnessing a search for new symbols, and while this exploration can be a liberating experience for those involved in it, the uncertainty and anxiety inevitably accompanying the death and rebirth of symbols of identity will be significant and widespread. There is a hint of the problem in Florence Howe's "Introduction" to the anthology containing Piercy's poem:

> We are not men, nor do we want to be. We are interested in our differences, in the range and possibilities of our development. We want to know ourselves and our history. We want to examine our relationships with men, with our children and our parents; we want to discover our relationships with women.
>
> Most of all, we want to shout NO MORE MASKS! . . . No more masks, especially not the oldest of these, the mask of maleness.[19]

With all of the negatives, this is a positive statement of purpose. At the same time, there is an implicit recognition that women are not sure of themselves nor certain of their roles, their history, and their relationships with others. Why should they be? The search for authentic, workable symbols to redefine new roles and for the expressive forms which women can use to create new social relationships is and will continue to be a formidable and at times dangerous task. We should expect wide-ranging experimentation with different life styles.

Furthermore, while all institutions will be involved in this search—if for no other reason than to make certain that the search does not threaten the institution's interests—it is in art where most of the experimentation will be carried out. We develop forms of social relationships in communication, but it is in art that these forms are perfected. Indeed, if one accepts a definition of art as the "conscious exploration through the imagination of the *possibilities* of human action in society,"[20] then art becomes *the* institution within which the new roles will be created and their meanings explored. Already women writers are seeking to chart what it means to be a woman and what it means to act in specific roles in specific social institutions. These artists will become increasingly significant as they create specific roles which give expressive form to the values, beliefs, and desires of women acting out these roles in various phases of social action. These writers will examine the meaning of these new roles. They will inspire their audiences to take the practical action necessary to realize specific ends. They will create the forms by which women can express their deepest fantasies and wishes which at present may appear a threat to their oppressors. They will depict the necessary struggle for freedom and social justice. They will point out the incongruity between the means and the ends in social action. They can point to the contradictions between methods and goals because art is one of the few institutions which sanctions the expression of doubt, ambiguity, irony, and disrespect. Hence, it is within art that the old roles will be destroyed and new roles created. Ultimately, it will be the symbolic acts of the artist which will legitimate these new roles. Artists will glamorize those symbols which transcend hierarchical conflict based on sex. They will dignify, ennoble, and spiritualize the symbols which stand for equality and justice in male-female relationships and give these symbols such a sacred aura that institutional, status, or national demands will become intimately linked with women's liberation.

If the ERA is passed and if, as we suppose, the symbolic prestige of the Constitution is able to "spill over" and attach itself to other areas of social life, then we will enter upon a new and radically different period of human relationships. For the first time on any large scale, men and women will be able to relate as "friends." Historically this has been impossible because, as one sociologist notes: "Friendship, the most profound of freely given social relationships, is possible only among equals, as Confucius ('Have no friends not equal to yourself.') and Aristotle remind us. It cannot be taken, forced, demanded, bought or sold, but must be given, and given by equals."[21] Has there ever been a work of art depicting men and women relating as *friends,* relating not sexually, not Platonically, not romantically, not in roles of submission and dominance, but as friends? I think not. Friendship has been possible only between children not between mature adults, for by the time we become adults, our roles are fixed. And in the interaction of the sexes, these roles have always been ones of superiors and inferiors, not equals. Finally and most significantly, because the ties of friendship are self-imposed and can be sundered by either party, it is only as men and women relate as friends that they can both come to understand what it means to be free and equal.

Footnotes

1. *The New York Times Magazine,* April 19, 1970; reprinted in *Futures Conditional,* ed. Robert Theobald (Indianapolis and New York: Bobbs-Merrill, 1972), pp. 157-66.

2. Quoted in *Juxtaposition,* ed. J. Burl Hogins and Gerald A. Bryant, Jr. (Palo Alto, Calif.: Science Research Associates, 1971), p. 101.

3. Much of the above discussion is taken from Theodore Thass-Thienemann, *The Subconscious Language* (New York: Washington Square Press, 1967), pp. 324-25.

4. Kenneth Burke, *A Grammar of Motives* (1945; reprint ed., Berkeley and Los Angeles: University of California Press, 1969), p. 341. Those familiar with the work of Kenneth Burke and Hugh Duncan will recognize my obvious dependence upon them throughout this paper.

5. Cf. George Herbert Mead, *Mind, Self and Society* (Chicago, 1934). Mead argues that the "self" arises in the communication of significant symbols.

6. "Faustian Powers and Human Choices: Some Twenty-First Century Technological and Economic Issues," in *Futures Conditional,* pp. 56-57.

7. "The Moral Order and the Legal Order," in *The Concept of Order,* ed. Paul G. Kuntz (Seattle and London: University of Washington Press, 1968), p. 385.

8. Ibid., p. 402.

9. *The ERA: What It Means to Men and Women,* Pub. No. 272 (Wash., D.C.: National League of Women Voters, September 1974), p. 2.

10. Pp. 397-98.

11. Ibid., p. 398.

12. Ibid., p. 396.

13. *Roles: An Introduction to the Study of Social Relations* (New York: Basic Books, 1965), p. 2.

14. *Social Relations and Social Roles* (San Francisco: Chandler, 1965), p. 203.

15. Ibid., pp. 203-204.

16. Ibid., pp. 204-205.

17. P. 401.

18. In *No More Masks!: An Anthology of Poems by Women,* ed. Florence Howe and Ellen Bass (Garden City, New York: Anchor-Doubleday, 1973), p. 247.

19. Ibid., p. xxviii.

20. Hugh Duncan, *Language and Literature in Society* (Chicago: University of Chicago Press, 1953), p. 3.

21. Hugh Duncan, *Symbols in Society* (New York: Oxford University Press, 1968), p. 87.

PSYCHOLOGICAL IMPACT

Introduction to Psychological Impact

The connection of attitudinal to legal change must be made. In view of the somewhat overwhelming obstacles to the implementation of ERA charted by our writers thus far, it might seem that the ERA's symbolic impact is its only claim to efficacy. While this is perhaps a pessimistic projection, we should not underestimate the social and psychological power of symbols.

The very length and complication of the state ratification process of a constitutional amendment effectively dramatizes its significance and the gravity of its sanction. The difficulty which the ERA's 52 year career has encountered will, ironically, increase its symbolic power when it is finally ratified. There will be no way to "sluff it off" lightly in view of the herculean effort marshalled to legally recognize its necessity. The entire drama of ratification is an elaborate *rite de passage* for women, and, indeed, it will literally mean the initiation of women into society, the coming of age of women heretofore considered legal minors.

Symbols are not static icons; they *act* to create social order. A social system ordered by hierarchies of different types needs to find some way to ensure the contentment of those at the bottom of each hierarchical ladder, to prevent their dissatisfaction with an order which dooms them to receive little of the rewards most valued by the society. To quell the dissatisfaction of the lower classes with their lack of access to monetary rewards, for example, our society invented the powerful symbol of the Horatio Alger myth, which dramatizes individual freedom and unlimited opportunity in a free enterprise system as the dominant American principle. Faced with "failure" the individual blames him/herself, not the society. The myth creates social order. In the sex hierarchy, where women are the devalued "class," our society invented such myths as sacred motherhood and the "natural" biological differentiation of the sexes to mystify and pretend to value that which is actually not valued, to make women content with and even glory in "woman's place." The myths create social order.

Dramatize a change in the symbolic structure of society, especially at the hallowed constitutional level (the Constitution itself being a powerful symbol of order for the American people), and you have an effective weapon for transforming social order, for changing the social and

235

psychological ways people interact with each other.

The limitations to psychological ERA implementation, i.e., female and male fears of equality, are evidence of the viselike hold these myths have on the American imagination. Nothing short of the collapse of social and sexual relations between the sexes is feared as a result of giving women equal rights under the law. The relationship between the sexes at all stages has been ritualized to the point of paralysis. It is appropriate that Jean Mundy's antifeminist is a married woman, since the institution of marriage is the most ritualized form of that relationship. Marriage is certainly a prominent factor militating against participation in a movement for equal rights insofar as women fear their husbands and the loss of their "comfortable," if not "valued," status and insofar as marriage itself often prevents the development of a strong individual identity and self-concept in women. Ironically, though, it has been shown that the mental strain of traditional marriage (i.e., inequality between partners) has placed married women in the second unhappiest category of people. Married women, weakened by their one and only self-defining role, unwittingly nail their own coffins by opposing equality. While it is true that psychological stress also results from their fears of equality and independence, this is only because women have been overly trained in dependence—not because equality is unhealthy! There is further irony in the fact that married female professionals, who are not dependent on their husbands for status and identity, are among the happiest of married women. It would seem that there is nothing to fear and much to gain from equality for married women, but Dr. Mundy's Mrs. X articulates well the power of a myth which can effectively hide the realities of traditional marriage and concomitant social inequalities to make women harm themselves.

While female fears of the ERA originate in a sense of dependence and a desire for protection, male fears of equality derive primarily from the prospect of sharing power, a prospect frightening to anyone who does not perceive commensurate benefit from that sharing. The difficulty men have in perceiving the benefits to them of equality are rooted even more specifically in the nature of the male stereotype and the masculine ideal. A change in even the legal nature of the relationship between the sexes would disorient men who have been taught only the traditional scenario. Already active male fears of and hostility toward women are aggravated by the prospect of equality in the sexual, occupational, and marital spheres of interaction.

Marc Feigen Fasteau believes that men perceive in the ERA more than a threat to their economic and social power; they see their sexuality threatened. There is, however, a great deal of evidence to prove that equality in nonsexual roles does not de-eroticize the sexual one and that, as Fasteau points out, the expansion of shared experience can make sex more meaningful. According to Alice Rossi, "The salience of sex may be enhanced precisely in the situation of the diminished significance of sex as a differentiating factor in all other areas of life."[1] Moreover, Abraham Maslow's exploration of the connection between sexual experience and the conception of self among women shows that, contrary to traditional notions of femininity and psychological theories, the more "dominant" the woman, the greater her enjoyment of sexuality and her freedom to be and give herself totally. Again, the facts belie the myths, allegiance to which produces fears of change and implementation setbacks for the psychological impact of the ERA.

A relaxation of these regressive fears and an openness toward the ERA concept would have an enormous utopian impact on the psyche of America. The possibilities of salutary change lie particularly in the expansion of woman's ideal role beyond motherhood into other areas of creativity and achievement. The mandate for such role changes arises not only from the symbolic effect of the ERA but from its very practical and tangible effect of giving women the legal opportunity to prove the myths myths.

As women are granted equal rights, they will begin to demand equal rights. The importance of this psychological growth cannot be overemphasized, for the development of self-esteem and the internalization of society's "expectations" create the *real* difference between the sexes. Boys quickly give up their dependence on the response of others for self-esteem and turn to objective achievement in work to fulfill this psychological need; girls are taught to be conformists, to depend on others (primarily males) for their self-esteem, measuring their personal worth by the degree of their conformance to male expectations rather than by objective criteria, like creative achievement. Moreover, the absence of objective success in achievement focuses girls' attention on interpersonal relationships; they are forced to use success in this arena to determine self-esteem. The conflict which may develop in women between the two standards is often resolved by defining "affiliation" *as* achievement[2] and counting themselves "different from but equal to" men. Hence, motherhood equals achievement equals creativity equals self-esteem. This "natural" equation is merely an attempt at compensation, at the recovery of some basis for self-respect, even if it is only biological. And, of course, it is the only role sanctioned for them. Thus, insofar as any person can be independent of society in creating an identity, men are freer to do so than women; for while men are also subject to social expectation, the direction of their achievement is freely chosen and their individual worth can be measured objectively by *what* they achieve rather than their conformance to a nonindividual, biological function. Furthermore, society values their kind of achievement more than women's, assuring them greater self-esteem from the beginning.

Consequently, we must explore the possibility of psychological changes wrought by the ERA from two points of view: a change in the definition of woman's current "creativity" as strictly affiliative or biological and in the development of self-esteem which has created this definition. The ERA can affect these processes both legally, by providing opportunities for women independent of their affiliative roles, and psychologically, by creating new social expectations of women, offering objective achievement as a socially sanctioned criterion for measuring self-worth. Beverly Chiñas and Naomi Weisstein consider these complementary perspectives of creativity and self-esteem, of woman as mother and professional.

Dr. Chiñas discusses the redefinition of parenthood likely to result in an ERA utopia. A quantitative redefinition of time to allow men to be parents and women to pursue careers, a likely if indirect effect of the ERA, will eventually lead to qualitative innovations in the very models of creativity that men and women choose to define their identity. If achievement is not the exclusive domain of men and childbirth is only one more role of women, the terms of "fulfillment" will be redefined sex neutrally. Future projections might anticipate a decrease in the male drive to achieve, as the creativity of fatherhood becomes a viable life choice, and an increase in the female need to achieve, as creativity outside motherhood becomes a viable life choice and childbirth is no longer sufficient to develop self-esteem. The cross movement need not apply to everyone, but the availability of choice is crucial: some of each sex will opt for other kinds of creativity.

While Dr. Chiñas describes the psychological changes relative to motherhood necessary to the development of woman's potential, Dr. Weisstein suggests the psychological changes relative to objective achievement that will permit this development. Using her own experience in the psychology profession as well as social psychological evidence that behavior is determined by expectation, she demonstrates the effect of low self-esteem and the social proscription against achievement goals for women on their career possibilities. Dr. Weisstein's own impetus toward achievement is explained by her early socialization in a context in which neither her competence nor her aspiration was questioned. She did not know women were *supposed* to be incompetent and hence unfit for professional careers, so she did not live up to those expectations. Self-esteem is necessary to aspiration; people seldom aspire to what they are told they cannot achieve. In an ideal world, where the expectations of women are the same as those of men, women would think better of themselves, expect more from themselves, and therefore achieve more. The relevance of discrimination here is not so much that it insures professional death for competent women but that, by encouraging low self-esteem through the expectation of incompetence, it prevents the very development of women's competence, and the myth is perpetuated. The ERA, by symbolically sanctioning achievement goals for women, increases society's respect for their potential, thus enhancing their self-esteem, the very prod necessary to achievement. We are speaking not only of a quantitative change in self-esteem but a qualitative one in that the availability of objective achievement as a measure of self-worth will eliminate the need for women to depend totally upon others for their self-esteem or to define their biological role as creativity par excellence.

Thus the ERA can, by means of increased options and psychological symbolism, redefine the roles of parenthood and career sex neutrally, making either or both viable options for each sex. Ruth Benedict's concept of "congenial responses"[3] is, perhaps, indicative of the way ERA will operate in the psychological arena: every individual has innate and personal tendencies that a culture may exploit constructively or underplay according to their synchronization with its value system. The ERA will assure a more viable and reasonable link between these individual tendencies, regardless of sex, and the social use made of them.

Footnotes

1. "Equality between the Sexes: An Immodest Proposal," in *Roles Women Play: Readings toward Women's Liberation,* ed. Michele Hoffnung Garskof (Belmont, Ca.: Brooks/Cole, 1971), p. 163.

2. Judith M. Bardwick and Elizabeth Douvan, "Ambivalence: The Socialization of Women," in *Woman in Sexist Society: Studies in Power and Powerlessness,* ed. Vivian Gornick and Barbara K. Moran (New York: New American Library, Signet Books, 1971), p. 234.

3. Discussed by Margaret Adams, "The Compassion Trap," in *Woman in Sexist Society,* p. 570.

Female Fears of Equality

Jean Mundy*

American Psychologist Association   9 September 1969

Dear Members:

When I read the article in the September 3rd *Washington Post* about your convention in the Statler-Hilton, I was completely disgusted and appalled! What is the matter with you women? Are you ashamed of your rolling figures—do you want to be men? Women have always been inferior in the business world and will always be, and rightly so!!! Women are too emotional, too illogical to ever have the same positions that men do. Women don't stay as reasonable as long as men do. Married men are just reaching their peak in their late 40s and 50s. By that time married women have passed their peak and are on their way down, and getting a bit silly and sentimental. The same thing goes for single people. I spent 3 years in the Armed Forces and had a good opportunity to observe the single senior military women at work. By the time they get into a fairly responsible job these "career women", with only a few exceptions, have gone daffy and spend their time doing unimportant things.

In the news article a group discussing "Alternative to Marriage" came up with the idea that the basic problem of women today is that "Women who are not married feel guilty about not being married and women who are married feel guilty about being married." I would say that the small number of women that *might* feel guilty about being married are divided into two parts. First there are the women who never should have been married in the first place; and second, there are the women who listen to clinical "psychologists" like you who keep telling them that they should feel guilty. I have never felt guilty about being

*The author wishes to thank Rita M. Sherr, A.C.S.W., for her contribution to this manuscript.

240

married, for I feel that it is my duty and indeed a great privilege as a woman to make a home where my husband can come back to at night and feel like a man. With true love and devotion to him I clean our home and cook, and will bear his off-spring and try to raise them to be normal and useful adults. How can a woman feel like a woman if she never does these womanly chores? Men have no experience in life that can compare in magnitude to the privilege we women have of bearing children. This is something that women, and women alone, can do. No man will ever come close to knowing the excitement, the closeness and the emotional feelings involved with child birth. Then think of the responsibilities involved after the birth of this child. What more of a challenge can a woman have in life than that of raising a child to adulthood? Is there any job with more responsibilities and more rewards than that of a mother? This is more than a nine to five job—it goes 24 hours a day!! A mother is responsible for the upkeep of the home; she must take on the majority of the training and raising of the children. These children will be only as good as she makes them. She will determine how successful they will be and what they will contribute to this world, because they reflect her every thought and idea. And did you ever think that those women who feel guilty about not being married might feel that they are missing something in this life by staying single????

This discussion group also says that the alternatives to marriage include:

1. Change in the law to make marriage a looser contract
2. To abolish marriage completely
3. To permit polygamy

In order to feel secure women and men must have the feeling that they are needed and in a safe situation. This is one reason that living with a person that you are not bound to by law—marriage—cannot be nearly as successful a relationship as one in which you are married. The security is there; he has promised in front of witnesses that he will stay with you for life. To abolish marriage completely would be to destroy our whole society and probably our civilization, though things might be more convenient for those of you who wish for unfertility or who are planning state-rearing of children. In our culture how could you expect to have normal children who would become responsible and well-balanced adults if they are not raised in a home-type atmosphere? (Maybe you learned something from the ancient Pueblos about child-rearing?) They will never be able to experience one of our most wonderful emotions—LOVE. And to permit polygamy in our society would indeed be to our disadvantage, because women out-number men. We would become numbers, no longer people with identity and personality. And we could then really be taken advantage of for there would be plenty more women who would want to take our place in the harum [sic].

Don't we have enough violence in this world without you women trying to stir up a possible revolution over a few silly ideas? Do you really think you could ever win? Don't be such fools!!!!

You women want to compete with your husbands. Did you ever stop to think that all day long your man is out fighting a competitive battle in the business world. Wouldn't it be nice for him to come home to a quiet place where his ego is no longer in danger—where his male desire to be superior is fulfilled?

Now, I conclude that women are not discriminated against; that they do need to do the prescribed motherly and wifely things to be a woman; and finally, our culture is suffering, but it's because women like you are ignoring your responsibilities and playing silly games.

So ladies (hope that term doesn't offend you), go out and fight your crusade; push your way into this Man's World. And when the men get tired of being pushed around and you fall flat on your faces, we real women will still be in our homes, happy and secure.

Go out and play your game—we'll fight you every step of the way!!

Signed (Mrs.) _____

Mrs. X wrote this letter in response to the A.P.A. Symposium on Women held in Washington, D.C., which discussed, among other issues, alternatives to traditional marriage. The letter was reprinted in its entirety in *Who Discriminates against Women?* (Sage Contemporary Social Science Issues, Beverly Hills/London, 1974) and discussed in the chapter "Women Who Discriminate against Other Women."

The letter was written in an attempt to stop the Women's Liberation Movement. Mrs. X used both exhortation and threats. The exhortation was "to stop being such fools . . . trying to stir up a possible revolution over a few silly ideas." The threat was that "we real women . . . will fight you every step of the way."

The correspondent did not intend to be autobiographical, but in the course of giving her argumentative sermon she tells us certain facts about herself.

1. "I spent three years in the armed forces where most of the single senior military women have gone daffy and spend their time doing unimportant things."

2. She is married: "He swore in the presence of witnesses to stay with me forever." She further comments, "If it were not for the marriage laws we would become numbers, no longer people with identity and personality."

3. "I clean our house and cook," adding, "How can a woman feel like a woman if she never does these womanly chores?"

4. She doesn't have any children, but "will bear his offspring who will be only as good as I make them and who will reflect my every thought and idea."

By reading between the lines, I can reconstruct her psychological syllogisms. Mrs. X joined the military and there could have explored the possibility of finding nonhousewife values for women, but she was disappointed. She saw the older single women as quite "daffy." Is it being single that makes you daffy? If so, better to marry. But if doing unimportant things is related to daffiness, then one must somehow make daily tasks very important. Mrs. X does just that. She speaks of keeping house as "my duty and indeed a great privilege." Mrs. X writes a lengthy letter, but tells us nothing about Mr. X except that he once swore.

Perhaps he is away a lot, but never mind; the fact that he exists turns the housework into "homemaking." Chores are baptized into nobility. If single, preparing dinner may deteriorate into eating a sandwich over the sink. Without a mate, cleaning regresses into exactly what it is—a necessary nuisance. Even if the soap liquid is labeled "Joy," using it does not expand consciousness or enlighten one. If you are doing housework alone, for yourself, it isn't worthwhile unless you are worthwhile and deserve pleasantly ordered surroundings.

Mrs. X has it backwards. She must glorify housework to glorify herself. How else can she "feel like a woman?" And, she must attack women who do not see housework as a chance to fulfill one's destiny. Hence, her protest against women's liberation.

Being married may be Mrs. X's attempt to secure the much needed identity; having children is another. Her children, she hopes, will "reflect her every thought." Mrs. X is authoritarian, fully intending to make her children, his offspring, a carbon copy of herself. Her children will not be allowed individuality. She cannot give what she has not yet learned to keep for herself.

Those without the precious gift of autonomy have to fall back on an external structure to give them identity. The rules of marriage, always the delight of anthropologists because of their cultural relativity, are considered within the culture to be sacrosanct. Without rules, titles, role models, discrimination by sex, "everybody," to quote another letter writer—Mrs. Mina Morello, Public Relations Director of the STOP E.R.A. in Northeast Philadelphia—"would be just a person."

Mrs. Morello, formerly of South Philadelphia, is more explicit about what Mrs. X fears. Without sex roles we will "break up the family unit and have immorality." Equality blurs sex identity lines and causes pervasive anxiety because the old rules and regulations must be reexamined. It is much easier to be told who you are, to be given your insignia. Equality for women means change, and transition periods are always difficult. Mrs. X's fears are real. She may lose her husband, her financial and emotional support, and her work.

It is safer not to ask for equality and not to challenge men. Women do not openly challenge men because they are afraid of the consequences. There is no deep, convoluted psychological mechanism here; it is simplicity itself. Women often do not oppose men because they are afraid they will be beaten, or put down, or not liked. "Women," Mrs. X pleads, "do you really think you would ever win?" No one can challenge the reigning heavyweight champion while expecting to lose.

One way to avoid all competition with men is to stick to bearing children. Mrs. X reminds us, "Bearing children is something that women, and women alone, can do." Women can safely claim childbirth as their right because it does not compete with men. Accordingly, women reiterate that they are in no way taking anything away from men, that they are supporting, preserving, and nurturing male schemes and male offspring. As long as one is womanly, wifely, feminine, "a real woman" (as Mrs. X describes herself), one runs no risk of competition—and possible failure. Maybe she is saying that as long as women stick to the jobs that nobody else wants or no one else can do, they will be secure and successful in keeping hubby home.

Why the need for security? Mrs. X writes, "Wouldn't it be nice for him to come home to a quiet place where his ego is no longer in danger?" She sees the world, particularly the business world, as a battlefield in which one risks not just economic failure but loss of identity. She opts for a safer plan: stay home, produce a child and make that child an alter ego. Identity is always at the core of her rationale.

There is a second kind of loss involved in challenging men. Fear of defeat is, ironically, accompanied by fear of losing the opponent himself.

Viveca Lindfors does a scene in her one-woman show, "I Am a Woman," which goes:

> I lie next to him at night wishing I had the courage to bash in his head with the frying pan. I don't bash in his head with the frying pan—not because he may over-power me but because if I do—he may leave me.

Ms. Lindfors, interviewed about this show, said that no matter what part of the country and what type of audience, be they college students, housewife Wednesday matinee groups, or New York sophisticates, there is always a chorus of responsiveness, groans and laughs to this scene and, in the more vocal groups, loud shouts of "Right On!"

This loss of a husband can mean freedom or an existential crisis resulting from the equivalent loss of a familiar and protective identity. It is his existence which sanctifies her household duties and provides her with an assigned identity. The anxiety which comes when identity is threatened blurs the thinking of Mrs. X and Mrs. M. Fear of loneliness, isolation, confusion about what part to play can severely disrupt the psychological system and may lead to mental breakdown. (See Phyllis Chesler's *Women and Madness*). Mrs. X is fighting for her familiar life and for her sanity. Indeed, she should fight; sanity is something worth fighting for, but unfortunately she doesn't know how to fight.

Women want identity and power exactly as much as men but are not trained to fight for it. In fact, they are trained not-to-fight, the reason being that fighting isn't ladylike. The real reason is the assumption, "You ain't got a prayer. You'll last about as long as an ice cube in hell." Again, fear of defeat is operative.

There are at least two serious side-effects of learning not-to-fight. One is that you never learn to face your fears and so are condemned to live with them for a lifetime. The other is that you miss the closeness of fighting. Hand-to-hand combat brings the contestants within arm's length. Boys that fight together become chums and buddies, loyal to the gang and to each other. Women don't start using fighting for closeness until after they are married a while, and then they do it very clumsily. Women will pick a fight over trivia just to get some response, any response, from the silent partner. And, never having learned to fight properly with other women, they do not know how to befriend other women. Quite the contrary.

Mrs. X warns that "there would be plenty more women who would want to take our place in the harem." She senses dangerous competition from other women—but what to do? Should she go the route of keeping her figure, staying youthful with expensive clothes and elaborate make-up, and being great in bed? Should she worry about the young secretaries in his office, the women he meets on his business trips? Should she indulge his affairs, pretend they don't happen, or scream like a banshee? Mrs. X does none of these things but takes refuge in the law, "He promised in front of witnesses." No wonder she is enraged at a group of psychologists who would tamper with the law. The alternative, making friends with women in their social circle rather than treating them as the enemy, is not viable for Mrs. X. When she was in the military service she "had a good opportunity to observe other women at close hand." This doesn't sound like friendship. Ms. Lindfors states in her interview that it simply never occurred to her to have women friends until she was matured. She realized that all her life she had been acting on the assumption—"Women! who needs them?"

Mrs. X has reason to be angry. She is in danger of being beaten if she enters the business world or being replaced by another woman if she stays home. What do you do with that anger? As a woman she was taught to express anger only in the cause of other people, never for herself. Only when it serves others can a woman really feel justified and be angry without feeling guilty. Mothers can fight for their children, nurses for their patients, teachers for their pupils, etc. So Mrs. X writes a letter, never telling us that she is suffering, but with other-directedness she justifies her anger by saying that "our culture is suffering because of women like you."

It is interesting that, although Mrs. X addressed her letters to "Dear Members," she attacks mainly the women in A.P.A. She blames "psychologists" and the women who listen to them for making other women feel guilty. Is it safer to attack women than men, or is she really more threatened by women? Sometimes women attack other women to show they are not one of them. By being male-defined, one opts for male protection. Mrs. M from Philadelphia stated that "My husband is behind me all the way." Is she boasting or reassuring herself?

Mrs. X's letter documents where we are today. We women are afraid of being unfeminine and we are afraid to risk loss of ego. We lack the training in how to fight fairly and openly. We don't understand that it is good to befriend other women. Instead, we run scared, valuing security above all, swallowing humiliation if need be rather than risking defeat. We brainwash our girl children into believing the same old cultural myth. "Women have always been inferior," and its counterpart, "Housework is really a glorious opportunity to fulfill women's destiny."

Psychologists would rather analyze letters than answer them. When Mrs. X asks, "Women, do you want to be men?," a psychologist would wonder if it is Mrs. X herself that wants to be a man. And if she asked me that question I would say, "No, I want to be a woman, but I don't want to be inferior to any man or any woman."

Being equal is hard work. It means defending ourselves instead of being defended, being pretty intelligent instead of just pretty, being physically strong, earning our own money, being success-oriented instead of love-oriented, and coping with more of the world than can be seen out of the kitchen window.

The best answer, I suppose, to her question is to want to be oneself.

Male Fears of Equality*

Marc Feigen Fasteau

If the twists and turns of definition as to what behavior can be considered masculine and what feminine can sometimes be obscure, the basic assumptions and imperatives which shape men's attitudes toward women come through loud and clear. First, we—men and women both—believe in the either/or theory of human personality even if we do not always conform to it: a person who is tough is always tough; a person who is tender and soft is always tender and soft; we do not expect people to be tough in one situation and tender in another according to the demands of the occasion, to have both responses in their repertoires.

Second, men believe that to be masculine they have to be radically different from women. Third, men believe they are better than women and that, in order to retain their masculine self-image when they deal with women, they must dominate and outperform them in every area except child rearing, homemaking, amateur culture, and the management of social life. Fourth, the areas assigned to women are thought of as less important and difficult than those assigned to men, and men, to keep their masculine identification and status, try to stay out of them.

Changes in men's beliefs about women have so far been superficial, at the level of intellect rather than feeling. Under pressure from our egalitarian ethic and the women's movement, more socially conscious men are beginning to agree in general terms to ideas about women which they are emotionally unable to accept in their personal relationships. The realization that they may not in fact be superior to, or even very different from the women they live or work with is frightening—and fear produces hostility

*Excerpted from *The Male Machine* by Marc Feigen Fasteau. Copyright © 1974 by Mark Feigen Fasteau, with permission of McGraw-Hill Book Co.

This reaction, as one would expect, is strongest among men who most need the prop of male superiority. . . . Antagonism to the aims of the women's movement has also triggered a resurgence of efforts, scholarly and otherwise, to prove that sex roles are "natural," the result of genetic and hormonal differences between men and women rather than social learning.

Our ideal of masculinity affects nearly every aspect of man's contact with women, including sexual relationships. The sex act is the only intimate contact many adult men ever have with women; it is as close as they come to crossing the barrier between the sexes. "As close as they come" because men take all their conditioning, all their ingrained ideas about how they should act and feel, to bed with them, where they tend to stifle the freedom and spontaneity that make sex personal and give it meaning. The deadening effect of the masculine stereotype is particularly poignant here because of the potential for intimacy that is being lost. . . . This pressure, this potential, in an act to which we are powerfully drawn is frightening to men who have to keep their psychic distance from women and from their own feelings. . . . It is the reason why men view sex as a dangerous encounter, not in the Victorian sense of its being sinful or unhealthy but as one of the ultimate tests of their masculinity: to get this close to a woman, to the feminine in her and—because of the emotions evoked—in oneself, and still be in command. For men who are most heavily steeped in the masculine ideal, often the same men who are most fearful of not measuring up, the sex act has a nasty edge of hostility.

A friend told me of the time when he and another man were playing tennis with an energetic woman friend. First she played against him, then against the other man. Finally, both were worn out and she was still going strong. "How dare you not satisfy me?" she said teasingly. The double meaning made both men uncomfortable. "What men are really afraid of in women's liberation," my friend explained, making explicit the point of his story, "is that women will make sexual demands that men can't meet."

The "bad woman" today is the one who is not sexually satisfied and who complains—of inadequate technique, of the absence of feeling, of anything that puts some of the responsibility for her unhappiness on the man. Even the woman of genuine passion whose only demand is for a response of matching intensity is a secret object of fear as well as attraction for men. Women who call men's bluffs by refusing to follow the bold-male-pursuer/shy-female-prey roles also tend to frighten men. We have in effect a new covert sexual ideal of "nameless, cooperative, uncritical women," who are sexually responsive but do not openly take the initiative.

But the fundamental problem of performance-ethic sexuality is that it is self-defeating, even on its own terms. . . . Although statistical evidence is not available to prove it, psychiatrists, family counselors, and other professionals in the field overwhelmingly believe that the rate of impotence has jumped substantially in recent years. . . . One psychiatrist has attributed it to the more open and more exacting demands of newly liberated women for sexual performance. . . . It is probably true that some women, in response to years of self-abnegation and sexual frustration, are overreacting and hostilely demanding depersonalized machinelike performance aimed only at their own gratification. But all the feminists with whom I have discussed the matter are convinced that such women are a small minority, that most are still a long way from even healthy self-assertion in bed. The increase in reported impotence, it seems to me, is due to other factors, factors in which male stereotypes about sex play the central role:

First, given that men's basic model for relationships is dominant-submissive/superior-subordinate, some men undoubtedly interpret women's demands for satisfaction as attempts to "take over and run the show," to reverse the traditional arrangement. Naturally, this can be a turnoff.

Second, some men are unable to relate sexually to women who participate as equals in the initiation and pleasures of sex. Sexual behavior, like other behavior in human relationships, is mostly learned, and the only script many men know is the one where they initiate, direct, and judge the performance. The new scenario is disorienting and does not stimulate the previously developed erogenous zones of their psyches. Not being on top, in "missionary position," for example, is upsetting to many men.

Third, it does not take much in the way of demands from a woman for a man who views sexuality as largely a matter of mechanics to begin to believe that she, also, values him solely for machinelike efficiency.

Fourth, because men expect themselves to be always ready and able, they probably count as impotence the times when, for one reason or another, they really didn't feel like sex but tried anyway. Since they are no longer the only initiators of sex, this is happening more than in the past.

Fifth, women are not letting men get away with totally inadequate performances as much as they used to.

Today, most men can acknowledge and satisfy sexual need fairly freely, but the masculine stereotype puts eros beyond their reach. For a man to allow himself to feel the passion of eros, the flight of imagination which fuses sexual attraction and the impulse toward intimacy with the partner, is to make himself vulnerable. It would mean that he wants, and cannot help but show that he wants, recognition of his uniqueness, an affirmation that he is known and that in the intimate world of the other person he counts, something every man, every human being, needs and desires. But once we acknowledge this desire we run the risk of having it denied; for the moment we are very much in the power of another individual. And for a man to be dependent—in particular, upon a woman—is a forbidden emotional state. It does not matter that the vulnerability, the dependence in the relationship is mutual—equality in love is not one of the values of the masculine ideal.

Of course, being human, men do care about certain women as more than sex objects, but in part to protect themselves, men have ritualized the gestures of deference and involvement. We call the system, what remains of it, Chivalry. The surviving gestures—opening doors; letting women out of elevators first (a particularly stupid exercise in stepped-on toes and kicked ankles in crowded office buildings during rush hour); lighting cigarettes; paying in restaurants, theaters, taxis, etc.; shielding women from headwaiters and drunks; ostentatiously allowing oneself to be governed by the women's whim (known after marriage as "humoring the old girl")—are so standardized that they are absolutely safe. A man may perform them without indicating that he has "lost control." But, like all such solutions, chivalry doesn't really work. Ritualizing acts of courtesy depersonalizes them, destroys their ability to convey feeling for the particular person at whom they are directed. And because these gestures are depersonalized, men are required to extend them to every woman, further draining them of meaning. It is not surprising that genuinely helpful acts that involve real effort or sacrifice—like carrying heavy packages or giving up a seat on a crowded subway to a mother and baby—have atrophied as ritual courtesies. That some women still value the remaining impersonal gestures shows only that they get very little else in the way of demonstration of involvement and respect from men.

Chivalry serves men better as a weapon. In situations with an undercurrent of hostility or bargaining, courtesies which force a woman into a position of having received consideration and personal favors put her at a disadvantage. Men can make chivalrous gestures without personal exposure, while women are expected to receive them as though they were personal and thus feel personally obligated. The woman "owes" a response, but since there are very few ritualized courtesies for her to return, the appropriate response for her can only be personal, whether it is being pleasant when she is angry or something more tangible—the feeling of obligation is itself a burden.

Men have also been taught that they and they alone are supposed to take the initiative in relationships with women. Men ask women out; women, traditionally, have had to wait to be asked. They have taken covert steps to help the process along, but in the end they, not men, have sat waiting for the telephone to ring. The breakdown of this custom, like the breakdown of the practice that in bed men do it and women have done it to them, is both unnerving and to a lesser extent, a relief to men. It's a relief to know that you are not always the one who has to make the effort, take the first step to expose yourself to being turned down. But a woman who straightforwardly takes the initiative upsets the only script most men know how to play: "If I am not in control, is she? Am I, therefore, less of a man?" A more flexible middle ground, where control is a central issue for neither the man nor the woman, is hard for men to conceive. Dominance over others is such an important part of the male ideal that men find it hard to imagine that women who refuse to behave as tradition prescribes aren't seeking dominance for themselves—most of them are not. And, most important, any convergence of sex roles threatens men's sense that they are different from women, the linchpin of the masculine self-image.

Why does the ceremony of brandy and cigars lose its power when women are in the room? Why does the idea of a woman participating as an equal in a senior action group of the National Security Council so jar men's sensibilities? For the same reason, I believe, that the gang of boys I once belonged to kept girls out of their treehouse: not because there were secret male activities to hide, but because if a girl could join then membership would no longer prove anything about masculinity. This is the magic, the reassurance of virility by reflection, the "atmosphere" that men fight so hard to protect. The determination with which men fight to keep this prop suggests how fragile their sense of masculinity is and how hard to maintain.

When men do venture forth from their clubs, taverns, and workplaces run by male hierarchies, they face certain hazards. One of these is encountering women who are both attractive and openly intelligent and worldly. From this kind of woman most men beat a hasty retreat. Imagine a business man approaching an attractive woman at a cocktail party and telling her, as part of his opening gambit, what a tough day he has had with his board of directors, meeting all day to decide whether to merge his ten-million-dollar plastics company into a much larger four-hundred million-dollar chemical producer. Imagine that, instead of opening her eyes wide at the large numbers and murmuring something appreciative and impressed sounding, she says something like, "Yes, that kind of decision can be tough. In fact, I just closed a similar deal for a small manufacturer of electronic components. The antitrust problems with these vertical mergers are getting worse all the time." If our protagonist had been talking to a man, the odds are that he would pursue the conversation eagerly. To the woman, his first reaction would be surprise (natural enough, since few women have this kind of power). Next would come confusion—he didn't really open the subject of his deal to talk about it substantively or to compare notes but mainly to impress. Should he switch gears and get into the substance, or continue to try to impress her? What if her company was worth fifty million dollars; suppose she knows more about this kind of deal than he does? The usual response to all this is a quick exit: "Excuse me, I'm going to get a refill." But men can be frightened away even by a show of critical intelligence on nonprofessional matters—a thorough and perceptive analysis of the character of other people at the party, for example. Only if the woman is old or unattractive or firmly attached to a close friend and thus out of the game preserve, not a challenge, is it possible for men to talk to her without concern about dominance.

A great depth of fear and hostility underlies even the more polite and civilized attempts to assert control over an independent woman or, especially, a feminist woman. Resistance only brings it out into the open; it does not create it. One indication of this fear is that men tend not to want to marry or establish close relationships with such women.

Most men who feel the appeal of independent women are in a particularly unhappy position. They are bored with women trained into the more traditional, passive, dependent mold, but so committed to the conquest of the women they find more interesting that they cannot open up enough to make real contact with them. They are unwilling to commit themselves to anyone they can't control.

The larger number of men look for and find women to whom they are superior—or let them believe they are superior—on the basis of occupational status in the middle and upper-middle income range, on the basis of the fact of maleness alone in lower income groups. The contempt they can then feel for women allows them to feel safe. "I feel more comfortable talking about my troubles to women," a member of a men's consciousness-raising group said, "because I don't really care what they think of me."

———————

For men to play their roles, women have to play theirs—or be kept in them. This is true in every area where men and women interact, but most of all at work. Participation in work has been the mainstay of men's sense of superiority and difference. Until recently, interesting, well-paid, and prestigious work—more than any other area of life—has been almost exclusively the province of men. Where the work is less rewarding, the aura of masculinity created by keeping women out is even more important: if holding a job as a steelworker proves nothing else, it at least proves that you are a man.

The connection between the masculine stereotype and the way men treat women at work came through in a survey by the *Harvard Business Review* of its subscribers' attitudes. Executives in defense, industrial-manufacturing, construction, and mining companies were more negative than men in "less masculine" industries about working with women. There are fewer women in the "more masculine" industries and male executives in them have less of a chance to unlearn their prejudices. But it also seems likely that they attract men whose stronger-than-average need for a masculinity-certifying atmosphere makes them more hostile to having women as colleagues.

Among the professions, the most prejudice and the fewest women are found in engineering, law, and medicine—traditionally thought of as masculine callings. And inside each profession, women are most strongly resisted in the more "masculine" specialties—corporate law and surgery are examples. Instead, they are tracked into family law or estates and trusts ("women bring personal warmth to working with widows and orphans"), and pediatrics or child psychiatry. At the non-professional level as well, women are especially resented in the occupations which have the greatest cachet of manliness. This resentment and fear is so strong that over the ages it has crystallized into superstitions, some of which still linger: a woman in a ship's crew jinxes the voyage; women in mines are such bad luck that workmen walked out of a Colorado tunnel-construction job several years ago when one woman mine inspector entered the excavation. The supernatural explanations for these beliefs have fallen away, but the hostility that created them remains.

The form of responsibility men are most reluctant to grant women is, of course, supervisory authority over men. The idea sends sympathetic vibrations of humiliation and outrage through every man in the office: "Gail could do the job, probably better than Cal. But we can't put her over all those guys . . . would you like to work for a woman?"

The men who are most concerned about proving their competitive masculine worth, younger men who haven't yet made it, are more threatened by having female colleagues and competitors than older men whose positions are assured at a level above that likely to be attained by women or who, either through success or failure, have lost some of their competitive zeal.

There is one way for women to get themselves taken seriously at work, and that is to become more like men than men themselves. A woman who is supercompetent, "older," devotes herself exclusively to her work (which usually means she is unmarried), who, although she may be attractive and pleasant, represses every vestige of genuine warmth and sexuality in favor of the approved front of impersonal efficiency, may eventually be accepted as one of the "boys." She doesn't pose the sexual challenge men usually read into their relationships with women. This makes her less complicated for men to deal with. Men also find her professional ability easier to take because they think of her as sexually deficient and therefore, on balance, still safely inferior: "She's great on the committee, but I'll bet she hasn't been propositioned in ten years." Even these women, however, face condescension from men, in fact *because* they have repressed their sexuality. They are perceived as somehow not quite real women.

On the other hand, any women who does not conform to this machinelike standard finds it impossible to get men to take anything but her sexuality seriously. Most men cannot accept the fact that a sexy woman is also tough and competent. The male sexual ideal of "nameless, cooperative, and uncritical" women, and the standard of invulnerability which fosters the ideal, do not permit it.

A man working with an attractive woman may view every encounter, no matter how businesslike in purpose, as sexually charged. The obligation to make at least a perfunctory pass is reinforced by the predominant view of sexual attractiveness as a relatively impersonal matter of physical assets —one woman with good breasts and nice legs is more or less interchangeable with any other. Men don't actually come on seriously to every attractive woman they work with, but they do expect a show of ritual, ego-satisfying flirtation. And when they have the power, as with a subordinate, they often insist on it, implicitly viewing it as part of her job. This byplay is especially manageable with a secretary: if she doesn't play the game—or when an affair goes sour—she can be fired or transferred with no more explanation than that a "personality conflict" has developed. But if the woman is an equal, someone who must be dealt with seriously, these same sexual overtones and obligations become unwanted complications. This is one of the subtler reasons why men keep women out of key decision-making groups. They know that in these situations it is essential to focus without distraction on the problems to be solved. At the same time, men are aware that, if an attractive woman is part of the group, they will feel compelled to play another game as well, that at the very least they will be distracted to the extent of having to make a conscious decision to ignore her "as a woman." It's simpler just to exclude her.

Some men recognize that most of the human warmth in their lives is created by women. And they are afraid that if women go to work at the same jobs they will lose the capacity and desire to perform this service.

[This attitude is based on] two assumptions, both associated with our sexual stereotypes: first, that women's primary purpose in life is to make men happy; and, second, the familiar "either/or" view of human personality, the idea that if a person has the capacity to be tough and objective, he or she cannot also be warm and caring. The net result is one more source of resistance to recognizing women's abilities to handle positions of responsibility and power.

To break [the] traditional pattern [of marital division of labor], basic assumptions have to be challenged: that the only kind of worthwhile career is an all-consuming one; that the social side of an executive job requires the full participation and services of the spouse; that the wife is the only person qualified to assume major responsibility for the care of children; that the additional money, glory, or benefit to humanity derived from the concentration of energy and time (both his and hers) on his career is always more valuable than the money, glory, or benefits to humanity and the personal satisfactions to her (or, possibly, to both) that a reallocation of time and effort freeing her to pursue a career would bring; and, all else failing, that their prize masculine and feminine identities depend on his superiority and her subordination. Only when these assumptions begin to be stripped away, do men have to face their unwillingness to tolerate, much less welcome, having an equal—in status, in competence, in earning power—as a mate.

Many blue-collar or clerical workers, forced by economic circumstances to accept the fact of a working wife, are unhappy about it. This opposition, according to sociologist Mirra Komarovsky, is based on possessiveness —the men want to keep their wives away from the sexual opportunities provided by outside employment—and "anxiety over loss of power." The relatively low status of blue-collar and clerical jobs makes almost any work by the woman a threat to the man's superiority, which is founded mainly on his position as sole breadwinner.

When upper-middle-income men face the prospect of their wives pursuing full-fledged, time-consuming, high-status careers, what emerges explicitly is their need to feel superior and to reaffirm the higher priority automatically accorded their work and emotional requirements.

Few men are willing to make significant concessions to a wife's career. Any commitment outside the home that threatens their position as the only major focus for their wives' energies and emotions is unacceptable.

Since the Victorian era we have been the victims of the motherhood myth, the idea that the mother, above the father and all other women, is particularly well-suited to care for the children. However contradictory and confusing, the myth still has a substantial hold on women and is thus available to men as a weapon. It is the first, seemingly selfless, line of defense when mother wants to get a job. The uncritical zeal with which men seize on this argument suggests strongly that it masks other sources of resistance. A very real one is the apprehension that if the woman holds a job outside the home, especially if it is a full time job, he will probably come under pressure to take a greater role in caring for the children than if she were to devote herself exclusively to home and children. It may be difficult for him to take time from his work, either because his conception of a career demands that he do nothing else or because he has a job with inflexible hours.

There is another level of resistance, however, to masculine involvement with child care. Being a father, in the sense of having sired and having children, is part of the masculine image; but fathering, the actual care of children is not. Part of the feeling that care of children is inappropriate as a strong commitment for men comes from the fact that it is a diversion from men's "real" work, the building of a successful career.

The rewards of caring for a child are real, but essentially personal, hard to measure or hang on to. This is not the kind of experience men are taught to value. It does not lead to power, wealth, or high status. As we have seen, the male stereotype pushes men into seeking their sense of self-esteem almost exclusively in achievement measured by objective, usually competitive standards.

Perhaps in the future, our lives will be shaped by a view of personality which will not assign fixed ways of behaving to individuals on the basis of sex. Instead, it would acknowledge that each person has the potential to be—depending on the circumstances—both assertive *and* yielding, independent *and* dependent, job *and* people-oriented, strong *and* gentle, in short, both "masculine" *and* "feminine"; that the most effective and happy individuals are likely to be those who have accepted and developed both these "sides" of themselves; and that to deny either is to mutilate and deform; that human beings, in other words, are naturally androgynous.

Creativity and the Demystification of Motherhood

Beverly Newbold Chiñas

THE MOTHERHOOD MYSTIQUE IN 20TH CENTURY AMERICA

The ''motherhood mystique'' is here defined as the supposition that the *biological potential for motherhood,* which of course distinguishes all women from all men, and the social behavior of *mothering* are somehow inherently linked in the female sex. Only very recently in human history and only in relatively affluent societies has mothering been regarded as woman's major role. For almost all of our history and in almost every human group, women have been expected to carry the lion's share of the economic burden as well. That they were able to do so and rear generation after generation of children should dispel any last vestige of the ''motherhood mystique'' which has permeated both popular and professional circles in the United States for so long.

The extent of the mystique of motherhood in American culture can be better understood when one considers that mothering has almost never been discussed as a separate and very different phenomenon from the biological event of motherhood. All women are assumed to possess mothering talents or ''instincts'' which propel them inexorably toward the role of mothering, whether or not they happen to become biological mothers. The motherhood mystique assumes that women are inherently superior to men at mothering and that women *must* mother someone or some thing for their own emotional well-being. Like the old racist argument that certain ethnic groups were more suited for stoop labor because of their short stature, the motherhood mystique serves as a convenient rationalization for placing the whole burden of child rearing on women and for excluding women from other occupations.

In the past, when biological mothers breast-fed infants for two or more years and could expect to begin a new gestation period about the time the

257

nursling was weaned, there was a lengthy period when a baby's life depended very directly on its biological mother. In such circumstances, it was very easy for the biological function of providing breast milk and the biological event of motherhood to be closely connected in people's minds with the social function of mothering. In areas of the world with modern technology the formula-fed infant is not thus biologically dependent on its mother after birth, and even the breast-fed infant can be switched to prepared formula if it is necessary. In any case, there is no necessary connection between the act of breast feeding and the quality or quantity of mothering which the nursing mother provides her child. Some individuals have tried to establish motherhood-mothering links by claiming that the act of breast-feeding stimulates the "mothering instincts" in the mother and establishes a firm mother-child bond which endures throughout their lives. This is utter nonsense. If it were true, we should be able to isolate and measure some behavioral and personality differences between adults who were breast-fed in infancy and those who were formula-fed and their respective mothers. Not surprisingly, no such differences have been noted, or, to my knowledge, even proposed.

On the other hand, there is some evidence that mothering is not carried in the genes but is learned behavior and that there is a considerable degree of variation in individual adaptation to the mothering role, both in humans and in nonhuman primates.[1] Among human mothers one would be very hard put to make a case for instinctive mothering behavior or for affectional ties developing in the mother during gestation. In fact, there are some data which would tend to disprove such theories. For example, it is well known that most foragers practice infanticide as a means of limiting family size. In such societies, it is usually the mother of the newborn infant who makes the decision and commits the act of infanticide.[2] If mothering were inherent, it would be difficult to understand how mothers could systematically practice infanticide.

In our culture, the motherhood mystique assumes that women who have abortions suffer great emotional damage for "going against their natures." Recently, a study attempted to test the validity of this assumption by comparing two groups of young women, one of which had requested and received induced abortions and the other of which had carried their unwanted pregnancies to term and given up their infants for adoption. The tests showed no differences in numbers and kinds of emotional problems between the two groups. As with other forms of sin, one has to feel guilty in order to suffer emotional damage for committing an act. The guilt must be socialized into the individual first, however.

Evidence such as this seems to indicate that the motherhood mystique serves "carrot-stick" purposes. It acts as a carrot which society holds out to pacify and delude women into believing that childbirth and motherhood are comparable to intellectual creativity and that mothering is not only "natural" but necessary to a woman's mental and emotional health. For centuries women have been lectured from pulpit, podium, soapbox, and marriage bed that they need nothing more than motherhood to make them complete fulfilled human beings and that, indeed, a woman cannot be a complete human being without motherhood. However, the ties between competent mothering and fulfilled hopes are tenuous in the extreme. Recent studies of elderly women show that those who accepted and tried to act out the motherhood mystique are the most unhappy. Society promised them something it could not deliver, and in old age they feel cheated and disillusioned.

The other face of the "motherhood mystique" coin is the idea that women *cannot* do anything but mothering or, if they do, they do it less well than men. While patently absurd, this idea has destroyed women's confidence in themselves so that they do not try very hard to succeed in careers and professions. Yet if one digs through obscure sources in search of lost "herstory," one is struck by how very much women have been able to accomplish in almost every human endeavor with little or no encouragement from society and often with active, hostile, and even violent discouragement. Individual women from every race and ethnic group, from every walk of life, have overcome tremendous odds to become great in their chosen endeavor only to be totally ignored, actively discredited, and even vilified for their efforts by the records of "history." One cannot begin to reconstruct women's history without gaining a profound respect for the intellectual creativity and stamina of women everywhere and in every time. Their great achievements against almost insuperable odds can only be viewed as monuments to the invincibility of the human spirit and a resounding denial of the motherhood mystique.

What Women Can Achieve. Women in the United States during the last quarter of this century must be living in one of the most exciting and challenging eras of history for our sex. The excitement lies in the fact that we do not know what women can achieve when the tremendous barriers and prejudices which have surrounded them are finally removed. We do not know the potential of women's physical or intellectual abilities because there have been no women who have grown to adulthood in an open, optimal environment for women's self-development.

One can make some predictions if one is sufficiently intrepid to risk the derision of people who fear change. One prediction I would make is that women's physical abilities will be found to be surprisingly similar to those of men, given the same amount and types of training. I do not mean that women's and men's bodies will develop similarly, but that women will be able to accomplish approximately the same feats according to height and weight as do men. Intellectually, the argument was settled long ago. Today, only the most uninformed individual could believe that one sex is intellectually superior to the other. If the two sexes perform differently in particular intellectual tasks in adulthood, it is because they have been trained from the cradle to categorize certain branches of learning as either masculine or feminine pursuits and to avoid those areas socially defined as inappropriate to their sex.[3]

An interesting hypothetical experiment on the interchangeability of the sexes in all roles (except reproductive ones) is to imagine two modern nations of approximately equal population and similar culture exchanging persons according to sex for, let us say, a five-year period. X nation would send all their male citizens over the age of 12 to Y nation and Y, in turn, would send all its female citizens to X. The result would be that each nation would have essentially one sex for a period of five years. Would society collapse? Would the whole situation become totally chaotic? I would predict that, after an initial period of adjustment to unaccustomed jobs and roles, things would proceed much the same with regard to day-to-day jobs which keep society functioning. Each sex might develop different styles of accomplishing the same things, especially in those roles they had not previously filled, but the end result would not be significantly different.

THE FATHERHOOD MYSTIQUE

Fatherhood and fathering are not so closely linked in the popular mind as are motherhood and mothering. Yet there is, I believe, a fatherhood mystique which reinforces male dominance and the right of males to "rule the roost" by assuming that dominance, assertiveness, and aggression are inherent male traits. In recent years, several male authors have enriched themselves considerably by claiming to prove what male readers want to hear—that male dominance, "bonding," aggression, and so forth, are genetically based and, therefore, men not only have the right to rule but *must* rule others because of their genes.[4]

Fatherhood and fathering have not been so closely linked as motherhood and mothering probably because of the time-space gap between the act of male procreation and birth. Social fatherhood is so important in all societies because biological fatherhood is not necessarily determinable. Furthermore, fatherhood does not imply fathering. Few people believe that fathering, meaning the supportive nurturing aspects of the parenting role, "comes naturally.'' In virtually all cultures, fathering has been qualitatively and quantitatively different from mothering; that is, fathers and mothers have provided their children with different, complementary services and training. In many cultures, fathering is a role which is split among several adults, as when the social father has an affectional and supportive role while the mother's brother takes the disciplinarian-trainer role. Commonly, the role of fathering does not become important until the child is weaned and often not until the child is six or more years old.

In the United States the ideal and actual roles of father have changed through time. The father as patriarch, an ideal strongly supported throughout the 19th century, has gradually given way to a less authoritarian, more egalitarian ideal—the ''buddy'' father of boys, the ''kindly advisor and protector'' father of both sexes. Despite the ideals, the actual father roles in urbanized America vary over a wide range from the father who is indifferent to or abandons his children to the emotionally detached and largely absent provider father, often found in middle-class suburban families, to the ''buddy'' father who tries to approach the post-World War II cultural ideal. Neither has the domineering, patriarchal father of earlier days passed from the scene entirely, although it is much more difficult to maintain this role in today's social system.

Since fatherhood is only peripherally connected to male identity, contrary to motherhood, fathering has been a role which can be participated in by degrees or even abandoned while a father figure continues to be present in the child's household. Whether or not they recognize it, many urban American fathers have nearly abandoned the role of fathering, except for the aspect of economic support. Perhaps the isolation of young children from fathers reached its peak with suburban commuter living. In general, the most important aspect of fathering in America has been economic support; our conceptions of fathering have not included actual day-to-day care, emotional support, nurturance, and guidance. Many men have not realized that our present definitions of fatherhood and fathering have cheated them of some of the most rewarding affectional roles in human experience. Now there are increasing numbers of young fathers who are beginning to recognize the importance of prolonged contact with their young children and who are reorganizing their lives to provide such contact.

PREDICTIONS AND PROSPECTS

As we enter the last quarter of the 20th century, I believe men's private, familial roles will become more important and more interesting to men who choose to become fathers, with their provider roles expanding to include provision of emotional support and guidance and diminishing in the economic sense, as women and men work together to provide the several kinds of support necessary to the successful rearing of children.

Parenthood and Parenting. As in other roles now segregated by sex, I believe that fathering and mothering will converge more and more into "parenting," a word already in use by a number of child psychologists. Parenting will combine fathering and mothering into a single role in which the gender of the parent is largely irrelevant.

For women, this change will signal the end of the trapped housewife syndrome. To feel trapped a woman must feel that her job is unrewarding and that she cannot escape it. Women in the future will exercise choice in their lives, selecting professions and careers that please them as well as parenting. Most women will not expect to be economically supported by a man when they marry, although some women will be. That is, expectations in marriage will change, and they will change for men as well as women. Accordingly, most women will not expect to have the entire burden and rewards of parenting through the preschool years, and women's choices of occupations and professions will reflect this change. Women will become must less ambivalent about their roles when they are expected to provide both partial economic support and partial emotional and affectional support for their children. When women are convinced that mothering is learned behavior, they will begin to feel much more comfortable about choosing to forego the role entirely.

Of course, all of these changes do not imply a "break-down" of the family. Anthropologists are not in the least concerned about the family and its future. Children will continue to be born and adults will continue to establish families, whether or not children are part of the plans. The form of the family may change. Probably there will be much more variability in the composition of the unit, so that family will not mean only a nuclear family (usually defined as including two parents and their minor children) but any group of people living together and cooperating in an economic and affectional unit over a period of time. Perhaps the old nuclear family will still prevail, perhaps not; it will depend upon what type of family organization fills the needs of the members of the unit most effectively for the most people. There is nothing sacred, from the anthropological perspective, about the conventional nuclear family as it is defined in America. Anthropologists are well aware that there are many types of families in many different cultures around the world. But they are also aware that urbanization has tended to favor small family units over larger ones. This may be merely a stage in urbanization, as urbanization itself may be a stage in our social evolution. Perhaps "posturban" society will encourage larger family units again, such as the communes which are now appearing, but it is highly unlikely that the traditional monogamous marriage and its nuclear family will disappear entirely from the social scene. I think most anthropologists anticipate that the conventional nuclear family will probably continue to be the prevalent type in the United States into the foreseeable future.

Parenting and Children. The new role of parenting should be most advantageous for the preschool child because it will mean that she or he has two adults and thus two distinct personalities on which to depend for the same types of support and training. Thus, a child will not be so severely handicapped by a mother who finds herself trapped in a parenting role thrust upon her by the social system. Nor will a small child suffer as much emotionally from the loss of a mother through death or divorce. The child will have two interchangeable parent figures with whom to interact instead of an ideally close and supportive mother figure and an ideally less nurturant and socially more distant father figure. Single parent families will not be at so great a disadvantage in the social system as has been the case, and single parent families headed by women will have an improved chance of remaining economically independent rather than becoming helplessly entangled in the degrading, dehumanizing mesh of public welfare. Day care facilities near the parents' work sites will provide substitute parenting of a better quality than is generally now available, and parents will utilize substitute parenting for fewer hours per day and for less total time in the child's life than lower and middle-class working parents presently do.

Parenting and Homemaking. Just as parenting replaces the sex-segregated roles of mothering and fathering, making a home will no longer be the exclusive domain of women but will be the role shared more evenly between the sexes. Some men will choose the homemaking role (which will be taught to and required for both sexes in the public schools) for long periods of time, others for short periods, and still other couples will share the role on a day-to-day continuing basis. Through the desexing of the homemaking role, men will gain a greater appreciation of the contributions women have always made to the family, and the role of homemaking will attain more stature and respect as a vital and important part of life. I anticipate that many of the trappings considered vital or desirable in homemaking today will not survive because they are not functional. Homes will become more functional, efficient, and comfortable and less opulent and ornate, as women cease to view their homes as an important creative expression of themselves, about the only one which society has allowed them.[5] Probably men will take more interest in seeing that the home provides for their comforts, hobbies, and interests and reflects something of their own personalities too.

Creativity. The desexing of parenting, homemaking, and occupational roles will open up significant new avenues of creativity for both sexes. Women will be able to learn skills such as carpentry, plumbing, electrical wiring and repair, and automobile repair, which have traditionally been done (or left undone) by the "man of the house." Men will have the opportunity to develop skills connected with homemaking which have always provided women with a degree of creative satisfaction, skills such as cooking, sewing, needlecrafts, and gardening. I have always felt that men miss a significant source of relaxation and creative satisfaction in our culture by not practicing needlework and other mind-relaxing handicrafts which are defined as "women's work."

As homemaking is desexed, I expect that more men will discover these sources of satisfaction for themselves and that a whole new genre of homecrafts and needlework will develop as men put their own personalities and creative imaginations into these pursuits. I do not see men and women entirely converging in their creative imaginations and interests anymore than I see them converging in personality. Just as women artists choose different subjects and depict similar subjects in different ways or as men's and women's creative writing differs, I think men will perform traditionally female pursuits in their own unique ways and bring their own experiences and world views to bear on their work. In other words, there will be distinct styles and methods which each sex will be free to develop and incorporate into every realm of creative activity. In the long view, as children are reared in desexed environments, I expect creativity patterns to converge more between the sexes. As long as children are reared as "men" and "women" first, and individual personalities second, I think we shall continue to see differences in world view according to sex expressed in creative endeavors.

In conclusion, it appears to me that converging sex roles, both within and outside the family, can vastly enrich human experience for all people of all ages. The individual will come to be valued for the qualities which make every personality distinct and human and to be criticized and pressured to change those qualities which society finds undesirable, regardless of one's biological sex. Of course, there will be many people who will refuse to try new roles and who will tenaciously cling to the conventional sex-segregated roles. It is difficult to change one's behavior and attitudes in adulthood, although not impossible. Many people, no doubt, will fear the challenge. It seems to me that the personal rewards of the changes discussed in these pages will be very great and will more than repay the sacrifices and adjustments necessary to effect them. In the long run, those persons with the courage, curiosity, and concern to try new actions, new behaviors, and new ways of thinking about themselves and others will gain immeasurably as individuals, and society itself will gain much from them.

Footnotes

1. The famous Harlow experiments with rhesus monkeys showed that females reared in isolation were usually insufficiently socialized to conceive, and in the rare cases where such a female produced a live infant, she rejected it completely at birth. They also found that "monkey mothers, like human mothers, vary greatly in behavior toward their infants —ranging from highly devoted and protective to neglectful and even abusive." [Harry Harlow and Margaret Harlow, "A Study of Animal Affection," in *Primate Social Behavior,* ed. Charles H. Southwick (New York: Van Nostrand, 1965).] Phyllis Jay found this same variation in mother aptitude among common langurs in their natural habitat, noting also that older females who had borne several infants were more capable mothers than very young female langurs, and that there were notable differences in female langurs' temperaments. ["The Common Langur of North India," in *Primate Behavior,* ed. Irven DeVote (New York: Holt, Rinehart and Winston, 1965).]

2. Infanticide is not limited to foraging societies but also occurs rather commonly in other societies lacking modern contraceptive techniques. Some anthropologists make a strong case for the prevalence of systematic human infanticide all through the Pleistocene epoch [e.g., Steven Polgar, "Population History and Population Policies from an Anthropological Perspective," *Current Anthropology* 13, no. 2(1972): 203-11; and Joseph Birdsell, "Some Predictions for the Pleistocene Based on Equilibrium Systems among Recent Hunter-Gatherers," in *Man the Hunter,* ed. Richard B. Lee and Irven Devore (Chicago: Aldine, 1968), pp. 229-39.]

3. Although newborn infants exhibit a few different responses according to their sex, there is no evidence that these relatively insignificant differences would limit adult role performance in any way.

4. The latest attempt along these lines is *The Inevitability of Patriarchy* by Steven Goldberg (New York: William Morrow & Co., 1973). His arguments have engendered a spirited debate between anthropologists and Goldberg [see *American Anthropologist* 77, no. 1 (March 1975): 69-77].

5. I base this prediction on personal observations of the contrast between the homes of male and female college professors of my acquaintance. There is a noticeable trend for women college professors to maintain significantly more modest homes than male college professors whose wives are homemakers. Presumably college professors of either sex can pay for the same accommodations if they desire to do so. The difference in living accommodations lies, I believe, in the fact that women professors do not gain their primary identity nor seek their major self-expression through their homes, as do wives of male college professors. There is also the very practical consideration that the larger and more ostentatious the home in today's servantless world, the more work is involved in maintaining it, and women college professors have significantly less time to devote to homemaking than do women who are full-time homemakers.

Social Expectation, Self Esteem, and Achievement*

Naomi Weisstein

INTRODUCTION: PERSONALITY PSYCHOLOGY
VERSUS SOCIAL PSYCHOLOGY

Women in our society are characterized as inconsistent, emotionally unstable, lacking in a strong conscience, "nurturant" rather than productive, hedonistic, submissive, "intuitive" rather than intelligent, "good at detail" rather than "creative," and if they are at all "normal," suited to the home and the family. These characterizations comprise a typical minority group stereotype;[1] but they are not simply part of our popular culture; they are fully incorporated into psychological theories about the nature of women. The latter part of this paper is an account of my struggle with the psychology profession over the very issue of whether or not it was proper, indeed conceivable, that a woman should be a scientist. I am an experimental psychologist—I do research in vision—and the profession had for a long time considered this activity on the part of one of my sex to be an outrageous violation of the social order and against all the laws of nature. But before dealing with the discriminatory effects of psychological theories on women, let me examine the underlying assumptions of those theories and the evidence which disproves them.

The basic reason that psychology (i.e., personality theory and, for the most part, theory from therapists and psychoanalysts) tells us next to nothing about human "nature"—male as well as female—is that it has been looking in the wrong place, assuming that what people do comes from some fixed, rigid, inner directive: sex organs, or fixed cognitive traits, or what happened up until but no later than the age of five. But this assumption has been shown

---

*An earlier version of this paper was delivered at the Biochemistry Biophysics Society meetings, June 1974 (Conference of the Federation of American Societies for Experimental Biology). Copyright © by Naomi Weisstein.

to fall again and again; a person will be assessed as possessing a particular constellation of personality traits and then, when different criteria are applied or a different judge is asked to judge or, more importantly, when that person is in a different kind of social situation, s/he will exhibit a completely different set of traits.[2] One might argue that personality is a somewhat subtle and elusive thing and that it would be hard to get a set of measures which would distinguish personality types; this is a reasonable argument. But even when one looks at what would be expected to be gross differences in a population—the difference between a certified schizophrenic, say, and a normal,[3] or between a male homosexual and a male heterosexual,[4] or between a "male" personality and a "female" personality,[5] we find that the same judges who claim to understand human personality and treat patients on the basis of this understanding simply can't distinguish one from the other. In one study,[6] judges who were wupposed to be experts at this kind of thing could not tell, on the basis both of clinical tests and of interviews (in which one is allowed to ask questions like: "When did you first notice that you had become Henry Kissinger?"), which of a group of people had been classified as schizophrenics and which as normals; and, even worse, some weeks later, when these same judges were asked to judge these same people, they reversed their judgments in many cases. Those judges (again, those in training to become and already established clinical experts) trying to distinguish between males and females or homosexuals and heterosexuals on the basis of what are assumed to be differences in their personalities have done no better.

In short, if judges can't agree on whether a person belongs to a certain personality category, even when those categories are assumed to be so different from each other as normal-crazy, male-female, straight-gay, and if the measurement depends on who's doing the measuring and on what time of day s/he's doing it, then theories which are based on these personality categories are simply useless.

What this means for women is that personality theory has given us no idea of our true "natures"—whether we were intended from the start to be scientists and engineers and thwarted by a society which has other plans for us or whether we were intended only to be mothers. But while personality psychology and clinical psychologists have failed miserably at providing any statements we can trust about women's "true nature"—about anyone's "true nature"—the evidence is collecting from a different area of psychology—social psychology—that what humans do and when they will do it are highly predictable; that what a person does and who s/he believes her/himself to be will, in general, be a function of what people around her/him expect her/him to be and what the overall situation in which s/he is acting implies that s/he is.

Let me describe four types of experiments which have made this clear.

The experimenter bias experiments.[7] These studies have shown that if one group of experimenters has one hypothesis about what they expect to find and another group of experimenters has the opposite hypothesis, both groups will obtain results in accord with their differing hypotheses. And this is not because the experimenters lie or cheat (although occasionally some do); of course, in the studies cited, the experimenters are closely observed and they are made outwardly to behave in identical fashion. The message about their different expectations is somehow picked up through nonverbal cues, head nods, ways of communicating expectations which we don't know much about yet. The moral here is that even in carefully controlled conditions, when we are dealing with humans (and even, in some cases, rats),[8] the hypotheses will influence the behavior of the person we are studying. It is obvious how important this would be in assessing the validity of psychological studies of the differences between men and women.

Inner physiological state versus social context. Schacter and Singer[9] injected subjects with adrenalin and showed that those subjects who were then placed in a room with somebody (a confederate of the experimenter) who acted euphoric became euphoric themselves and those subjects who were then placed in a room with somebody (another confederate of the experimenter) who acted angry became angry themselves. This seems to indicate that the far more important determinant of how a person will act is not her/his physiological state but the social context in which s/he is acting. Thus, no matter how many physiological differences we can find between men and women, we must be very cautious in assigning any fixed behavior to the physiological state. The point is made even more strongly, perhaps, in studies of hermaphrodites with the same diagnosis (the genetic, gonadal, hormonal sex, the internal reproductive organs, and the ambiguous appearances of the external genitalia were identical), where it was shown that one will consider oneself male or female depending simply on whether one was defined and raised as male or female.

The obedience experiments. In Milgram's experiments,[10] a subject is told that s/he is administering a learning experiment and that s/he is to deal out shocks each time the other "subject" (in reality, a confederate of the experimenter) answers incorrectly. The equipment appears to provide graduated shocks ranging upwards from 15 volts through 450 volts; for each of four consecutive voltages there are verbal descriptions such as "mild shock," "danger, severe shock," and finally, for the 435 and 450 volt switches, a red XXX marked over the switches. Each time the stooge answers incorrectly, the subject is supposed to increase the voltage. As the voltage increases, the stooge begins to cry in pain; s/he demands that the experiment stop; finally, s/he refuses to answer at all. When s/he stops responding, the experimenter instructs the subject to continue increasing the voltage; for each shock administered the stooge shrieks in agony. Under these conditions, about 62½% of the subjects administered shocks that they believed to be possibly lethal.

No tested individual differences between subjects predicted how many would continue to obey and which would break off the experiment. When forty psychiatrists predicted how many of a group of 100 subjects would go on to give the lethal shock, their predictions were orders of magnitude below the actual percentages; most expected only one-tenth of one percent of the subjects to obey to the end.

But even though *psychiatrists* have no idea how people will behave in this situation and even though individual differences do not predict which subjects will obey and which will not, it is easy to predict when subjects will be obedient and when they will be defiant. In a variant of Milgram's experiment, two stooges were present in addition to the "victim"; these worked along with the subject in administering electric shocks. When these two stooges refused to go on with the experiment, only ten percent of the subjects continued to the maximum voltage. This is critical for understanding human behavior. It says that behavior is predicted from the social situation not from the individual history.

Internalization of social expectations. The experiments discussed offer overwhelming evidence for the proposition that people act in ways expected of them and that they believe they are what others expect them to be. In the case of women, this is damaging: we internalize society's expectations that we are inferior. There are numerous examples—for instance, the classic experiment by Goldberg[11] in which *women* judging the quality of an article found it to be excellent when they thought that a man wrote it and found the *same* article to be "poor to indifferent" when they thought that a woman wrote it. Thus, society's stereotypes become our own; we expect little from other women and think little of ourselves.

Summary of the social psychological evidence. In brief: if subjects under quite innocuous and noncoercive social conditions can be made to kill other subjects and under other types of social conditions will positively refuse to do so; if subjects can react to a state of physiological arousal by becoming euphoric because there is somebody else around who is euphoric or angry because there is somebody else around who is angry; if subjects will act one way because experimenters expect them to act that way and another group of subjects will act a different way because experimenters expect them to act that different way, then it is obvious that a study of human behavior requires, first and foremost, a study of the social contexts within which people move, the expectations as to how they will behave, and the authority which tells them who they are and what they are supposed to do.

As mentioned, the relevance to males and females is obvious. We don't know what immutable differences in behavior, nature, ability, or possibility exist between men and women. We know that they have different genitalia and different sex hormone levels; perhaps there are some unchangeable differences; probably there are a number of irrelevant differences. But it appears that all these differences may be trivial compared to the enormous influence of social context. And it is clear that until social expectation for men and women is equal and just, until equal respect is provided both for men and for women, our answers to the question of immutable difference, of "true" nature, of who should be the scientist and who should be the secretary, will simply reflect society's prejudices. And as long as society maintains these prejudices, women will continue to be the secretaries and men will continue to be the scientists—because that's the way the rules are set up and also because both women and men will internalize these prejudices and assume that these represent the just and natural order of things. To demonstrate these theories in action, I am going to describe the difficulty of entering the scientific profession and staying there if one is a woman, of fighting the stereotypes and the discrimination accompanying them and avoiding their internalization by women themselves.

PSYCHOLOGY AND THE WOMAN PROFESSIONAL

First, then an account of the early years: how I *discovered* that what I wanted to do constituted unseemly social deviance. It was a discovery that I was not prepared for. I would like to summarize my early credentials to give some idea of how difficult it was for me to understand that the profession thought all women were stupid and incompetent: I graduated Phi Beta Kappa from Wellesley; got my Ph.D. in psychology at Harvard University in two and one-half years, where I was first in my graduate class. So, when I was unable to obtain an academic position when I got out, I was somewhat startled. The job market wasn't tight at all then—this was in 1964, when most universities were expanding and jobs were everywhere. Yet, at places where I was being considered for jobs they were asking me questions like, "Who did your research for you?" (David Bakan, University of Chicago) and "How can a little girl like you teach a great big class of men?" (Donald Lewis, Rutgers) At that time, still unaware of how serious the situation was, I replied, "Beats me. I guess I must have a talent."

As I mentioned, I wasn't prepared for this. A number of factors contributed to my lack of preparation. First, I went to the Bronx High School of

Science in New York City, and there gender didn't enter very much into intellectual pursuits; the place was a nightmare for everybody. We were all, boys and girls alike, equal contestants: all of us were competing for that thousandth of a percentage point in our grade point average which would allow entry into one of those high class out-of-town schools where we could go, get smart, and lose our New York accents.

I ended up at Wellesley, and this further retarded my discovery that women were supposed to be stupid and incompetent: the women faculty at Wellesley were brilliant. (I learned later on that they were at Wellesley because the schools that had graduated them, like Harvard and MIT and Yale and Cal Tech couldn't, or didn't care to, place them in similar schools, where they could continue their research.) So they are our brilliant unknowns, unable to do research because they were laboring under enormous teaching loads, unable to obtain the kinds of minimal support necessary for scholarship—graduate students, facilities, communication with colleagues. But whereas I was at the time ignorant about women's lot in the academy, others at Wellesley knew what it was like. Deans from an earlier, more conscious feminist era would tell me that I was lucky to be at a women's college where I could discover what I was good at and do it. They advised me that women in a man's world were in for a very rough time; they told me to watch out when I went to graduate school; they suggested that men wouldn't like my competing with them. However, I didn't listen to them, and when I listened, I didn't believe them. I thought what these women were telling me might have been true in the nineteenth century but not now. Or then, in the early sixties.

So my discovery that women were not welcome in psychology started for real at Harvard. At first, since I was so ignorant about what men thought about women, my reaction to what was happening at Harvard was something like: "This certainly is one weird university." I had few other ways to explain it.

For instance, on the first day of class, the entering graduate students had lunch with the chairman of the department. After lunch, the chairman leaned back in his chair, lit his pipe, began to puff, and announced:

"Women don't belong in graduate school."

And the male graduate students (as if by some prerranged signal) then leaned back in their chairs, puffed on their newly bought pipes, and cheered and nodded and added:

"Yeah."

"Yeah," said the male graduate students. "No man is going to want you. No man wants a woman who is more intelligent than he is. Of course, that's not a real possibility, but just in case. You are out of your *natural* role; you are no longer feminine. You belong at home. Etc.''

My mouth dropped open, of course, and my big blue eyes (they have since changed back to brown) went wide as saucers. An initiation ceremony, I thought. Like a freshman beanie. Very funny. Next lunch, for sure, the male graduate students will get it.

But the male graduate students never were told they didn't belong. They were nurtured and trained, groomed and run. After all, before long they would take up the white man's burden and expand the empire. (At least the empire of whomever they were working for.) Meanwhile for me and for the women in my class, things got—what shall I say?—weirder.

Even though I was first in my class, when I wanted to do my dissertation research, Harvard would not provide me with access to the equipment necessary for the research: the excuse was that I might break the equipment. (This was certainly true. The equipment was eminently breakable, and the male graduate students who were working with it broke it every week; I did not expect to be different.) I collected my data elsewhere, came back to Harvard, was awarded my Ph.D., and, as I mentioned, I couldn't get any of the dozen or so jobs I was considered for. The same chairman who asked me whether I could teach a great big class of men told my advisor that (although they were impressed with me) they had decided not to risk hiring a woman. It was simple.

Meanwhile, I was hanging on by getting NSF Postdoctorals and trying to do some research. Prior to my second postdoctoral year, the University of Chicago began negotiations with me for what I thought, at that time, was something like a real job: an instructorship jointly in the undergraduate college and the psychology department. The negotiations appeared to be proceeding in good faith, so I wrote to Washington and informed them that I would not be taking my second postdoctoral year. Then, ten days before classes began, when that option as well as any others I might have had were closed down, Donald Levine, the Master of the Social Sciences Collegiate Division at the University of Chicago, called me and told me that, because of a nepotism rule, I could not be hired as faculty at the University of Chicago. If I wanted, I could be appointed lecturer, teaching general education courses in the college; there was no possibility of an appointment with psychology. The lectureship paid very little for a lot of work, and I would be teaching material I hardly knew. In addition, there was a university rule that lecturers could not apply for research grants (because their position in the University was so insecure). He concluded by asking me whether I was willing to take the job: ten days before the beginning of classes he asked me whether I was willing to take the only option still available to me.

I took the job and sat in, so to speak, in the office of the Dean, Wayne Booth, until he waived the University restriction on applying for research grants. Describing my presence, he told a colleague: "This is Naomi Weisstein. She hates men." I had simply been telling him that women are thought to be "unproductive" because of nepotism rules like the one being applied to me and that the least they could do was to let me apply for a grant. I had also inquired whether the nepotism rule was written down anywhere; he said, "No, it's an informal rule. We feel we need flexibility in applying it."

Now, lecturers at the University of Chicago are generally women. They are generally married to men who teach at the University of Chicago. And, as at Harvard, *weird* things happen to them. They are not granted faculty library privileges; in my case, I had to *get a note* from the secretary to Donald Levine each time I wanted to take a book out for an extended period of time. Their classrooms are continually changed; at least once a week, I would go expecting to teach my class and find a note pinned to the door instructing me and my class to go elsewhere: across the campus, down the hall, over to Gary, Indiana.

So I left the University of Chicago. I had gotten my grant, and Loyola University in Chicago had offered me a job. I was on my way.

Well, not exactly. Although the psychology department was at first very supportive—the chairman, Ron Walker, was especially helpful and especially enlightened about women at a time when few others were—the other kinds of support one needs to do experimental psychology (machine and electrical shops, physics and electrical engineering departments, technicians, a large computer) were not available. And, when you are a woman and you are at an "unknown" place, you are isolated. Nobody informs you about meetings. Nobody sends you prepublication drafts, so you wait two or three years to find out what the current research is. You are not in those inner reaches of your professions where debate and exchange are occurring, where you have access to the informal networks of communication, to the news, to the comment and criticism, to what's going on. These inner reaches, I might add, are not just metaphorical and intangible. For instance, there actually exist, at least in psychology, two secret societies of which I am aware where fifty or so of the "really excellent" young scientists get together to make themselves better scientists.

But the intangibles are there as well. Women are treated in ways in which men are hardly ever treated. Let me give you one stunning example. I sent an article to a journal editor whose interests I knew to be close to what was reported in my paper. My paper described an experiment I had done that I thought was really good. The editor replied that there were some control conditions that should be run and some methodological loose ends, so they couldn't publish the paper. Fair enough. Then he went on to say that they had much better equipment over there, and they would like to do the experiment themselves. Would I mind? I told them I thought it was a bit unusual, asked them if they were suggesting a collaboration, and said that I would be most happy to visit with them and collaborate on my experiment. The editor then wrote back a very angry letter telling me that the experiment was trivial, that they only collaborated with distinguished scientists, and that they were too busy to pursue the matter further.

In other words, what they meant by "did I mind" was did I mind if they took my idea and did it themselves. Now as we all know, instances of taking someone else's idea and pretending it's your own are not at all uncommon in science. But the striking thing about this exchange was that the editor was arrogant enough, assuming that I would be submissive enough, to openly ask me whether I would agree to this arrangement. Would I mind? No, of course not. Women are joyful altruists. We are happy to be able to give of ourselves. After all, how many good ideas do you get in your lifetime? One? Two? Why not give some of them away?

And outright discrimination is tolerated and understood. Loyala hired a man to head an institute of audition connected to the psychology department and funded by a private grant. The psychology department promised me that he would purchase a small digital laboratory computer on this grant and that we would share this computer. When Terrence Dolan, the man they hired, took the job and bought his computer, he refused me access to it, although I offered to put in money for peripherals to make the computer faster and easier to work with for both of us. Dolan told the chairman that he simply couldn't share the computer with me: he had difficulty working with women. To back this up, he indicated that he'd been "burned twice." And the chairman, although he had been, as I mentioned, previously very helpful towards me and not bothered in the least about women, accepted that as an explanation! Dolan's difficulties in working with women weren't a problem *he* had that *he* should work out; apparently, it was *my* problem. Colleagues thought no worse of him for his problem; he got tenure quickly and is a powerful force in the department. Yet, if a woman comes to *any* chairman of *any* department and confesses that she has difficulty working with men, she does so at her grave peril.

What this meant for me at the time was that my research was hurt: I could not get my experiments done as quickly or as well. So there I was, doing research with stone-age equipment, trying to get by with wonder woman reflexes and a flashlight, while a couple of floors below, Dolan, who had been burned twice, was happily playing with his computer. It's like we women are in this totally rigged race: a lot of men are driving souped-up, low-slung racing cars, and we're running as fast as we can in tennis shoes we managed to salvage from a local garage sale.

Besides the atmosphere of hostility, derision, expectations of inferiority, and isolation from communication with colleagues, there is a peculiar kind of social-sexual assault. Let me illustrate this with a recent letter to *Chemical and Engineering News* from a research chemist:

> There are differences between men and women. . . . Just one of those differences is a decided gap in leadership potential and ability. . . . This is no reflection upon intelligence, experience, or sincerity. Evolution made it that way. . . . Then consider the problems that can arise if the potential employee, Dr. Y, (a woman) [*sic*, he could at least get his chromosomes straight] will be expected to take an occasional trip with Dr. X. . . . Could it be that the guys in shipping and receiving will not take too kindly to the lone Miss Y?

Now what Dr. McGauley is saying here, very simply, and to paraphrase the old song, is that women are *trouble*. And by trouble he means sexual trouble. And somehow, some way, it's our fault. Women are universally assigned by men, first, no matter who they are and what they have in mind, to sexual categories, and then they are accused by men of taking men's minds away from work. When women's liberationists say that women are treated as sex objects, they are compressing into a single, perhaps rhetorical phrase, an enormous area of discomfort, pain, harassment and humiliation. This is especially clear at conventions: conventions are harassing and humiliating for women because women, by and large, cannot have male colleagues. Conversations, social relations between men and women at conventions, are viewed as sexual not professional encounters.

I have been at too many professional meetings where the "joke" slide was a woman's body, dressed or undressed. A woman in a bikini is a favorite with past and perhaps present presidents of psychological associations: Hake showed such a slide in his presidential address to the Midwestern Psychological Association, and Harlow, past president of the American Psychological Association, has a whole set of such slides which he shows at the various colloquia to which he is invited. It's his whole act. This business of making jokes about women's bodies constitutes a primary social-sexual assault: the ensuing raucous laughter is at the shared understanding of what is assumed to be women's primary function to which we can always be reduced. Showing pictures of nude and sexy women insults us; it puts us in our place. "You may think you are a scientist," it is saying, "but what you really are is an object for our pleasure and amusement. Don't forget it."

So much for my own experiences. I could continue with numerous additional examples, as can almost any woman who has ever been in science, but I will simply conclude with a story about Rosalind Franklin, the X-ray crystalographer who was treated so cruelly by Watson, as described in his book, *The Double Helix*.[12] It seems apparent that Watson and Crick could never have developed their model had it not been for the data provided by Franklin's X-rays. They needed her data, they needed her cooperation; but they never thought about the possibility of treating her like a colleague and collaborating with her. They just kept making fun of her, trying to sneak looks at her data, and assuming she was wrong when she opened her mouth. Only at a late point in the story does Watson remark:

> For the first time Crick was able to see how foolproof was her assertion that the sugar-phosphate backbone was on the outside of the molecule. Her past uncompromising statements on this matter thus reflected first-rate science, not the out-pourings of a misguided feminist.

I have not been able to check this out yet, but I seriously doubt that Rosalind Franklin was a misguided feminist: I seriously doubt that she was a feminist at all. And this is probably the most tragic part of the story because, as we have seen, humans act in ways people expect them to act, and they believe they are what other people assume they are. It is only when there are countervailing beliefs, countervailing social contexts, that we can begin to question the assumptions about who we are and how we are supposed to behave. So if Franklin had been a feminist, she might not have had to endure all that isolation, all that ridicule, all that abuse, without knowing where it was coming from and what it was all about. She might even have said to Watson and Crick: "Listen, you two. You need my data, I can use your theories. Let's work together, the three of us, and maybe we'll all share the prize." She might have had women to help say it with her.

WHY HAVE THERE BEEN SO FEW GREAT WOMEN SCIENTISTS?: SOCIAL EXPECTATION AND SELF-ESTEEM

The answer is that there have been many great women scientists but few have been allowed to achieve even a tiny fraction of their potential. A couple of us manage to survive in the profession for one improbable reason or another, and most of our energy is spent not at science but at survival. And while we're struggling against the overt discrimination—the really blatant stuff—the covert stuff creeps in: we begin to feel that we're not as good as the men who are getting the recognition, the information, the promotions, the awards, and the honors—recognition, in many cases, for what we did while working with them or "under" them.[13]

But most of us don't make it through at all. And we don't make it through, not because we don't have the ability, but because the odds against us are simply too great. The scientific community doesn't want us, and we begin to believe what the scientific community thinks. And so when the n'th door is slammed shut in front of us, we stop thinking it's unfair; we stop contemplating trying to kick it open.

If we are to change what women will and can be, we must change the whole system of informal and formal social structures which discriminate against women. We must change both the structures which are overt and blatant—like nepotism rules in universities—and the structures which are covert and subtle—like the whole set of expectations which tell women that they don't have the ability men have. Otherwise, it is inevitable that we will internalize what others think of us and act in ways appropriate to their expectations. We will stop being scientists, or more likely, we will never even try.

Anybody offering the great-woman-scientist routine as proof of women's lack of scientific potential ought to be deeply embarrassed and ashamed: there is something gravely wrong with a society which tolerates fewer great women scientists than great men scientists.

Social Expectation and the Equal Rights Amendment

The Equal Rights Amendment deals specifically with rules and action: it will make certain kinds of overt discrimination illegal. But covert and overt discrimination reinforce each other, and a fight against one is a fight against the other. One of the deepest effects of the Equal Rights Amendment may be in the area of social expectation. The passage of such an amendment says, in effect, that the expectations of what women are supposed to be and what they are supposed to do are changing. What we know about human behavior leads us to predict that once these expectations change, women's behavior will change. When women are assumed to be as capable as men, as smart, as responsible, as creative, as fully human, then we will be on our way to realizing some of that infinite potential that should be the birthright of all humans—men and women alike.

Footnotes

1. H. M. Hacker, "Women as a Minority Group," *Social Forces* 30 (1951): 60-69.

2. J. Block, "Some Reasons for the Apparent Inconsistency of Personality," *Psychological Bulletin* 70 (1968): 210-12.

3. K. B. Little and E. S. Schneidman, "Congruences among Interpretations of Psychological and Anamestic Data," *Psychological Monographs* 73 (1959): 1-42.

4. E. Hooker, "Male Homosexuality in the Rorschach," *Journal of Projective Techniques* 21 (1957): 18-31.

5. N. Weisstein, "Psychology Constructs the Female; or the Fantasy Life of the Male Psychologist (with Some Attention to the Fantasies of His Friends, the Male Biologist and the Male Anthropologist)," *Journal of Social Education* 35 (1971): 362-73.

6. Little and Schneidman.

7. R. Rosenthal, "On the Social Psychology of the Psychological Experiment: The Experimenter's Hypothesis as Unintended Determinant of Experimental Results," *American Scientist* 51 (1963): 268-83, and *Experimenter Effects in Behavioral Research* (New York: Appleton-Century-Crofts, 1966).

8. R. Rosenthal and R. Lawson, "A Longitudinal Study of the Effects of Experimenter Bias on the Operant Learning of Rats" (Manuscript, Harvard University, 1960).

9. S. Schachter and J. E. Singer, "Cognitive, Social, and Physiological Determinants of Emotional State," *Pyschological Review* 63 (1962): 379-99.

10. S. Milgram, "Some Conditions of Obedience and Disobedience to Authority," *Human Relations* 18 (1965): 57-76; and "Liberating Effects of Group Pressure," *Journal of Personality and Social Psychology* 1 (1965): 127-34.

11. P. Goldberg, "Are Women Prejudiced against Women?," *Transaction* 5 (1968): 28-31.

12. (London: Weidenfeld and Nicholson, 1968).

13. To give just one recent example: "Some surprise was expressed among astronomers here last year when the Nobel Prize was shared by Dr. Hewish and Sir Martin Ryle, with no recognition of Mrs. Burnell's well-known role in the pulsar discovery. Some suspected she had been omitted because she was no longer active in radio astronomy. . . . Asked if she felt her results had been 'pinched' Dr. Burnell . . . said from her Sussex home: 'No, I don't. I am quite delighted that Hewish and Ryle got the prize. I think it's marvelous!' " (*New York Times,* 22 March 1975)

Index